MONEY AND BUSINESS CYCLES

ASSOCIAZIONE SIGISMONDO MALATESTA

The Associazione Sigismondo Malatesta is a private cultural Association founded in 1988 and run by a group of scholars working in different fields and coming from different Italian universities: Naples, Rome, Venice and Bari.

The Association promotes meetings, conferences and seminars in the fields of economics, history of ideas, comparative literature and history of theatre. The home of the Association is the Rocca Malatestiana in Sant'Arcangelo di Romagna – Rimini.

Money and Business Cycles

The Economics of F.A. Hayek
Volume I

Edited by

M. Colonna

Università degli Studi di Napoli
Italy

H. Hagemann

Universität Hohenheim
Stuttgart, Germany

Edward Elgar

Published by
Edward Elgar Publishing Limited
Gower House
Croft Road
Aldershot
Hants GU11 3HR
England

Edward Elgar Publishing Company
Old Post Road
Brookfield
Vermont 05036
USA

Printed in Great Britain at the University Press, Cambridge

British Library Cataloguing in Publication Data
Economics of F.A. Hayek. – Vol.1: Money
and Business Cycles
  I. Colonna, M.   II. Hagemann, H.
  330.1

Library of Congress Cataloguing in Publication Data
The Economics of F.A. Hayek / edited by M. Colonna, H. Hagemann.
    Includes index.
    Contents: v. 1. Money and business cycles — v. 2. Capitalism,
socialism, and knowledge / edited by M. Colonna, H. Hagemann, O.Hamouda.
    1. Money.   2. Business cycles.   3. Capitalism.   4. Socialism.
5. Economic man.   6. Hayek, Friedrich A. von (Friedrich August),
1899–1992.   I. Hayek, Friedrich A. von (Friedrich August), 1899–1992.
II. Colonna, M. (Marina)   III. Hagemann, Harald.   IV. Hamouda, O.F.
HG221.E254   1994   93–42575
330.1–dc20   CIP
                                                             r 94
ISBN 1 85898 011 9 (Volume I)
     1 85898 012 7 (Volume II)
     1 85278 545 4 (2 volume set)

Contents

Contributors

Richard Arena, Université de Nice, Sophia-Antipolis, France
Marina Colonna, Università degli Studi di Napoli, Italy
Meghnad Desai, London School of Economics and Political Science, UK
Gilles Dostaler, Université de Québec à Montréal, Canada
John Eatwell, Trinity College, Cambridge, UK
Harald Hagemann, Universität Hohenheim, Stuttgart, Germany
David Laidler, University of Western Ontario, London, Canada
Murray Milgate, Harvard University, Cambridge, Mass., USA
Paul Redfern, London School of Economics and Political Science, UK
Christof Rühl, University of California at Los Angeles, USA
Mario Seccareccia, University of Ottawa, Canada
Hans-Michael Trautwein, Universität Hohenheim, Stuttgart, Germany
Giancarlo de Vivo, Università degli Studi di Napoli, Italy

Introduction

Friedrich August von Hayek was born in Vienna on 8 May 1899 and died in Freiburg on 23 March 1992. Hayek was a leading figure both in the tradition of classical liberalism and in Austrian economics. His scientific work covered seven decades, and it explored several academic disciplines, including economics, philosophy, political science, history of thought, jurisprudence, epistemology and theoretical psychology. Examination of the most important aspects of his extraordinarily intensive activity shows quite clearly that all were focused on the ultimate goal of explaining the spontaneous order of a free market society and the ways to preserve it. In recent reappraisals of Hayek's life work, the great variety of his contributions has been sometimes seen as a complex system of ideas of such coherence that it seems to have sprung from an ambitious architectonic programme.

Over seven decades, undeterred by sharp fluctuations in the relative acceptance of his thought, Hayek was a prolific promoter of his ideas. As a young scholar he drew tremendous attention from his academic peers after his arrival at the London School of Economics. Subsequently, he lost ground over his abrasive clash with Keynes and the Cambridge school, and his early promise seemed overshadowed in the period immediately following World War II. With the onset of the cold war, however, as other economists focused their attention on the optimism of growth and the stimulus or stabilization of effective macroeconomic demand, economic developments in communist countries presented Hayek with a platform from which to reissue his pessimistic warnings of the dangers and inefficiencies of centralized planning. Later, in the 1970s, when industrialized nations suffered both financial instability and high rates of inflation, the time was ripe for an alternative voice. First, monetarism became attractive as a rival to Keynesian remedies. Then, as new conservative governments took power, politicians and their officials increasingly sought the advice of Hayek and his disciples. For many observers, the decade of the 1980s can be characterized by the revival of Hayek's influence on economic policy, by the promotion of individual enterprise and by the desire to remove many trappings of the interventionist era – although Hayek enjoyed only a quite modest support among academic economists. Finally, in recent academic debates on trade cycle, money and equilibrium, economists of several different schools of thought have begun to refer to Hayek's early contributions, despite the fact that substantial disagreements remain as to their interpretation and merit.

When Hayek was a student at the University of Vienna, attending courses in law, economics and psychology, his interest in economics had already been stimulated by some early reading (before and during the war) in philosophy, methodology and economic planning. From the very beginning the need to understand economics was seen by Hayek as a necessary step in the understanding of wider problems of the political order and the organization of society. At the university Hayek got his main general introduction to economics from the last lectures of Friedrich von Wieser and from reading Carl Menger's *Grundsätze der Volkswirtschaftslehre*. But the research programme which led him to become first an economist, and later a social and political philosopher, was originally conceived under the influence of Ludwig von Mises who introduced Hayek to two of the topics which would become a prominent part of the first stage of that programme: monetary and trade cycle theory and what at that time was called economic calculation under socialism. Hayek met Mises at the Österreichische Abrechnungsmat (a government office for settling prewar debts) where he was appointed to a temporary job in 1921, and at the Miseskreis of which he was a member from 1924 to 1931. In 1927 they both founded the Österreichisches Institut für Konjunkturforschung.

From 1924 to 1942 Hayek made important contributions to price theory, monetary theory and capital theory. But the ultimate aim of his work in each of these fields was to integrate them into a unified theory which could explain industrial fluctuations. This aim originated in Hayek's discontent both with static general equilibrium theory and its evident inability to explain recurrent trade cycle, and with the then dominant monetary trade cycle theories and their exclusive focus on general price level.

According to Hayek the proper task of monetary theory was not to investigate the relation between the quantity of money and the general price level, but the relation between the variations in the quantity of money and their impact on relative prices. The integration of monetary and price theory was attempted in his first important theoretical essay in 1928: 'Das intertemporale Gleichgewichtssystem der Preise und die Bewegungen des "Geldwertes"' (translated into English in 1984) and became the basis of his 1929 *Geldtheorie und Konjunkturtheorie* (translated into English in 1933), where he gave a detailed methodological explanation of what should be a proper starting point for a satisfactory monetary theory of the trade cycle. Hayek's thesis was that money, when it is present, loosens the close interrelationships which are described by pure theory under the assumption of barter and creates the possibility that the price mechanism will not operate according to the self-regulating principles of price theory. Hayek claimed that any change in the volume of money formed the 'necessary and sufficient' condition for the emergence of the trade cycle. From the start, Hayek's trade cycle theory was unique: it differed from the monetary theories of the trade cycle then prevailing in the Anglo-Saxon world because of its rejection of even the notion of the general price level and its insistence on the influence of money on relative prices and real quantities. But it differed also from the real trade cycle theories then prevailing in continental Europe by its exclusive focus on money as *the* causal factor, explicitly refuting any causal role to changes in real data.

Hayek's next step in the working out of his trade cycle theory came two years later, when he was invited by Lionel Robbins to give four lectures at the London School of Economics. The content of those lectures was published in 1931 under the title *Prices and Production*. In the present revival of Hayek's work, the hostility of Keynes and Sraffa to that little book of 112 pages has become well known again.

In *Prices and Production* Hayek's main concern was with the changes in capital structure brought about by changes in the volume of money, in particular describing the self-reversing real effects of credit expansion. The burden of his theory was that all new capital goods which are created with the help of a credit expansion ('voluntary' savings being constant) will be destroyed during the crisis which necessarily follows the upward phase of the cycle. In other words, in a free market society newly created money can never take the place of true voluntary savings: money expansions do have temporary distorting effects on the price system and on the directions of production, but because these effects are not in harmony with the free choices of the consumers, money will never be able to change permanently the relative scarcity of capital. It is here that is to be found Hayek's first positive attempt at integrating monetary and capital theory, a line of research which Hayek himself regarded as an evolution of Wicksell's and Mises's contributions to monetary theory.

Although Hayek never repudiated the core of the trade cycle theory expounded in *Prices and Production*, he very soon came to realize some 'irremediable defects' of that 'exposition'. As he explicitly stated in the preface to the 1935 edition of *Prices and Production*, those defects were partly due to some highly simplified assumptions and, more importantly, to the fact that he had based his whole argument on the main propositions of the Austrian theory of capital before having developed it in greater detail and adapted it to the complex phenomena to which it was applied.

Under pressure from the criticisms of many contemporaries, Hayek wrote several articles in order to clarify, improve and defend specific aspects of his trade cycle theory. Among those articles, the two essays, 'Profits, Interest, and Investment' (1939) and 'The Ricardo Effect' (1942) can perhaps be regarded as the most relevant. At the same time, faithful to his original plan, he undertook the more fundamental task of recasting the Jevons–Böhm-Bawerk–Wicksell position in the field of capital theory in order to provide a satisfactory integrated theoretical foundation for his explanation of more complex phenomena. The publication in 1941 of his *The Pure Theory of Capital* was in fact only a partial answer to all the questions raised by his trade cycle theory: in the first chapter Hayek warns the reader that the content of the book is only an 'introduction' to a more comprehensive and more realistic study of the phenomena of capitalistic production – the full treatment of the economic process as it proceeds in time, and the monetary problems that are connected with this process being outside the compass of the book. Thus, in *The Pure Theory of Capital* Hayek confined himself to the limited, although extremely complicated study of what type of productive equipment is the more profitable to be created under various conditions, and how the different parts of productive capacity are made to fit together in any given moment of time. From the methodological point of view Hayek's approach, which entailed a detailed description of all capital goods in terms of their multifaceted characteristics (complementarity, reproducibility, substitutability, durability and specificity), marked an important change in the development of capital theory. According to Hayek, his new research in that field had the important advantage of putting capital theory 'in a form which would prove useful for the study of industrial fluctuations'. Within that approach, it was a matter of primary importance for Hayek both to reject the commonly used notion of capital as a homogeneous substance the quantity of which could be regarded as a datum, and to abandon one of the most inappropriate simplifications which he himself was responsible for in *Prices and Production*, namely the use of the notion of an average period of production. It could be interesting to remark that as early as in his 1927 essay 'Zur Problemstellung der Zinstheorie' (translated into English in 1984), Hayek criticized Böhm-Bawerk for having regarded the given structure of production in general as a datum. Quite surprisingly he even concluded that as long as this assumption was a necessary one, it 'would imply nothing less than a declaration of bankruptcy of the entire theory of value' (1984, pp. 61, 68). Hayek's first attempt at abandoning the oversimplified notion of the average period of production can be traced back to his 1934 essay 'On the Relationship between Investment and Output'.

The early 1940s marked the end of Hayek's first stage of research on formal economics, and the beginning of his commitment in two adjacent fields: social sciences methodology and the interweaving of the philosophy, jurisprudence and economics of freedom. Apart from several important articles, some of which have been reprinted in *New Studies in Philosophy, Politics, Economics, and the History of Ideas* (1978), his major works are: *The Road to Serfdom* (1944), *Individualism and Economic Order* (1949), *The Counter-Revolution of Science. Studies on the Abuse of Reason* (1952), *The Sensory Order. An Inquiry into the Foundations of Theoretical Psychology*

(1952), *The Constitution of Liberty* (1960), *Studies in Philosophy, Politics, and Economics* (1967), *Law, Legislation and Liberty* (1973–79), and *The Fatal Conceit. The Errors of Socialism* (1988).

This new line of research had roots in Hayek's previous work. Hayek's trade cycle theory, with all its monetary and capital theoretical implications, had the explicit role of providing a 'scientific' proof of the harmful effects resulting from the price stabilization policies which since the 1920s had gained almost general approval. By contrasting the smooth working of a free market economy with its hampered movements due to government interference, Hayek soon realized the 'contradiction' between the economic events described by all trade cycle theories and the fundamental principles of the equilibrium theory which they had to utilize in order to explain those events. According to Hayek this problem stemmed from the fact that the then prevailing 'elementary' general equilibrium models were far from clear on how the state of equilibrium was achieved, and how prices could perform their task of coordinating the production and consumption plans of individual economic actors in the real world. Hayek's first attempt at clarifying this point within a general equilibrium context was in his 1928 essay on intertemporal equilibrium (mentioned above) by introducing time and money under the assumption of perfect foresight. The problem was then tackled again in a series of writings whose innovative methodological content has been recognized only recently. Following this new line of research Hayek began to inquire into the nature of the market system, that is into the problem of what sort of information market prices transmit, and why the contribution of the price system to the social well-being is irreplaceable. Hayek's notion of prices as 'signals', of the 'division of knowledge' and of spontaneous order' are the most innovative offsprings of his research.

The earliest contributions to the topic ran parallel with his writings on trade cycle theory and originated from his involvement, together with Ludwig von Mises, in the debate over economic calculation under socialism. Hayek wrote three articles on this topic: 'The Nature and History of the Problem' (1935a), 'The Present State of the Debate' (1935b), both published in the book *Collectivist Economic Planning* he edited, and 'Socialist Calculation: The Competitive "Solution"' (1940). The articles were a response to H.D. Dickinson, O. Lange and A. Lerner, and more specifically to O. Lange's neoclassical economic theory of market socialism, where the pricing problem was supposed to be solved by a true market process for consumer goods, and by a central planning board through the trial and error process for the communally owned resources, while managers were supposed to act so as to equal the marginal cost of any product to its price and the price of any resource to its marginal value product. Hayek's rejection of the claim that market socialism would be morally superior and more efficient than capitalism started by pointing out Socialists' misunderstanding of the nature of the market economy and the complexity of the problems which the price mechanism solves by interacting with the spontaneous actions of the market participants. At the heart of his demonstration of the practical impossibility of conveying to a central board all the information which makes the free market society as efficient as it is there was a theoretical argument which Hayek would develop later: knowledge is a discovery process carried out by the individual participants in the market. Technical knowledge 'consists in a technique of thought which enables the individual to find new solutions rapidly as soon as he is confronted with new constellations of circumstances' (a similar argument would apply to the knowledge of consumers about their preferences). Thus, according to Hayek, because knowledge is dispersed among myriads of people and is in a continuous process of creation and revision, the advantage of the free market in 'decentralizing' the task of collecting all kinds of data by entrusting it to the price mechanism must be seen in its ability 'to react to some extent to all ... small changes and differences'. Only under such conditions is it possible to take a 'rational decision' even in questions of detail, a circumstance which in the aggregate decides the success of productive effort (1935b, pp. 210–13).

The challenge thrown down by market socialism forced Hayek to deepen his understanding of the functioning of a free market society and, in so doing, to undertake the systematic study which led him to write his first most important contributions to the problem of economic knowledge: 'Economics and Knowledge' (1937), 'The Use of Knowledge in Society' (1945), and 'The Meaning of Competition' (1946), all reprinted in *Individualism and Economic Order*.

The extensive literature generated by Hayek's ideas during the 60 years of his intense intellectual activity and after his death reveals a marked change of attitude by the profession. While during the 1930s a polite scepticism pervaded the comments of even those economists who were in the same camp as Hayek, nowadays the recognition of the significance of Hayek's work and of its attractions as a system of thought have become typical even among scholars basically out of sympathy with Hayek.

During the 1930s and early 1940s the most hostile criticisms of Hayek were concentrated on what was the most important, but also one of the most difficult points in Hayek's theory, namely his claim that any 'transition to more roundabout methods of production', or any 'lengthening of the structure of production' brought about by a credit expansion (which manifests itself during the upward phase of the cycle) contains the seeds of its own destruction, i.e. brings with it an inevitable crisis. Both the monetary theory and the capital theory embedded in Hayek's trade cycle analysis were put under severe scrutiny by a large number of scholars, either to show that there was no difference between such a transition being brought about by monetary expansion or by true voluntary saving, or that the crisis was not at all inevitable, or that monetary expansion was not the only, and not even the most important cause of the trade cycle, or that – under Hayek's assumptions of full employment and flexible prices – the cyclical movements described by him could not even exist. Nevertheless, in the early 1940s, because of the increasing interest in Keynes's *General Theory* and its economic policy implications, the debate on Hayek's trade cycle theory, and on trade cycle theories in general, died out. For 40 years it was almost forgotten that in the 1930s Hayek was the principal rival of Keynes.

The greater interest in Hayek's work reemerged in the late 1970s. This seems due not so much to the fact that Hayek was awarded the Nobel Prize for Economics in 1974, but more to the fact that Hayek's contributions after the early 1940s dealt with much wider topics than pure economic theory, thus raising and stimulating interest and debates in a large audience, which includes economists, but which has involved those interested in methodological issues and in analytical yet comprehensive explanations of the working of a capitalist society.

Part of this new work on Hayek has been devoted to a reappraisal of his trade cycle theory. Lucas's appeal to Hayek as the ancestor of his own business cycle theory has in fact provoked a considerable number of essays on whether, or within which limits this descent holds. Other authors have pointed out some misunderstandings of Hayek's theory by his early critics. Although there have been some authors who supported Hayek's trade cycle theory even on technical grounds, most of the present debate on his economics seems to be concerned mainly with his ability to inspire new research, and with his far-reaching insights into methodological issues.

The present collection of essays originated in the conference 'The Economics of Hayek', conceived by the editors in April 1990 in Cambridge, England and held in July 1992 at the Rocca Malatestiana in Sant'Arcangelo di Romagna (Rimini, Italy) under the generous auspices of the cultural organization Associazione Sigismondo Malatesta. While the conference and the essays are the consequence of the recent revival of interest in Hayek's work, several of them take up the ideas that engaged economists during the 1930s and early 1940s on Hayek's early work. This has entailed a twofold reevaluation. On the one hand, the essays examine the merits of arguments raised during that early debate; on the other hand they return directly to Hayek's early work that focused especially on capital, money and dynamics. They have been collected into two volumes, *Money and Business Cycles*, and *Capitalism, Socialism and Knowledge*.

Volume I, *Money and Business Cycles*, is devoted almost entirely to Hayek's trade cycle theory and the related dynamic economics. It contains three sections entitled: 'Money and the Trade Cycle', 'Hayek and Structural Theories of the Business Cycle' and 'Hayek and Equilibrium Business Cycle Theories'.

Part I contains the papers by David Laidler, Marina Colonna, Mario Seccareccia, Hans-Michael Trautwein, and John Eatwell and Murray Milgate, each of which, from a different point of view, assesses the role of money and monetary theory in Hayek's business cycle analysis. In 'Hayek on neutral money and the cycle', David Laidler describes and places in their historical context Hayek's contributions to macroeconomics in the 1920s and 1930s. He also appraises their importance relative to contemporary as well as to later work. Marina Colonna in her 'Hayek's trade cycle theory and its contemporary critics' sets Hayek's contribution to trade cycle theory in the context of past attempts to explore the relationships between economic instability and monetary policy. The paper attempts to clarify the important aspects of Hayek's analysis in order to show if and in what sense Hayek's theory is unique.

Also in Part I, Mario Seccareccia's 'Credit money and cyclical crises: the views of Hayek and Fisher compared' is a review of Hayek's and Fisher's versions of the monetary overinvestment cycle theory. It examines Fisher's favouring the 'nationalization' of money and Hayek's advocating of the contrary during the 1970s. In his contribution 'Hayek's double failure in business cycle theory: a note' Hans-Michael Trautwein identifies two fundamental flaws in Hayek's account of money and the trade cycle. The first flaw is a logical gap between Hayek's non-monetary equilibrium benchmark and the credit cycle; the second is his somewhat schizophrenic treatment of the banking system as endogenous and exogenous cause of cyclical fluctuations. John Eatwell and Murray Milgate argue that although Hayek's theory of competition and his attack on the orthodox concept of perfect competition are attractive and persuasive, his argument, nonetheless, contains an internal contradiction. A brief comment by Giancarlo de Vivo has also been included at the end of Part I.

Part II includes contributions by Harald Hagemann, and Meghnad Desai and Paul Redfern, in which the issue of the real nature of production is emphasized. In 'Hayek and the Kiel school: some reflections on the German debate on business cycles in the late 1920s and early 1930s' Harald Hagemann focuses first on the causal endogenous factors of money, credit and technological change found in Hayek's and Lowe's theories of the trade cycle. He then analyses the vertical and horizontal nature underlying their respective structures of production. Meghnad Desai and Paul Redfern in their paper, 'Trade cycle as a frustrated traverse' give an analytical reconstruction of Hayek's argument in *Prices and Production*. They construct a simple numerical account of the equilibrium traverse of a growing economy in order to clarify the analytical anatomy of Hayek's famous triangle diagrams.

Finally, in Part III, Gilles Dostaler in 'The formation and evolution of Hayek's trade cycle theory' examines the genesis and the evolution of Hayek's theory of business cycles in the 1920s and 1930s. Dostaler highlights the richness and the complexities of Hayek's theory even though, he claims, one can reject both his premises and his practical conclusions. Christof Rühl in 'The transformation of business cycle theory: Hayek, Lucas, and a change in the notion of equilibrium' investigates and challenges the claim that Hayek was one of the forerunners of modern equilibrium business cycle theory by analysing his contribution to the interwar business cycle debate and his technical approach in the light of today's new classical mode of analysis. In 'Hayek and modern business cycle theory' Richard Arena argues that even though there are specific common features in both Hayek and the new classical theory that would make them part of the same tradition, they also present striking differences that make the two conflict.

Volume II, *Capitalism, Socialism and Knowledge*, contains chapters that focus on three particular issues, 'Capital', 'Socialist calculation' and 'Methodology', topics less discussed by economists and related to Hayek's methodological and philosophical contributions.

Part I, the set of essays dedicated to Hayek's theory of capital, includes the papers by Ian Steedman and Ferdinando Meacci which both address Hayek's pure theory of capital. Ian Steedman focuses his analysis solely on Hayek's difficult book *The Pure Theory of Capital*. He briefly explains Hayek's objective: to correct and improve the theory of capital in the tradition of Jevons, Böhm-Bawerk and Wicksell. He then concentrates on the critical aspect of Hayek's own contribution. Steedman reviews the entire book section by section and shows how despite Hayek's caution and often his rejection of traditional tools, Hayek retained the conclusion his predecessors had built specifically on premises he rejected. Ferdinando Meacci in his 'Hayek and the deepening of capital' is concerned with the nature and role of time-consuming methods of production in a dynamic economy. His discussion concentrates on the concertina effect, the Ricardo effect and the input and output functions. He explains Hayek's weaknesses in attempting to grasp the dynamics of both effects, thus limiting considerably his input and output functions.

Part II contains chapters by Erich Streissler, Bruno Jossa and Laurence Moss that deal with the widely debated topic of Hayek's socialist calculation, a subject that occupied most of Hayek's attention. Erich Streissler in his erudite 'Hayek on information and socialism' not only situates Hayek's ideas in relation to those of Adam Smith and the Austrians and in contrast to those of Lange and Lerner; he also explains Hayek's analysis of information in planning and its implication for policy. In 'Hayek and market socialism' Bruno Jossa, on the other hand, uses Lange's notion of market socialism as a reference to discuss and analyse Hayek's market economy. Jossa makes a distinction between centrally planned economies and market socialism with autonomous firms. He argues that Hayek's attack on the latter is inappropriate. Laurence Moss considers in 'Hayek and the several faces of socialism' the impact that Hayek's attacks on certain variants of socialist thought had on the evolution of his economic ideas. The lesson one can draw, Moss maintains, is not that Hayek gave up economics, as his critics have asserted, but that he simply changed his emphasis from the study of the management of a household in an 'ordered structure' into the study of the 'catallaxy'. This explains the importance of his insistence on the notions of law, order and market structure.

Part III deals with various philosophical and methodological aspects of Hayek's thought, Hayekian issues far less discussed by economists than by other scholars; its four essays are by Bruce Caldwell, Tony Lawson, Stephan Böhm and by Omar Hamouda and Robin Rowley jointly. Bruce Caldwell begins his essay by placing Hayek's theory in the context of the development of Austrian methodological thinking. He then proceeds in his 'Four theses on Hayek' to discuss how Hayek's transformation involved a move away from equilibrium theory, how with a shift of emphasis from economics to more sociological and philosophical issues, Hayek set the stage for his methodology in his 'Scientism' essay, and finally how Popper had little influence on Hayek's methodology. In contrast Tony Lawson questions Terence Hutchison's and Caldwell's claim that Hayek's early changes in his methodology were significant. In 'Realism and Hayek: a case of continuing transformation', he maintains that Hayek struggled all along to overcome methodological difficulties, with the results of his struggle becoming only recently apparent in his 'Scientism'. From a realist perspective, Lawson relates Hayek's ontological presuppositions to the nature of the objects of natural and social science.

In the third essay of this final part, 'Hayek and knowledge: some question marks' Stephan Böhm has a twofold aim: first to draw attention to the profound differences between Hayek's notions of knowledge and the concept of information as usually understood in the recent economics of information and search, and second to explore some of the philosophical underpinnings and ramifications of the role of knowledge in economics as understood by Hayek. Omar Hamouda and Robin Rowley, for their part, are concerned with the role of information in 'Rational processes: markets, knowledge and uncertainty'. In their analysis of Hayek's rational processes, Hamouda and Rowley focus on the pertinence of Hayek's thinking on prediction and explanation, data and testing, and the reappraisal by economists of information sharing and the value of competition. They argue that Hayek's individualism and spontaneous order do not establish the only information system that yields efficient economic results. Brief comments by Riccardo Bellofiore,

Jack Birner, Andrea Salanti and Carlo Zappia have also been included at the end of Volume II.

The editors, as the organizing committee of the conference, 'The Economics of Hayek', wish to express their thanks not only to the contributors of papers, but also to the more than 60 participants in the conference. We would also like to thank Erich Streissler for his memorable dinner speech. Financial support came from Assessorato alla Cultura della Regione Emilia Romagna, the Banco di Napoli, and the Associazione Sigismondo Malatesta. Finally we would like to express our thanks to our publisher, Edward Elgar, for his interest and patience.

Marina Colonna
Harald Hagemann

PART I

MONEY AND
THE TRADE CYCLE

1 Hayek on neutral money and the cycle*

David Laidler

Friedrich von Hayek's work occupies an important place in recent political and economic thought. No one did more, and very few did as much, to preserve and then rejuvenate the liberal tradition that the Great War and the economic and political upheavals which followed it seemed, for three or more decades, to have destroyed. But Hayek's earliest contributions to economics were in a much narrower area. From the early 1920s until the late 1930s, he was primarily an economic theorist, working on problems of monetary theory and the cycle, what we would nowadays call macroeconomics. His reputation in this particular field has been uncertain: in the 1930s, so Deutscher (1990) tells us, Hayek stood third in citations in English language journal articles in the area of macroeconomics, behind Keynes and Robertson, but ahead of Hawtrey and Pigou; and Hayek, it should be recalled, was of a younger generation than any of these.[1] In Shackle's *Years of High Theory* which appeared in 1967, and purported to tell the story of the development of economic theory over the period 1926–39, Hayek's name appeared only as the editor of the 1933 volume in which the German version of Gunnar Myrdal's *Monetary Equilibrium* was published; but by 1974 the rehabilitation of Hayek's work on the cycle had proceeded far enough to help bring a Nobel prize (shared with Myrdal), and a widespread reputation for having anticipated Milton Friedman's (1968) 'accelerationist hypothesis' about the inflationary process.

This essay discusses Hayek's contributions to macroeconomics in the 1920s and earlier 1930s, and attempts to assess their importance relative to contemporary as well as to later work. It begins with a brief account of the roots of his analysis as they appear in the writings of Wicksell, Böhm-Bawerk and von Mises, and goes on to describe Hayek's own theory of the cycle. It then argues that, though there is much to admire in that theory, the features that most clearly distinguish it from the work of such contemporaries as Robertson, and indeed the Stockholm school, are also the least defensible, and indeed

*Peter Howitt and Mario Seccareccia made useful comments on an earlier draft of the paper, as did participants in this conference, including of course, the official discussants Jack Birner and Giancarlo de Vivo. I am indebted to all of them. This paper forms part of a broader study of the development of monetary economics in the interwar years being undertaken with the financial support of the Lynde and Harry Bradley Foundation whose aid is gratefully acknowledged. Mr Toni Gravelle has provided invaluable research assistance.

were recognized as such at the time. It also suggests that the links between Hayek's accelerationism and Friedman's are at best tenuous. It concludes that, though the significance of Hayek's work for the development of economics in the 1930s is amply confirmed, so is the view that his specific analytic conclusions have little *direct* relevance for more recent debates. Nevertheless many of the issues which he addressed figure prominently in those later debates, and if his contributions are judged with regard to the questions he raised, rather than the answers he gave, then a more favourable verdict is warranted.

Wicksell, Böhm-Bawerk and Mises

Wicksell's 'cumulative process' analysis provided the starting point for many attempts to model the business cycle in the interwar years, even though he himself did not think that it was of any particular importance for understanding the cycle.[2] Rather Wicksell believed he was providing a theory of secular inflation in an economy with a monetary system dominated by banks whose capacity to create credit meant that simple versions of the quantity theory of 'money' (which to Wicksell was synonymous with currency) were of little, or, in the limit, of no relevance. According to Wicksell, inflation would arise in such a system whenever the 'natural' rate of interest, to be defined in a moment, exceeded the 'market' rate at which banks stood ready to lend. Such a discrepancy would lead to an expansion of bank loans, and a bidding up of the prices of both inputs and output. In the limiting case of a 'pure credit economy', in which commodity currency had no role to play, such a discrepancy could persist and inflation could go on forever, but Wicksell, writing before World War I, treated this case as having only theoretical significance. As a practical matter he believed that rising prices would lead to a drain of currency from the banks, reduce their reserves, and force them to curtail their lending by raising the market interest rate. The latter would eventually reach equality with the natural rate, at which point inflation would cease.[3]

In the current context, the crucial feature of Wicksell's analysis is its association of inflation with a failure of the interest rate to coordinate intertemporal choices, to equate saving and investment, and its identification of this failure with the operation of the monetary system. This coordination failure was not inevitable. Money could be 'neutral' and, according to Wicksell, it would be: when the market rate of interest was equal to the natural rate defined as that which would equilibrate saving and investment if the economy under analysis operated by a hypothetical process of barter; when the market rate of interest was equal to the natural rate defined as the marginal product of capital per unit of capital; and when the market rate of interest was at a value compatible with the maintenance of zero credit and money creation on the part of the banks, and hence (again according to Wicksell) with price stability. But would saving and investment be equal to each other in a barter economy at a rate equal to the marginal product of capital even when their equilibrium values were positive? And if their values were positive, so that the economy was growing, zero credit creation would no longer involve a stable price level: which of the two conditions would then provide neutrality, zero credit growth or zero inflation? And, finally, if neutrality did not prevail, just what consequences would follow for real variables?

Here we have an intellectual muddle of impressive proportions but, as it turned out, a seminal muddle, for as I have already suggested, a significant proportion of the business cycle analysis of the 1920s and 1930s, not least that of Hayek, may be read as the outcome of attempting to come to grips with the puzzles bequeathed by Wicksell. The particular tack taken by 'Austrian' analysis, of which Hayek's work provides the most fully worked out example, began by investigating the real consequences of non-neutral money and bringing the insights yielded by this investigation to bear on the rival claims of zero credit creation and price level stability to characterize its neutrality. As Gunnar Myrdal (1931) remarked (tr. 1939):

> It is not surprising that it was the Austrians who found the connexions with Wicksell: Wicksell himself was a pupil of Böhm-Bawerk and he put his thoughts into forms and constructions based directly on Austrian habits of thought. (1939, p. 7)

The ideas which Wicksell had taken from Böhm-Bawerk (1884, tr 1890) lay in the area of capital theory and were therefore particularly suited to investigating the real consequences of a failure of the intertemporal allocation mechanism. In those 'Austrian habits of thought' consumption goods, known as 'goods of the first order', were produced with the aid of intermediate goods, known as 'goods of higher orders' by way of a 'roundabout' process in which the passage of time was of the very essence. A decision to save was simultaneously a decision to consume at some time in the future, and a decision to invest was a decision to devote currently available resources to the production of goods of a higher order which would then be used to produce goods of the first order at some future time.

According to Böhm-Bawerk, more roundabout methods of production were inherently more productive, but the productivity of roundaboutness diminished on the margin. It was the role of the rate of interest to coordinate saving and investment decisions so that the marginal productivity of the capital created by the latter was just sufficient to compensate for the sacrifice of current consumption implicit in the former. For example, a shift of preferences towards more saving would lead to a lower rate of interest and a more roundabout method of production would therefore be adopted; in due course, when it came to fruition, this would provide the extra consumption goods the demand for which had been implicit in the initial act of saving.[4] Wicksell had explicitly used this analysis of Böhm-Bawerk's to underpin the concept of the natural rate of interest in his most careful exposition of his views on the interaction of the monetary system with the real economy, that set out in Chapter 9 of *Interest and Prices* (1898), the only place in his work in which he completely and self-consciously abstracted from commodity money; and in his *Theory of Money and Credit* (2nd German ed. 1924, tr. 1934) Ludwig von Mises characterized the problem raised by Wicksell's work for Böhm-Bawerk's analysis of intertemporal allocation in the following way:

> ...it would be entirely within the power of banks to reduce the rate of interest... provided that in so doing they did not set other forces in motion which would automatically re-establish the rate of interest at the level determined by the circumstances of the capital market, i.e., the market in which present goods and future goods are exchanged for one another. The problem that is before us is usually referred to by the catch-phrase *gratuitous nature of credit*. (1934, p. 352, italics in original)

Wicksell had, as we have seen, usually argued that, where bank money was convertible into commodity money, the capital market equilibrating value of the rate of interest would always reassert itself eventually and he had treated this as the empirically relevant case. By 1924, however, in the wake of the widespread abandonment of the gold standard during World War I, his theoretical possibility, the 'pure credit economy', had acquired considerable practical relevance. Hence Wicksell's attempt to solve the problem posed by the 'gratuitous nature of credit' by focusing upon the behaviour of banks' reserves of commodity money could not be generally satisfactory. Thus, the problem which Mises raised, apparently referring to Chapter 9 of *Interest and Prices*, namely that

> ...if we start with the assumption, *as Wicksell does*, that only fiduciary media are in circulation and that the quantity of them is not legislatively restricted, so that the banks are entirely free to extend their issues of them, then it is impossible to see why rising prices and an increasing demand for loans should induce them to raise the rate of interest they charge for loans. (1934, p. 356, italics added)

was, in the postwar years, of more than merely theoretical interest.

Mises attacked this problem by focusing on a consequence of bank credit creation which Wicksell had assumed away, namely that '...if the rate of interest on loans is artificially reduced below the natural rate...then entrepreneurs are obliged to enter upon longer processes of production' (1934, pp. 360–61). This insight was not unique to Mises. Cassel (1923, p. 416) had made a similar point, but Mises went further. He asserted that, though investment would thus be affected, saving would not be, with the result that '[a] time must necessarily come when the means of subsistence available for consumption are all used up although the capital goods employed in production have not yet been transformed into consumption goods' (1934, p. 362). Such a dislocation of saving and investment could not persist, because the resulting excess demand for consumption goods would raise their price relative to that of intermediate goods. 'That is, the rate of interest on loans...again approaches the natural rate' (1934, p. 363).

But this view of the operation of banking, thought Mises, '...leads ultimately to a theory of business cycles' (1934, p. 365).[5] At the heart of that theory lay a vision of banks (even under commodity convertibility) engaging in credit creation and generating excess investment, which in due course would be cut short before coming to fruition by a shortage of saving. A further injection of bank credit could prolong the process but, according to Mises, would not prevent its ultimately coming to an end in a crisis characterized by a stock of partly completed investment projects. Indeed, the longer this outcome was delayed by continued inflation, the more severe was the crisis likely to be.

Intertemporal allocation, forced saving and neutrality

In 1924 Mises had provided only a sketch of what would in due course come to be known as Austrian business cycle theory. Though his insights were picked up by Hayek as early as 1925, it was not until the early 1930s that they were fully developed; and in the interim Hayek had brought a strong element of Walrasian general equilibrium theory into the analysis.[6] Indeed, in his important 1928 article 'Intertemporal Price Equilibrium and Movements in the Value of Money' (Hayek, 1984, ch. 4), the Walrasian influence is at least as apparent as the Austrian (even though Walras is not explicitly cited there). This paper is built on the notion, which we nowadays associate with Arrow and Debreu, that physically similar goods separated in time are appropriately treated as distinct entities whose relative prices are determined within a general equilibrium system which extends over time.[7] Its central message is first that '...given a general expansion of production, the maintenance of equilibrium requires a corresponding reduction in prices, and in this case any failure of prices to fall must give rise to temporary disruptions of the equality between supply and demand' (1928, tr. 1984, p. 74) and second that a monetary economy is highly likely to suffer such temporary disruptions.

> It would be possible to conceive of a structure of money prices at successive points in time being established which corresponds to the intertemporal equilibrium system, only if the monetary system was one in which any change in the quantity of money was excluded. In practice... it is impracticable to regulate the monetary system in this way. (1928, tr. 1984, p. 97)

Now the arguments advanced by Hayek *in this paper* for requiring falling money prices to maintain equilibrium in a growing economy are incomplete. They hinge on the outcome of a conceptual experiment in which nominal outlays upon inputs are held constant while nominal output prices vary, depending upon the behaviour of the quantity of money; but the prediction that variations in the quantity of money will distort *relative prices*, and its implication that the distortion in question will create disequilibrium between the supply and demand for output, are asserted rather than derived.

> If, during such a general expansion in output, the expectation is held with certainty that the prices of products will not fall but will remain stable or even rise, hence that at the point more distant in time the same or even a higher price can be obtained for the product produced at lesser cost, the outcome must be that production for the later period, in which supply is already at a relatively adequate level, will be further expanded at the cost of that for the earlier period, in which supply is relatively less adequate.' (1928, tr. 1984, pp. 92–3, italics in original)

This conclusion involved rejecting the Wicksellian identification of price level stability (Hayek, of course, objected to the very notion of 'the price level') with monetary neutrality in the context of a growing economy, and would remain central to Hayek's subsequent writings on the matter. What was missing in 1928, however, was an analysis of the mechanism known as *forced saving*, which lay at the heart of his subsequent accounts of how money creation in any amount affected relative prices, though it is clear enough that, at that time, he was well aware of how this would fit into the broader picture. His failure to deal with it in 1928 arose rather from the fact that this paper was not primarily a contribution to the monetary theory of the cycle: 'It is not our task here to elaborate these reflections into a theory of economic crises, especially since our neglect of the phenomena of credit would mean that any such theory at which we arrived would be completely lacking in reality' (1928, tr. 1984, p. 102). The elaboration in question was soon to follow, in *Monetary Theory and the Trade Cycle* (1929, tr. 1933) and *Prices and Production* (1931).

Hayek, like many of his contemporaries, was distinctly ambivalent towards the quantity theory of money. Though he told readers of *Prices and Production* that '…it would be one of the worst things which would befall us if the general public should ever again cease to believe in the elementary propositions of the quantity theory' (1931, p. 3), he also pointed out to them that '…it is on the assumption of a knowledge of the decisions of individuals that the main propositions of non-monetary economic theory are based' (1931, p. 4) and that those individual decisions were responses to relative prices. The quantity theory, however, dealt with '…aggregates or general averages, [and] this means that monetary theory lags behind the development of economics in general' (1931, p. 4). The proper focus for monetary theory was relative prices; and in particular the rate of interest, the intertemporal relative price. From this standpoint, the quantity theory was inadequate according to Hayek.

Now Marshall and Fisher among others had paid attention to the distorting effects of asymmetries between borrowers' and lenders' expectations about the time path of the general price level on saving and investment decisions and the rate of interest; and this analysis had provided a means for linking the quantity theory to the explanation of the cycle based on the behaviour of this intertemporal relative price.[8] Hayek was well aware of this line of reasoning. In his (1931–32) review of Keynes's *Treatise on Money* (1930) he used it to great effect in criticizing Keynes's discussion of the 'Gibson Paradox', and he also referred explicitly to it in *Prices and Production*, noting in passing that it had been anticipated by Henry Thornton in 1811. Even so, his discussion of it in this book ended with the remark that 'This theory, however, does not concern us here' (1931, p. 14). Rather, he told his readers, the relevant theory of how monetary factors distort the intertemporal relative price, and disrupt the coordination of saving and investment, was one in which

> ...everything depends on the point where the additional money is injected into circulation (or where money is withdrawn from circulation), and the effects may be quite opposite according as the additional money comes first into the hands of traders and manufacturers or directly into the hands of salaried people employed by the State. (1931, p. 11)

This theory too, as Hayek knew and drew to his contemporaries' attention, was a revival of classical ideas (see 1932b). Like the classics (and Wicksell for that matter) Hayek took for granted a commercial banking system whose monetary liabilities entered circulation by way of loans to the above mentioned traders and manufacturers; and he emphasized the potential implicit in this institutional fact for the creation of money to interfere with the capital market's coordination of saving and investment. In this view of things, banks played a dual role in the financial system, acting not only as creators of money, but also as intermediaries between savers and investors, and any expansion of credit on their part involved placing in the hands of investors newly created purchasing power which was not offset by an increase in voluntary saving. This purchasing power, however, would be used by investors to bid resources away from consumers, thus creating an involuntary cut in real consumption below its intended level, and the label 'forced saving' was attached to this phenomenon. For Hayek, it was this, as we would now term it, *first-round* effect of money creation that was critical in undermining the market's capacity to coordinate saving and investment, rather than the *ultimate* effect of money on the general price level and inflation expectations, which was stressed by cycle theories based on quantity theory. In his view, *any* net creation of credit on the part of the banks, whether in response to a cut in the market rate of interest engineered by the banks, or an increase in the natural rate arising from technical change that was not immediately matched by an increase in the market rate, was a potential source of disturbance. Thus, zero credit creation was established as the *sine qua non* of monetary neutrality, and one puzzle bequeathed by Wicksell was solved.

The logic of the argument up to this point cannot be challenged; nor however can any claim of originality be made for it. Among others, in England, Robertson (1926, 1928) and Pigou (1927) had come to similar conclusions – without, it should be noted, being at that time aware of Wicksell's work – while in Sweden, Lindahl (1929, 1930), building on similar Wicksellian and Walrasian foundations to Hayek (though writing in Swedish), had also done so. It was Hayek's next step which was both distinctive and more controversial. Whereas the non-neutrality of money had little or nothing to do with the cycle in Wicksell's analysis, and credit creation was only a *potential* source of trouble in the views of Robertson, Lindahl, and others, because they thought its effects could include the generation of *voluntary* saving by way of 'induced lacking' or changes in the level or distribution of income, for Hayek it was *always* disruptive, and provided the key ingredient to his explanation of the recurrence of economic crises.[9] In this, as we have seen, he was following the lead of Mises (1924).

The inevitable crisis
Hayek, unlike many of his contemporaries, was always careful to acknowledge the contributions of others of which he was aware, and he was clear that the predictions of his theory which set it apart from other analyses of forced saving involved the alleged

> ...tendency for capital accumulated by 'forced saving' to be, at least partly, dissipated as soon as the cause of 'forced saving' disappears. This latter point is...a peculiar characteristic of my own theory of the credit cycle, since it has, so far as I know, never been as explicitly stated before; and it is upon the truth of this point that my theory stands or falls (1932a, p. 239).

This prediction depended upon two characteristics of Hayek's analysis: his insistence on beginning all exercises from a state of full employment equilibrium; and his neglect of variables other than the rate of interest that might influence voluntary saving. According to Hayek's methodological principles, as set out in his *Monetary Theory and the Trade Cycle,*

> ...*we can gain a theoretically unexceptionable explanation of complex phenomena only by first assuming the full activity of the elementary economic intercon-*

nections as shown by the equilibrium theory, and then introducing, consciously and successively, just those elements which are capable of relaxing these rigid interrelationships. (1933, pp. 95–6, italics in original)

All of Hayek's analytic exercises, therefore, begin from a situation of full employment equilibrium with zero credit creation and the rate of interest at a 'natural' level at which saving and investment are equal. This equilibrium is then disturbed by an injection of bank credit to the business sector, caused either by an increase in the natural rate of interest or by a lowering of the market rate of interest. More roundabout methods of production are thus set in motion, using resources bid away from consumers, but no mechanism that might lead to a corresponding tendency on the part of consumers *voluntarily* to defer their consumption plans is allowed to intrude. In due course, therefore, consumption demand materializes before the new investments have borne fruit, and hence before the goods necessary to meet that demand are available.

At this point, unless there is a further injection of bank credit which creates another round of forced saving, the price of current relative to future consumption goods rises, which is, of course, the same thing as saying that the market rate of interest increases. However, resources already committed to lengthening the period of production are now locked into partially completed projects and cannot be reallocated to meet consumption demand. According to Hayek, such excess demand for consumption goods, coupled with the existence of a stock of partially completed capital equipment, are the essential characteristics of an economic crisis, the upper turning point of the business cycle. Moreover, given the restrictive assumptions with which he starts, namely that the economy is already at full employment and that only an increase in the rate of interest can bring about an increase in voluntary saving, these phenomena cannot help but materialize. Two questions arise at once: why would further injections of bank credit not enable the economy finally to achieve and then sustain indefinitely a more roundabout structure of production? And why should the appearance of uncompleted capital equipment on the scene bring with it a general downturn in economic activity and the onset of unemployment among the labour force? We shall discuss in turn the answers which Hayek gave to these questions.

Mises (1924), who was, it should be recalled, writing in the immediate aftermath of the great postwar hyperinflations, had answered the first of these questions by simply asserting that attempts to stave off trouble by further credit creation would lead to rising inflation and the ultimate collapse of the currency. This remained a standard Austrian argument, and Lionel Robbins's (1934) version of it is quite representative:

> Once costs have begun to rise it would require a continuous increase in the rate of increase of credit to prevent the thing coming to disaster. But that itself, as we have seen in the great post-war inflations, would eventually generate panic. Sooner or later the initial errors are discovered. And then starts a reverse rush for liquidity. The Stock Exchange collapses. There is a stoppage of new issues. Production in the industries producing capital-goods slows down. The boom is at an end. (1934, pp. 41–2)

Hayek discussed this all-important matter in a number of places, but though his treatment of it is far more complete than the brief arguments by assertion that we encounter in the writings of Mises or Robbins, it is not totally convincing. In *Monetary Theory and the Trade Cycle* he put things as follows:

> If the new processes of production are to be completed, and if those already in existence are to continue in employment, it is essential that additional credits should be continually injected at a rate which increases fast enough to keep ahead, by a constant proportion, of the expanding purchasing power of the consumer. (1933, p. 223)

But surely a constant *proportional* rate of credit expansion would enable the new higher *relative* price of capital goods to be perpetuated. There seems to be nothing here to require that inflation must *accelerate* to stave off a crisis. Hayek seemed to recognize this logic in *Monetary Theory and the Trade Cycle*, because he went on to claim only that '...a moment must inevitably arrive when the banks are unable any longer to keep up the *rate of inflation* [Note: not the *rate of increase in the rate of inflation*] required...' (1933, p. 223, italics added). It would be a travesty, nevertheless, to argue that, after all, Hayek did not believe in the necessity of accelerating inflation for sustaining a boom and staving off the crisis. In his most careful discussion of the matter, which occurs in an essay entitled 'Capital and Industrial Fluctuations – A Reply to Criticism', first published in *Econometrica* (1934) and subsequently appended to the second edition of *Prices and Production* (1935) he argued unequivocally that

> It is only a question of time when this general and progressive rise of prices becomes very rapid. My argument is not that such a development is *inevitable* once a policy of credit expansion is embarked upon, but that it *has to be* carried to that point if a certain result – a constant rate of forced saving, or maintenance without help of voluntary saving of capital accumulated by forced saving – is to be achieved. (1935, p. 151, italics in original)

He could hardly have been clearer about what he believed, then, but this still leaves open the question of whether the belief in question could actually be deduced from his analysis. The quotation from *Monetary Theory and the*

Trade Cycle discussed above suggests that it could not, as does the following quotation from an earlier passage of the 1934 '...Reply to Criticism':

> A constant rate of forced saving...requires a rate of credit expansion which will enable the producers of intermediate products, during each successive unit of time, to compete successfully with the producers of consumers' goods for constant additional quantities of the original factors of production. But as the competing demand from the producers of consumers' goods rises (in terms of money) in consequence of, and in proportion to, the preceding increase of expenditure on the factors of production (income), an increase of credit which is to enable the producers of intermediate products to attract additional original factors, will have to be, not only absolutely but even relatively, greater than the last increase which is now reflected in the increased demand for consumers' goods. Even in order to attract only as great a proportion of the original factors, i.e., in order merely to maintain the already existing capital, every new increase would have to be proportional to the last increase, i.e., credit would have to expand progressively at a constant *rate*. But in order to bring about constant additions to capital, it would have to do more: it would have to increase at a *constantly increasing rate*. (1936, pp. 149–50, italics in original)

The argument is logically correct. If capital is to become progressively deeper, inflation must accelerate, but note that the above discussion also appears to repeat that of *Monetary Theory and the Trade Cycle* and to concede that a constant proportional rate of monetary expansion would suffice to sustain and render viable a once and for all step change in the time structure of production.[10]

Hayek had, as we have noted, argued continuously for the preceding decade that neutrality of money in Wicksell's sense required zero credit creation, and that, in a growing economy, any credit expansion even at a rate necessary only to maintain price level stability would eventually lead to a crisis. This argument was not advanced merely for the sake of logical completeness. It was relevant to an important fact of recent economic history which Hayek and his colleagues in Vienna had predicted before the event, namely that 1929 had seen the onset of a severe crisis in the United States after almost a decade of non-inflationary expansion. Hayek's analysis certainly appeared to imply that, with new money being injected into the economy through loans to producers, a stable price economy, such as that of the United States in the 1920s, would end up with a deeper capital stock than one characterized by zero money growth and falling prices; but, as Haberler (1937) argued specifically with respect to this situation, it is less obvious that the process was bound to collapse into crisis and disequilibrium. If Haberler was correct, and the passages quoted above suggest that Hayek's own logic could not dispose of this possibility, then, even though he had predicted it, Hayek's explanation of the 1929 crisis was nevertheless inadequate and an important empirical element of the case that both he and his supporters made for his theory was discredited.[11] And Haberler's 1937 criticism was all the more telling, coming as it did from someone who, in 1932, had been an exponent of Hayek's position. Though Haberler did not also raise the issue of the sustainability of forced saving through a constant rate of price inflation in an economy growing more slowly than the rate of money creation, the 'critics' to whom Hayek was replying in 1934, namely Hansen and Tout (1933) had, and it would appear, once again on the basis of Hayek's own words, that the logic of his reply was not sufficient to dispose of their arguments.[12]

Other commentators too, even those who, unlike Keynes (1931), treated Hayek's work with respect, pointed to a logical weakness at just this point in his argument. Thus Bresciani-Turroni (1934) who found much merit in Hayek's (1933) discussions of forced saving, noting that the analysis accounted for certain phenomena observed during the great hyperinflations, nevertheless found the conclusions for cycle theory that Hayek drew from those discussions to be '...too sweeping...' (1934, p. 345). Hawtrey in his (1932) review of *Prices and Production* complained about the '...intolerably cumbersome theory of capital...' that Hayek deployed there, and concluded that '...he himself has been led by so ill-chosen a method of analysis to conclusions which he would hardly have accepted if given a more straightforward form of expression' (1932, p. 125); and in his subsequent (1933) review of *Monetary Theory and the Trade Cycle*, Hawtrey remarked that

> Professor Hayek finds the explanation of the trade cycle in the characteristic of a growing community, that the banks must be constantly putting the rate of interest below the equilibrium level to induce the appropriate increase in the means of payment. But he does not explain why this cause should operate *periodically* rather than continuously... (1933, p. 671 italics in original)

Piero Sraffa (1932) too observed that, in his view, as in the case of capital accumulation induced by voluntary saving, '...equally stable would be the position if brought about by inflation; and Dr. Hayek fails to prove the contrary...' (1932, p. 47). The original element in Hayek's theory, in his own view, was the claim that any rate of credit creation on the part of the banking system, other than zero, would lead to *unsustainable* forced saving, and hence to an *inevitable* crisis. But as Colonna (1990, p. 56) has noted, and as the above examples illustrate, he was unable to produce a foundation for this claim logically tight enough to convince his contemporaries of its validity. I shall return to this matter below when I assess Hayek's contribution in the light of more recent analysis.

First, however, something must be said about Hayek's answer to the second of the two questions posed earlier, namely why, given that forced saving could not be sustained indefinitely, its collapse would lead to an economic crisis marked by declining employment. There can be no doubt that Hayek attached great importance to this question. As he remarked in *Prices and Production*,

> To provide an answer to this problem [of how it comes about at certain times that some of the existing resources cannot be used, and how, in such circumstances, it is impossible to sell them at all – or, in the case of durable goods, only to sell them at a very great loss] has always seemed to me the central task of any theory of industrial fluctuations... (1931, p. 85)

Why could labour that had been misdirected to producing capital goods during the upswing not simply return to producing consumption goods, and why, in the real world, were complete and usable capital works, such as factories, standing idle even though the labour necessary to run them was readily available? Hayek's attempts to deal with these issues in the first edition of *Prices and Production* were perfunctory. They rested on the assertion that the degree of substitution between labour and similar inputs on the one hand, and capital on the other, was sufficiently small that a shortage of finished and hence usable capital equipment would make it impossible to employ existing supplies of those other inputs:

> In the actual world...the single workman will not be able to produce enough for a living without the help of capital and he may, therefore, temporarily become unemployable. And the same will apply to all goods and services whose use requires the co-operation of other goods and services which, after a change in the structure of production of this kind, [i.e., incomplete capital deepening] may not be available in the necessary quantity. (1931, p. 84)

The *ad hoc* character of this argument will make it appear unsatisfactory indeed to a modern reader, but in the context of the 1930s literature it is fairly typical. Before 1936, *everyone* had difficulty explaining unemployment. Even so Hayek himself must have been dissatisfied with this treatment, because the section of *Prices and Production* in which it appears was considerably extended in the second (1935) edition. It now incorporated an argument to the effect that the existence of unused capital equipment, far from demonstrating the feasibility of increasing the economy's output,

> ...is a symptom that we are unable to use the fixed plant to the full extent because the current demand for consumers' goods is too urgent to permit us to invest current productive services in the long processes for which (in consequence of 'misdirections of capital') the necessary durable equipment is available.' (1935, p. 96)

In this edition also, there occurs a brief reference to downward stickiness of money wages as a possible contributing factor to the onset of unemployment, a phenomenon not mentioned in the first edition, nor in the earlier *Monetary Theory and the Trade Cycle*. This addition presumably reflects the influence of British discussion on Hayek's thinking, for the phenomenon was much invoked there.[13] Haberler's (1937) verdict on Hayek's analysis of these matters was nevertheless that 'This...explanation of the depression is...incomplete and unsatisfactory.' (1937, p. 54) and it is hard to disagree with that verdict; though, as I have already remarked, it is one which can be applied with equal justice to virtually all of the pre-*General Theory* literature.

Policy pessimism

It has already been noted that there was nothing unique about Hayek's emphasis on forced saving as an important phenomenon of the business cycle. What set his analytic work apart from that of most of his contemporaries was his insistence that a change in the rate of investment engendered by credit expansion was unsustainable and bound to lead to an economic crisis characterized by the simultaneous occurrence of an excess demand for consumption goods and an excess stock of incomplete and unemployable capital goods. There is a parallel contrast to be drawn between Hayek's policy views and those of the majority of macroeconomists writing during the 1930s, because the very characteristics of his positive analysis that set it apart from the mainstream also yielded policy implications that placed him in opposition to prevailing orthodoxy.

In Britain, though there were many differences of opinion among them, not all of them minor, Hawtrey (1919) Robertson (1926, 1928), Pigou (1927), and Keynes (1930) all believed that monetary policy, whose principal weapon was bank rate, could, and by and large should, be deployed for stabilization purposes. In the United States too, the policy pessimism expressed by the contributors to Brown et al. (1934) (who included Schumpeter) was a minority position, as readers of Wright (1932) are soon aware. And the Stockholm school, with some of whose work, namely that of Myrdal, Hayek was undoubtedly familiar from the beginning of the 1930s onwards, were equally convinced not only that the maintenance of monetary neutrality required the active participation of the monetary authorities, but that activist monetary policy could be used to the good.[14] As to what we would nowadays call fiscal policy, though coherent *theoretical* arguments in its favour are hard to find in the British literature before the publication of the *General Theory*, the majority of British economists had nevertheless favoured 'public works' as a means of combating unemployment since before World War I; Hawtrey was, as Deutscher (1990) has shown, a rare exception here. American economists often saw deficit finance as a means of bringing about monetary expansion. And a theoretical case for deficit-financed public expenditure was developed by Swedish economists in the early 1930s, and made available to English readers by Brinley Thomas in (1936).

In short, contrary to the mythmaking that would later accompany the 'Keynesian revolution', the prevailing climate of opinion about macroeconomic policy in the early 1930s was profoundly activist. Hayek and his associates, notably Robbins (1934), were very much in a minority in their views on these issues, which, of course, followed directly and inevitably from the very aspects of Hayek's positive analysis which made it unique, and which have been discussed in the preceding section of this paper. To begin with, as Hayek pointed out in his review of Keynes's *Treatise on Money*, if economic crisis was the inevitable consequence of forced saving, and if credit creation on the part of the banking system created forced saving, then once an economic downturn had begun

> Any attempt to combat the crisis by credit expansion will...not only be merely the treatment of symptoms as causes, but may also prolong the depression by delaying the inevitable real adjustments. (1931–32, part 2, p. 44)

So much for the feasibility of using monetary policy actively to counter a depression!

It might, though, seem that Hayek's analysis at least provided a recipe for avoiding crises inasmuch as it implied that holding the quantity of money constant would prevent forced saving occurring in the first place. Though the purely theoretical exercises which Hayek presented to his readers led to this result, it was, nevertheless, in his view, too simple to be translated directly into a policy doctrine. To begin with, changes in the degree of vertical integration in the economy would complicate matters:

> ...changes in the demand for money caused by changes in the proportion between the total flow of goods to that part of it which is effected by money...should be satisfied by changes in the volume of money if money is to remain neutral towards the price system and the structure of production. (1931, p. 105)

Nor was this

> ...the only exception to which our original maxim of policy, that the quantity of money should remain invariable, may be deemed to be subject. There is another occasioned by changes which are more familiar...any change in the velocity of circulation would have to be compensated by a reciprocal change in the amount of money in circulation if money is to remain neutral towards prices. (1931, pp. 106–7)

These difficulties, combined with distributional effects arising from the fact that the above-mentioned changes would occur in specific sectors of the economy, and not across the board, and hence needed to be offset by injections (withdrawals) of money into (out of) the sectors in which they had taken place, meant that the maintenance of monetary neutrality was, as a practical matter, impossible.[15] Furthermore

> ...it could be attempted only by a central monetary authority for the whole world: action on the part of a single country would be doomed to disaster. It is probably an illusion to suppose that we shall ever be able entirely to eliminate industrial fluctuations by means of monetary policy. The most we may hope for is that the growing information of the public may make it easier for central banks both to follow a cautious policy during the upward swing of the cycle, and so to mitigate the following depression, and to resist the well meaning but dangerous proposals to fight depression by 'a little inflation'. (1931, pp. 108–9)

And if conventional monetary policy could not be expected to help much, nor could other more innovative measures designed to influence aggregate demand. For example, since a defining feature of economic crisis was an excess demand for consumption goods '...the granting of credit to consumers, which has recently been so strongly advocated as a cure for depression, would in fact have quite the contrary effect' (1931, pp. 85–6). In general the only cure for depression

> ...is the most speedy and complete adaptation possible of the structure of production to the proportion between the demand for consumers' goods and the demand for producers' goods as determined by voluntary saving and spending...The only way permanently to 'mobilise' all available resources is, therefore, not to use artificial stimulants – whether during a crisis or thereafter – but to leave it to time to effect a permanent cure by the slow process of adapting the structure of production to the means available for capital purposes. (1931, pp. 86–7)

Advice to the effect that the only way to deal with the worst depression ever experienced was to await its end was hardly calculated to contribute to the popularity of those who offered it, and indeed there is some anecdotal evidence, including that recounted by Friedman (1974, pp. 162–3), that Hayek's policy pessimism was a powerful factor in undermining the influence of the whole body of his macroeconomic analysis, not only, but particularly, among the younger members of the academic community. This willingness to court unpopularity surely implies that Hayek's theoretical beliefs were honestly and strongly held, and provides an early example of the intellectual integrity which has been the hallmark of his career; but this still leaves open the question of whether the beliefs in question were in fact defensible. I shall attempt to deal with this issue in the final section of this essay, both from the standpoint of the state of knowledge as it stood in the 1930s, and as it stands now.

An assessment of Hayek's contribution

It cannot, I think, be questioned that Hayek's policy pessimism was indeed implicit in his positive analysis, and that questions about whether or not it was justified must be answered with reference to the logical and empirical validity of that analysis. As we have seen, his conclusion that the neutrality of money involved not price level stability, but rather zero credit creation, solved an important theoretical puzzle that had been left unresolved by Wicksell, but as we have also seen, Hayek was neither the first nor the only economic theorist to reach such a conclusion. What was unique to the 'Austrian' business cycle theory, which he did so much to create, was not the proposition that credit creation involving loans to the business community would lead to a deepening of the economy's capital stock, but that in this particular effect were to be found the seeds of an inevitable economic crisis. The latter conclusion in turn stemmed from Hayek's view that credit creation would bring about no corresponding change, or because of its effect on the rate of interest even a fall, in voluntary saving, and hence could not help but dislocate the coordination of intertemporal choices; and this view in turn derived from his insistence on beginning his analytic exercises at full employment and from his ignoring the possibility of factors other than the rate of interest affecting voluntary saving.

It is now a commonplace that, if saving depends upon real income, and if the latter is free to vary, then variations in the rate of investment induced by credit creation, among other factors, will bring about changes in the level of real income and therefore the rate of voluntary saving as an integral part of the mechanisms that re-equilibrate intertemporal choices. But this commonplace was not fully worked out until the *General Theory,* and Hayek should not be faulted for being unaware of this possibility before it was fully developed by others. Even so, in their writings of the early 1930s, Swedish economists had analysed Wicksellian cumulative processes in which output varied and had suggested that, in the course of such processes, changes, for example in the distribution of income, might be engendered which would transform initially forced into voluntary saving. Myrdal, the German version of whose work Hayek edited for publication in 1933, was one of these, and Hayek's own colleague Brinley Thomas had also introduced these Swedish ideas to the London School of Economics between 1934 and 1936, as his book of the latter date makes clear.[16] Moreover, as early as 1926, Dennis Robertson had suggested that, if inflation created by forced saving eroded the real value of consumers' cash balances, then this would induce them to increase their saving in order to maintain their value; *Banking Policy and the Price Level* should have been known to Hayek, having been cited by Robbins in his introduction to *Prices and Production* as the '...one work...in English since the war with which...[*Prices and Production*] can be compared.' (1931, p. xi)[17]

To be sure, these lines of enquiry were not fully worked out by their exponents, and I am not suggesting that the arguments advanced in support of them were sufficiently compelling to have required Hayek to abandon his own model as a vehicle for further research. Even so, the possibility of the voluntary saving rate responding in an equilibrating fashion to the very type of monetary non-neutrality that Hayek analysed was sufficiently widely entertained among his contemporaries that a little scepticism about the necessary truth of results which hinged on assuming away this possibility was perhaps in order.

Hayek was strictly deductivist in his theoretical method, believing that if one starts from self-evidently true premises, and applies valid logic to deriving conclusions from them, then the latter too must be true. The trouble with deductivism, however, is that the self-evident truth of the premises lies in the eye of the beholder. A little more willingness to entertain alternatives might have caused Hayek to be less certain about his conclusions than his method of presenting them suggests that he was. Or perhaps that fact that, beginning in 1937, he began to propagate a very different view of market processes to the Walrasian equilibrium approach which underlay his business cycle theory should be taken to indicate that Hayek did after all, at about that time, come to just this conclusion for himself.[18] Moreover, to push a particular line of reasoning a little further than its logic will bear is hardly a unique fault among economic theorists, especially those as young as Hayek was in the 1930s. There is, then, nothing in the record I have presented to suggest that Hayek's work did not merit the attention which his contemporaries gave it; though there are grounds enough to justify the scepticism that many of them expressed about some of his conclusions.

An assessment of Hayek's work in the light of more recent developments must surely begin with the relationship between Hayek's 'accelerationist hypothesis' and that developed by Friedman in the course of the 'monetarist controversy' of four decades later, and it should be apparent that there is little if any *logical* connection between the two doctrines. Friedman's hypothesis was derived from a consideration of the interaction of the effects of an excess demand for labour on the time path of money wages, and therefore prices, relative to their expected time path, with the influence of the actual time path of inflation on those same expectations. Hayek's hypothesis, as we have seen, was based upon an analysis of the role of the relative price of capital and consumption goods in the forced saving process. Labour market behaviour never entered his discussion of the issue, nor did endogenous inflation expectations. This latter omission is especially notable, because the Stockholm school in general, and Myrdal in particular, with whose work Hayek was familiar, made much of this phenomenon, showing that its influence on the nominal rate of interest had important implications for the analysis of 'neutral money'. Even the Stockholm school, however, did not take the crucial step of incorporating inflation expectations into their treatment of the money–wage–price formation process; and Hayek, who had explicitly denied the relevance of Marshall and Fisher's analysis of the influence of inflation expectations on the business cycle, systematically downplayed the significance of expectations in his work, a matter for which he was criticized by some of his contemporaries.[19]

In the light of all this it is hard indeed to make a strong case for Hayek as having anticipated Friedman. We must be careful, though, about how far we push this point. Qualms about the manner in which he derived the conclusion in question cannot alter the fact that Hayek did frequently and clearly state the opinion that attempts to prolong a cyclical upswing by continued credit creation would lead to accelerating inflation, nor can it alter the fact that Friedman was later to make exactly the same claim. This is by no means the only occasion in the history of economic thought in which a conclusion, later agreed to be valid on the basis of subsequent developments in economic theory, has been propounded on the basis of an intuition that was sounder than the logic deployed in its defence. Malthus's denial of Say's law of which Keynes (1936) made so much, is a famous example of just this phenomenon. It is not clear that the Hayek of the 1930s, who took such pains to base his analysis on careful deductive reasoning, would have been very pleased had he foreseen that the most durable of his contributions to macroeconomic analysis was the result of his intuition running ahead of his logic.

There is, nevertheless, a little more to be said about the importance of Hayek's analysis. He and his associates undoubtedly lost the debates of the 1930s, and as we noted at the outset of this essay, for a while his contribution vanished from view altogether, probably because much of the powerful simplicity of the 'Keynesian' macroeconomic orthodoxy which emerged from the debates in question stemmed from assuming away precisely those, as we would now call them, 'supply side' phenomena to which he paid particular attention. Subsequent developments in economic theory have however demonstrated beyond any reasonable doubt the importance of confronting and analysing those same phenomena. Once economists had developed more fully than they had in the 1930s the notion of anticipated inflation and its effect on the demand for real balances, and once the basic neoclassical growth model had been created, then it became possible to analyse the effects of nominal money creation on the economy's capital–output ratio, not to mention the level of economic welfare it generates. The answers which the literature on what we nowadays call the 'super-neutrality of money' has provided are not those that Hayek envisaged, but they are nevertheless answers to questions closely related to those which he was posing. And once the possibility of incorporating price anticipations as an argument in an aggregate supply curve was appreciated, and combined with the notion of rational expectations, it also became possible to develop a logically viable Walrasian approach to the analysis of the business cycle.[20]

Now Tobin (1965), Johnson (1967), Sidrauski (1967), Friedman (1968, 1969), and Lucas (1972) did not begin from explicit consideration of problems left unsolved by Hayek, in the way in which Hayek did with respect to Wicksell.[21] But Hayek's work nevertheless takes on an attractive appearance when viewed in the light of their work. In the longer run macroeconomists had to rediscover for themselves the problems on which Hayek had worked, and, now that we have the results of their efforts to guide us, we can see clearly that, whatever we may think of his answers, Hayek at least asked good questions, and that the neglect into which his contributions fell in the immediate postwar period was undeserved. Perhaps, then, after a lapse of 60 years, Lionel Robbins's assessment of Hayek's contribution is again, and will henceforth remain, apposite:

> I would not urge that Dr. Hayek has solved all the riddles of cyclical fluctuations. I am sure that Dr. Hayek himself would be the first to repudiate such a suggestion. But I do think that he has advanced considerations which any future work on this problem will have to take very seriously into account. (1931, p. xi)

Notes

1. The relevant numbers, based on Deutscher's Tables 7.2 and 7.3 (1990, pp. 190–191), are Keynes: 191, Robertson: 92, Hayek: 57, Hawtrey: 55, and Pigou: 51.
2. I have discussed Wicksell's analysis in considerable detail in Laidler (1991a) ch. 5., and therefore deal with it only briefly here. The reader is also referred to Leijonhufvud's essay on 'The Wicksell Connection', (1981) ch. 7, for an alternative account of the importance of Wicksell's work on the coordination of intertemporal choices for the development of macroeconomics in the twentieth century.
3. Note that Wicksell did not systematically incorporate the so-called 'Fisher effect' of inflation expectations on the nominal interest rate into his analysis. On this matter see Laidler (1991a) pp. 139 et seq..
4. The reader will note that the foregoing analysis takes it for granted that an aggregate production function characterized by diminishing returns to 'capital' exists. There are of course grave difficulties here. Wicksell was aware of them, but he set them to one side when discussing monetary matters. His Swedish successors, for example Lindahl (1929, 1930, tr. 1939) and Myrdal (1931, tr. 1939) paid much more attention to these issues, and as I argued in Laidler (1991b), this is one reason why they made no attempt to ground their development of Wicksell's idea of a 'natural' rate of interest in the technical properties of a production function. Sraffa (1932) made much of the absence of a unique 'natural' rate of interest in a multi-good world in his review of *Prices and Production*, and in his (1934) review of Myrdal, Hicks also drew attention to this matter, reminding his English speaking readers that this particular criticism of Austrian capital theory had also been raised by Piero Sraffa. As I noted in (1991b), and as Steedman also demonstrates in his contribution to this conference (reproduced as Chapter 1 in Volume II of this series), Hayek had, by (1941) become fully aware of these problems. I do not make more of this point in this essay because I do not believe that it is necessary to rely on it in order to mount an effective critique of Hayek's earlier work.
5. Mises (1924) is of course the second edition of a book first published in 1912. Its seminal

arguments about the relevance of Wicksellian analysis to the understanding of business cycles, which are what concern us here, were not developed in its first edition.

6. See Hayek (1925), reprinted as ch. 1 of Hayek (1984) fn. 4, pp. 27–8 for his first sketch of the theory which he developed from the insights of Mises. Hayek does not refer explicitly to Walras in his writings on the trade cycle, but a footnote on p. 42 of the English translation (1933) of *Monetary Theory and the Trade Cycle* makes it clear that by 'equilibrium theory' he meant the theory developed by what he termed 'the Lausanne school'. Hagemann's contribution to this conference (Chapter 6) analyses the relationship between Hayek's concern with equilibrium analysis and the views of his German contemporaries.

7. This paper is, therefore, an important contribution to the development of general equilibrium theory per se. Note that Lindahl (1929) presented a similar extension of Walrasian analysis to encompass the passage of time.

8. That is, Hayek was unfair to suggest that quantity theory-based approaches to cycle theory, utilizing what we now call the Fisher effect, neglected relative price behaviour.

9. 'Induced lacking' is Robertson's idiosyncratic label for the tendency of agents who see that inflation is eroding their cash balances to cut down consumption in order to maintain the real value of their money holdings. In modern vocabulary, it represents the voluntary payment of an inflation tax. Robertson, who tended to treat this phenomenon as arising along with, and in addition to, forced saving, was unable to integrate this insight into his analysis in a manner that we would now regard as satisfactory. The missing ingredients were a clear conception of the distinction between anticipated and unanticipated inflation, and the effect of the former on the demand for money. Although Robertson's Swedish contemporaries did know about anticipated inflation and its effect on nominal interest rates, the complete story here was not worked out until the contribution of Martin Bailey (1956). See also n. 12 below.

10. All in all, it is hard to allay the suspicion that Hayek was not always clear about the distinctions among, first a constant arithmetic rate of change of money and prices and a constant proportional rate of change, and second among rates of change and rates of acceleration, both arithmetic and proportional, of the relevant variables.

11. Thus Robbins referred explicitly to the 1929 US crisis as confirming Hayek's analysis in his introduction to *Prices and Production*, as did Haberler (1932); while Hayek himself cited the events of 1927–33 in his (1934) 'Reply to Criticism'.

12. Nowadays, armed with the concept of fully anticipated inflation, we would hardly bother to distinguish between these two cases, arguing correctly that they were essentially the same. Credit creation which first put purchasing power into the hands of firms would, provided its effects on the price level were fully anticipated, appear in a modern 'money and growth' model as a redistribution of the proceeds of a tax on cash balances to firms, combined with a requirement that those proceeds be used to acquire capital equipment. It would have real consequences for the capital output ratio to be sure, whose magnitude would vary with the amount of the tax, but no tendency to destabilize the economy.

13. As Laidler (1991c, pp. 95 et seq.) argues, wage stickiness was a central feature of Cambridge cycle analysis from the late 1870s onwards, and figured prominently in the work of Marshall, Pigou, Robertson and Keynes, long before the publication of *The General Theory*. It plays at best a peripheral role in Austrian analysis, even in that version of the latter deployed by Robbins (1934).

14. And the Stockholm school knew enough about expectations to argue that if monetary policy was to be 'neutral' in the sense of equilibrating saving and investment at full employment, it had to set the money rate of interest at a level that was compatible with the inflation expectations which were in turn implicit in that monetary policy. Because they did not extend their analysis of expectations to wage formation, and because they did regard money wages as following a rather sticky time path, largely independent of market forces, they tended to opt for a monetary policy that would adapt price inflation to the rate of wage inflation. On this see Laidler (1991b).

15. Nowadays we would subsume both of the above effects under the heading 'shifts in the *income* velocity of circulation'. Hayek distinguished between them because, like most of

his contemporaries, when he used the term 'velocity' he thought in terms of a *transactions* concept.

16. And Brinley Thomas (1936) explicitly criticized Hayek for assuming away the effects of real income changes as a result of his insistence on always starting his conceptual experiments from a state of full employment.

17. Hayek's reference to Robertson (1926) in *Prices and Production* (1931, p. 30) suggests that he had not yet read it carefully enough to understand its contents fully. Moreover, in his (1931–32) review of the *Treatise*, Hayek was content to refer to the much less thorough account of Robertson's analysis contained in the (1928) edition of *Money*.

18. I am referring here to Hayek's 1937 *Economica* paper on 'Economics and Knowledge' which as I suggested in (1991b) seems to be the beginning of a new direction in Hayek's work. On this matter, see also Roy McCloughry's introduction to Hayek (1984) where he refers to the publication of this paper in 1937 as representing 'a watershed in Hayek's thought' (p. viii).

19. Brinley Thomas (1936) was particularly vehement on this point. Given his support for the analysis of the Stockholm school, this is hardly surprising. For my own views on this issue, see Laidler (1991b).

20. In (1991b) I argued that the similarities between what Hayek was attempting in the area of business cycle theory, and what Robert Lucas and his associates later accomplished, are sufficiently great to justify labelling the latter as 'neo-Austrians' rather than 'new-classicals'. Axel Leijonhufvud (1991), in his 'Comment' on my paper made the case against doing so. There was no difference about substance between us, only about the appropriateness of the label in the light of the evidence, and interested readers are invited to make up their own minds about this matter. See also the contributions of Arena and Rühl to this conference (chapters 10 and 9, this volume), which outline the similarities and differences between Hayek's analysis and that of Lucas.

21. But it is fair to draw the readers' attention to the fact that that perennial source of trouble for neoclassical economics, the assumption of the existence of an aggregate production function, underlies all these contributions, and makes it dangerous to claim any uncontroversial validity for their implications. All I claim here is that the above-mentioned authors took up problems similar to those addressed by Hayek, and that, using a framework in some respects the same as his, got a good deal further in analysing their logic.

References

Bailey, M.J. (1956), 'The Welfare Cost of Inflationary Finance,' *Journal of Political Economy*, **64** (April), 93–110.

Böhm-Bawerk, E. von (1884), *Capital and Interest* (1st ed., tr. into English 1890), London: Macmillan.

Bresciani-Turroni, C. (1934), 'Review of F.A. von Hayek: *Monetary Theory and the Trade Cycle*,' *Economica*, new series **1** (August), 344–7.

Brown, D.V. et al. (1934), *The Economics of the Recovery Program,* Cambridge, Mass.: Harvard University Press.

Colonna, M. (1990), 'Hayek on Money and Equilibrium,' *Contributions to Political Economy*, **9**, 43–68.

Cassel, G. (1923), *The Theory of Social Economy Vol. 2* (first English tr.), London: Jonathan Cape.

Deutscher, P. (1990), *R.G. Hawtrey and the Development of Macroeconomics*, London: Macmillan; Ann Arbor: University of Michigan Press.

Friedman, M. (1968), 'The Role of Monetary Policy,' *American Economic Review*, **58** (March), 1–19.

Friedman, M. (1969), 'The Optimum Quantity of Money' in *The Optimum Quantity of Money,* London: Macmillan.

Friedman, M. (1974), *Milton Friedman's Monetary Framework,* Chicago: University of Chicago Press.

Haberler, G. von (1932), 'Money and the Business Cycle' in Q. Wright, (ed.), *Gold and Monetary Stabilization.*

Haberler, G. von (1937), *Prosperity and Depression*, Geneva: League of Nations.

Hansen, A.H. and H. Tout (1933), 'Annual Survey of Business Cycle Theory: Investment and Saving in Business Cycle Theory,' *Econometrica*, **1** (April), 119–47.

Hawtrey, R.G. (1919), *Currency and Credit*, London: Longmans Green.

Hawtrey, R.G. (1932), 'Review of F.A. von Hayek: *Prices and Production*,' *Economica*, **12** (February), 119–25.

Hawtrey, R.G. (1933), 'Review of F.A. von Hayek: *Monetary Theory and the Trade Cycle*,' *Economic Journal*, **43** (December), 669–72.

Hayek, F.A. von (1925), 'The Monetary Policy of the United States after the Recovery from the 1920 Crisis,' (English tr. in Hayek, 1984).

Hayek, F.A. von (1928), 'Intertemporal Price Equilibrium and Movements in the Value of Money' (English tr. in Hayek, 1984).

Hayek, F.A. von (1931), *Prices and Production* (1st edn.), London: Routledge.

Hayek, F.A. von (1931–32), 'Reflections on the "Pure Theory of Money" of Mr. J.M. Keynes' (2 parts), *Economica*, **11** (August), 270–95, and **12** (February), 22–44.

Hayek, F.A. von (1932a), 'Money and Capital: A Reply,' *Economic Journal*, **42** (June), 237–49.

Hayek, F.A. von (1932b), 'A Note on the Development of the Doctrine of Forced Saving', *Quarterly Journal of Economics*, **47** (November), 123–33.

Hayek, F.A. von (1933), *Monetary Theory and the Trade Cycle* (English tr.), London: Routledge.

Hayek, F.A. von (1934), 'Capital and Industrial Fluctuations – A Reply to Criticism,' *Econometrica*, **2** (April), 152–67.

Hayek, F.A. von (1935), *Prices and Production* (2nd ed), London: Routledge and Kegan Paul.

Hayek, F.A. von (1941), *The Pure Theory of Capital* (reprinted 1975), Chicago: University of Chicago Press.

Hayek, F.A. von (1984), *Money, Capital and Fluctuations – Early Essays* (ed. R. McCloughry), Chicago: University of Chicago Press.

Hicks, J.R. (1934), 'Review of Myrdal's Contribution to F.A. von Hayek (ed.): *Beiträge zur Geldtheorie*,' *Economica*, new series, **1** (November), 479–83.

Johnson, H.G. (1967), 'Money in a Neo-classical One Sector Growth Model' in *Essays in Monetary Economics,* London: Allen and Unwin.

Keynes, J.M. (1930), *A Treatise on Money* (2 vols), London: Macmillan.

Keynes, J.M. (1931), 'The Pure Theory of Money: A Reply to Dr. Hayek,' *Economica*, **11** (November), 387–97.

Keynes, J.M. (1936), *The General Theory of Employment Interest and Money*, London: Macmillan.

Laidler, D. (1991a), *The Golden Age of the Quantity Theory,* Hemel Hempstead: Philip Allan, Princeton N.J.: Princeton University Press.

Laidler, D. (1991b), 'The Austrians and the Stockholm School – Two Failures in the Development of Modern Macroeconomics?' in L. Jonung (ed.), *The Stockholm School Revisited*, Cambridge: Cambridge University Press.

Laidler, D. (1991c), 'Wage and Price Stickiness in Macroeconomics – An Historical Perspective,' (the 1991 Henry Thornton Lecture), London: The City University.

Leijonhufvud, A. (1981), 'The Wicksell Connection – Variations on a Theme' in *Information and Coordination*, London: Oxford University Press.

Leijonhufvud, A. (1991), 'Comment' (on Laidler 1991b) in L. Jonung (ed.), *The Stockholm School Revisited*, Cambridge: Cambridge University Press.

Lindahl, E. (1929), 'The Place of Capital in the Theory of Price' (English tr. in Lindahl, 1939).

Lindahl, E. (1930), 'The Rate of Interest and the Price Level' (English tr. in Lindahl 1939).

Lindahl, E. (1939), *Studies in the Theory of Money and Capital*, London: Allen and Unwin.

Lucas, R.E., Jr. (1972), 'Expectations and the Neutrality of Money,' *Journal of Economic Theory*, **4** (April), 103–24.

Mises, L. von (1924), *The Theory of Money and Credit* (2nd ed., English tr. by H.E. Batson, London: Jonathan Cape, 1934; reprinted by Yale University Press, 1953).

Myrdal, G. (1931), *Monetary Equilibrium* (English tr. with minor emendations, 1939), London: W. Hodge.

Pigou, A.C. (1927), *Industrial Fluctuations*, London: Macmillan.

Robbins, L.C. (1934), *The Great Depression*, London: Macmillan.

Robertson, D.H. (1926), *Banking Policy and the Price Level*, London: P.S. King and Son.

Robertson, D.H. (1928), *Money* (2nd ed.), London: Nisbet.

Shackle, G.L.S. (1967), *The Years of High Theory*, Cambridge: Cambridge University Press.

Sraffa, P. (1932), 'Dr. Hayek on Money and Capital,' *Economic Journal*, **42** (March), 42–53.

Sidrauski, M. (1967), 'Rational Choice and Patterns of Growth in a Monetary Economy,' *American Economic Review,* **57** (May, papers and proceedings), 534–44.

Thomas, B. (1936), *Monetary Policy and Crises – A Study of Swedish Experience,* London: Routledge and Kegan Paul.

Tobin, J. (1965), 'Money and Economic Growth,' *Econometrica*, **33** (4), 671–84.

Wicksell, K. (1898), *Interest and Prices* (English tr. 1936), London: Macmillan.

Wright, Q. (ed.) (1932), *Gold and Monetary Stabilization (Lectures on the Harris Foundation)*, Chicago: University of Chicago Press.

2 Hayek's trade cycle theory and its contemporary critics

Marina Colonna

It has been commonplace to characterize Hayek's trade cycle theory as resting on the proposition that credit expansion is the only possible cause of trade cycles, and that capital accumulation brought about by credit expansion and the connected process of forced saving *always* contains within itself the seeds of its own destruction. At the end of the cycle the economic system is dragged back to its 'original' equilibrium: entrepreneurs return to their 'old' methods of production and their 'old' rate of accumulation, consumers return to their 'old' amount of savings by restoring their 'unchanged' time-preference schedules, while the market rate of interest rises to the 'unchanged' level of natural rate. This way of presenting Hayek's thesis is found in Ellis (1934, p. 426), but a similar picture was given also by Hansen and Tout (1933, p. 135), by Haberler (1937, p. 56), and by others.

This idea, that in Hayek's trade cycle theory the net result of forced saving is always nil, was initially derived from *Prices and Production* (1931, 1935), Chapters II and III. There Hayek was concerned with only two possible causes of an increase of industrial output, both of which, according to him, would require a transition to more capitalistic methods of production: first, changes in the volume of voluntary saving, a downward shift of the time-preference schedules, and second, changes in the quantity of money at the disposal of entrepreneurs, a credit expansion at a rate of interest below the level of the natural one. Hayek made clear that the changes in the methods of production he had in mind were 'changes in the use made of the existing resources. [...] *not* changes [...] made possible by the progress of technical knowledge' (1935, pp. 35, 72). By analysing the adjustment processes involved in the two cases, Hayek's aim was to show that while in the former case the process would result in a new equilibrium characterized by a permanent increase in the amount of real capital (a permanent 'lengthening of the structure of production'), in the case of a credit expansion the structure of production would be lengthened only temporarily, to be shortened again as soon as the true underlying data of the economic system (the unchanged time-preferences of the consumers) were allowed to manifest themselves by the restoration of the 'natural' working of the price mechanism. The results of Hayek's analysis, together with the monetary policy recommended by him on the basis of that analysis, generated a very strong reaction and a debate which lasted for more than ten years.

The main purpose of this paper is to examine the criticism of some contemporaries in order to determine if the arguments which they used against Hayek's theory were either appropriate or decisive. The review will focus on those authors who were mainly concerned with the monetary aspects of that theory. In a rather fundamental sense, this choice would appear unjustified, because Hayek's approach had the peculiarity of stressing the necessary integration between monetary, price and capital theories. Indeed, Hayek's trade cycle theory was so deeply rooted in his capital theory that it would seem to be impossible to provide a critical assessment of the former without starting from an evaluation of the latter. An evaluation of Hayek's capital theory can be found in Steedman's and Meacci's contributions to Volume II of this series (Chapters 1 and 2). Here an alternative approach will be used, showing how deeply the results of Hayek's monetary and trade cycle theory are rooted in his capital theory, without making any attempt to go further in an evaluation of the latter one.

The first two sections deal with Hayek's critique of the quantity theory of money and with the methodological issues he raised in order to justify his own approach to monetary and trade cycle theory. In the third section, Hayek's criticisms of non-monetary trade cycle theories are considered in order to point out his ambivalent attitude towards the relative importance of non-monetary factors in explaining the emergence of trade cycles. In the final part of this section an attempt is made to clarify the relation between Hayek's research in the 1920s and his contributions in *Prices and Production* and in subsequent writings on trade cycle theory. The next section recalls the main features of the analysis of the cycle provided by Hayek in *Prices and Production*. The fifth section contrasts Hayek's theory with the arguments of some of his contemporaries, and in particular with Robertson's *Banking Policy and the Price Level*. On many important points Robertson's trade cycle theory has often been regarded as very close to that of Hayek. Keynes was the first to associate Robertson and Hayek on the basis of their common mistake in believing that inequalities between saving and investment only arise as a result of changes in the amount of money (Keynes, 1931, p. 246). More recently, Presley has asserted that Hayek's forced saving was 'identical' to Robertson's automatic lacking (Presley, 1979, p. 128), and he went so far as to ascribe to Robertson's trade cycle theory changes in the structure of production very similar, if not identical, to those described by Hayek (1979, p. 107). Nevertheless, two differences between the two authors are repeatedly recalled: Robertson's notion of induced lacking, and their respective views about the more appropriate policies which could help the economic system to get out of depression.

The quantity theory of money

Hayek's theory was based on a redirection of research in monetary theory which, by rejecting the 'superfluous' concept of the general price level and substituting for it investigations into the effects of money changes on relative prices and real quantities, seemed *prima facie* to entail the rejection of the quantity theory of money.

The first attempt to incorporate money into price theory was made in his essay 'Intertemporal Price Equilibrium and Movements in the Value of Money' (1984; originally published in German in 1928). There Hayek pointed out that in order to explain actual 'concrete problems', economic analysis had to '[go] on to a consideration of the monetary economy, with prices which necessarily are set at successive points in time' (1984, pp. 71, 72). In this new perspective, Hayek undertook the task of investigating the exchange relations between all kind of goods at and between each successive point in time within the overall time period under consideration. His analysis was directed towards a demonstration that, under dynamic conditions, the then proposed price stabilization policies would distort the intertemporal structure of relative prices and, consequently, would lead 'to shifts in the structure of production which ultimately must call for a disparity between supply and demand' (1984, p. 90).

But, as pointed out by Laidler (Chapter 1, this volume), at this stage of Hayek's research the alteration of relative money prices, and the consequent misdirection of production, was asserted rather than explained. The new approach, however, was applied again to the theoretical explanation of the 'causes' of trade cycles in *Monetary Theory and the Trade Cycle* (1933; originally published in German in 1929), where his criticism of the 'naive' quantity theory was clear enough:

> In my opinion the most important step towards such a theory [of the money economy], which would embrace all new phenomena arising from the addition of money to the conditions assumed in elementary equilibrium theory, would be the emancipation of the theory of money from the restrictions which limit its scope to a discussion of the *value* of money. (1933, pp. 131–2)

Nevertheless, it was only in *Prices and Production* that Hayek provided a methodological argument in support of his new approach. Here, according to Hayek, the reasons for rejecting any '*direct* causal connections between the *total* quantity of money, the *general level* of prices and, perhaps, also the *total* amount of production' are that

> none of these magnitudes *as such* ever exerts an influence on the decisions of individuals; yet it is on the assumption of a knowledge of the decisions of indi- viduals that the main propositions of non-monetary economic theory are based. It

is to this 'individualistic' method that we owe whatever understanding of economic phenomena we possess; that the modern 'subjective' theory has advanced beyond the classical school in its consistent use is probably its main advantage over their teaching. If therefore, monetary theory still attempts to establish causal relations between aggregates or general averages, this means that monetary theory lags behind the development of economics in general. (1935, p. 4)

The application of an individualistic method of analysis to monetary theory by introducing money into price theory called for a redefinition of the task of monetary theory. Hayek stated it in the most striking way in *Prices and Production*:

its task is nothing less than to cover a second time the whole field which is treated by pure theory under the assumption of barter, and to investigate what changes in the conclusions of pure theory are made necessary by the introduction of indirect exchange. This first step towards a solution of this problem is to release monetary theory from the bonds which a too narrow conception of its task has created. (1935, p. 127)

The trade cycle

Hayek's new approach to monetary theory was directed towards the demonstration that monetary factors cause trade cycles but that the trade cycle itself is a real phenomenon. Hayek split the presentation of his theory into two parts, providing the most extensive explanation and defence of the monetary causes of the trade cycle in *Monetary Theory and the Trade Cycle*, while deferring to his next book *Prices and Production* a comprehensive though concise theoretical account of their effects on the price system and on the structure of production. But it is only by connecting these two contributions that it becomes possible to reach a better understanding of both Hayek's definition of the trade cycle phenomenon and his thesis on the 'inevitability' of the crisis. These clarifications are rooted in Hayek's methodological discussion about economic theorizing, and in his attempt to recast the foundations of trade cycle theory in a way which would make it 'scientifically satisfactory'. We shall briefly summarize the main points raised in *Monetary Theory and the Trade Cycle* and the solutions suggested.

Although Hayek regarded the trade cycle as a disequilibrium phenomenon – 'a general disproportionality between supply and demand' – it seemed imperative to him to explain it by using the 'purely deductive method' of analysis normally used in pure theory. The reason for regarding deductive analysis as a superior method was emphasized by Hayek again and again throughout his book. In many trade cycle theories, Hayek argues:

in place of such theoretical deduction, we often find an assertion, unfounded on any system, of a far-reaching indeterminacy in the economy. Paradoxically stated as it is, this thesis is bound to have a devastating effect on theory; for it involves the sacrifice of any exact theoretical deduction, and the very possibility of a theoretical explanation of economic phenomena is rendered problematic. [...] But the same procedure which in one case may only lead to a lapse from theoretical elegance, breaking the unity of the theoretical structure, may in other cases lead to the introduction of thoroughly faulty reasoning, against which only a rigid systematical procedure provides an effective security. (1933, pp. 96, 98)

According to Hayek the introduction of money among the assumptions of elementary pure theory was the very device which could meet the desired methodological requirement, thus saving trade cycle theory from problems of inconsistency. Hayek started by explaining why money should play such a role:

> If it is admitted that, in the absence of money, interest would effectively prevent any excessive extension of the production of capital goods, [...] then it must also necessarily be admitted that disproportional developments in the production of capital goods can arise only [...] from the elasticity of the volume of money. [...] [F]or, unlike all [other causes], [...] [m]oney, being a pure means of exchange, [...] must by its nature always be re-exchanged without ever having entirely fulfilled its purpose; thus, when it is present it loosens that finality and 'closedness' of the system which is the fundamental assumption of static theory, and leads to phenomena which the closed system of static equilibrium renders inconceivable. (1933, pp. 92–3)

This thesis was based above all on a demonstration of whether, how, and to what extent monetary factors might affect relative prices and real quantities. But in *Monetary Theory and the Trade Cycle* that demonstration was still lacking. Once again there were only vague explanations. The 'loosening' of the closedness of the system due to the existence of money was described by Hayek as 'a break [...] in that tendency towards equilibrium which is described in pure analysis', or 'deviations in individual price-relations [...] away from the position which is necessary to maintain the whole system in equilibrium', or a 'falsification of the pricing process', or '[the stultifying of] the automatic mechanism of adjustment which keeps the various parts of the system in equilibrium' (1933, pp. 70, 123, 140, 178). A still inadequate account of how monetary factors could produce such effects was presented by Hayek under the heading 'Unsettled Problems of Trade Cycle Theory' (1933, ch. V).

Hayek instead concentrated his attention on the further claim that the automatic and self-regulating mechanism of prices could be distorted *only* by monetary factors. This argument was submitted to detailed scrutiny in Chapter II of *Monetary Theory and the Trade Cycle*, where he tried to show that no other causes, either real or psychological, could produce such effects, and in Chapter IV, where 'credit expansions' were proved to be the 'automatic' outcome, or an 'inherent tendency' in an economic system with modern banking organization. Hayek's theory was thus an 'endogenous' trade cycle theory. This last step was of paramount importance for Hayek in order to present trade cycle phenomena in a theoretical framework of general validity: '[e]ndogenous theories, in the course of their proof, avoid making use of assumptions which cannot either be decided by purely economic considerations, or regarded as general characteristics of our economic system – and hence capable of general proof' (1933, pp. 3–4).

Once the decisive role of credit expansion was admitted, not only did it have a key position in trade cycle theory, but the theory itself would become 'self-sufficient' and would share the same deductive method of pure theory:

> [O]nce we have been compelled to introduce new assumptions foreign to the static system – it is [...] the first task of a theoretical investigation to examine all the consequences, which must necessarily ensue from this new assumption, and, in so far as any phenomena are thus proved to be logically derivable from the latter, to regard them in the course of the exposition as effects of the new condition introduced. Only in this way is it possible to incorporate Trade Cycle theory into the static system which is the basis of all theoretical economics; and for this very reason, the monetary elements must be regarded as decisive factors in the explanation of cyclical fluctuations. (1933, pp. 97–8)

On the basis of these arguments Hayek reached the twofold conclusion that endogenous money changes were the only 'necessary and sufficient' conditions for the emergence of the trade cycle, and that, by assuming the monetary starting-point, it would become possible to demonstrate, 'in a purely deductive way', the occurrence of disproportionate developments in the economic system which inevitably bring about a crisis.

Non-monetary trade cycle theories

In Chapter II of *Monetary Theory and the Trade Cycle* Hayek presented an extensive criticism of those theories of the trade cycle which were exclusively or mainly based on changes in real data and on real processes. The authors of such theories included Schumpeter, Aftalion, Robertson, Hardy, Pigou, Morgenstern, Spiethoff, Cassel, Lowe, Lederer, Lescure and Mitchell. The works of all these writers were regarded by Hayek as important and useful in many respects, but either incomplete or inconsistent. Hayek's criticism, which cannot be followed through here in all its detail, was essentially based on arguments which, in his opinion, are necessarily valid when one deals with an economy where credit expansions have only a secondary or no role at all, and in which, consequently, one has to assume that the automatic and self-regulating mechanism of prices is at work. Let us consider two cases only.

Hayek's confidence in the working of the price mechanism appeared first in his criticism of those non-monetary theories of the trade cycle which explained cyclical fluctuations by introducing the assumption of a 'general misconception' as regards the economic situation due to the entrepreneur's miscalculations, ignorance, or psychological errors of pessimism and optimism, and so on. All those factors justified some sort of break in the working of the price mechanism and hence the development of a trade cycle. But according to Hayek, the authors of such theories failed to explain why, in the absence of money, those factors should ever exist: why, for example, expectations should generally prove incorrect, or entrepreneurs should suddenly become pessimistic or optimistic. According to Hayek the fundamental error in all those theories arose from their misconception of the significance of the price mechanism for, he says, 'so long, at least, as disturbing monetary influences are not operating, we have to assume that the price which entrepreneurs expect to result from a change in demand or from a change in the conditions of production will more or less coincide with the equilibrium price' (1933, p. 69). Nevertheless, if we try to derive from Hayek's reasoning how, in a barter economy, entrepreneurs should succeed in their calculation of the expected price, we find that Hayek does not adopt the usual assumption of perfect knowledge. He assumes, instead, that the production of each entrepreneur is guided 'by the price which he can expect to get after the change in question has taken place', that the entrepreneur 'is not in the least concerned with the amount by which, in a given case, the total amount demanded will alter' (1933, pp. 68–9), and that 'in the exchange economy, production is governed by prices, independently of any knowledge of the whole process on the part of individual producers, so that it is only when the pricing process is itself disturbed that a misdirection of production can occur' (1933, pp. 84–5).

In a rather strange way this latter assertion seems to anticipate one of the issues which would be raised by Hayek in the most explicit way later on, in his discussion of competition and the division of knowledge in society. But what is strange is this: in all contributions specifically devoted to trade cycle theory Hayek had assumed that in a barter economy the working of the price mechanism would always 'automatically' lead the economic system towards the competitive equilibrium described by standard equilibrium theory. At the same time he was also considering the working of that price mechanism and the resulting competitive equilibrium as the inalienable point of reference in trade cycle theorizing. For, as will become clearer later, the same competitive equilibrium was also supposed to be the final point for a monetary economy after the cyclical movements caused by monetary factors were worked out. Yet, by dismissing the assumption of perfect knowledge in *Monetary Theory and the Trade Cycle*, Hayek did not seem to realize that he was dismissing one of the standard ingredients of the notion of perfect competition while, at the same time, persistently using that notion to support his thesis that only monetary factors could distort the natural and automatic working of the price mechanism.

This lapse in theoretical rigour may be regarded as a limited though persistent shortcoming (the same notion of equilibrium was retained by Hayek in 1941, in his book *The Pure Theory of Capital*). Hayek's criticism of those non-monetary theories of the trade cycle was not so sound and definite as he thought. On the other hand, contradictions, inconsistencies and similar shortcomings were just as frequent as new and enlightening ideas in many other authors who in that period were concerned with trade cycle phenomena. Nevertheless, in the case of Hayek it may be suspected that his rejection of the perfect knowledge assumption in his work on the trade cycle was not a temporary shortcoming. For in the two chapters included in *Collectivist Economic Planning* (1935a), he started to provide the theoretical foundation of such a rejection by discussing the role of knowledge in a competitive society. This discussion was based, *inter alia,* on the idea of the division of knowledge, an idea which was brought into greater clarity in his first important contribution on the topic 'Economics and Knowledge' (1937), and became one of the distinctive subjects in his subsequent works (cf. Eatwell and Milgate, Chapter 5, this volume).

Confidence in the working of the price mechanism also appears in Hayek's evaluation of those theories which explained cyclical fluctuations by introducing fluctuations in the real data of the economic system. According to Hayek, fluctuations in real data *as such* could not be regarded as determining factors of trade cycles because the nature of the fluctuations caused by them is completely different from those which characterize cyclical fluctuations. Changes in real data do not in themselves engender that particular boom which contains within itself the seeds of an inevitable reaction. On the contrary, they induce processes of adjustment which lead the economic system *towards* a new equilibrium.

Hayek was well aware that in a progressive or a dynamic economy fluctuations can arise out of irregular changes in economic data, thus involving the economic system in a continuous process of adaptation. But, according to him, any trade cycle theory which was concerned exclusively with those kinds of fluctuations was simply off the point:

> [t]he simple fact that economic development does not go on quite uniformly, but that periods of relatively rapid change alternate with periods of relative stagnation, does not in itself constitute a problem. It is sufficiently explained by the adjustment of the economic system to irregular changes in the data – changes whose occurrence we always have to assume, and which cannot be further explained by economic science. (1933, p. 55)

In sharp contrast with those kinds of fluctuation, Hayek provided a precise definition of cyclical fluctuations as 'developments leading away from equilibrium and finally, *without any changes in data*, necessitating a change in the economic trend' (1933, p. 55, emphasis added). And then he explained that '[t]he phenomena of the upward trend of the cycle and of the culminating boom constitute a problem only because they inevitably bring about a slump in sales [...] which is *not* occasioned by any corresponding change in the original data' (1933, pp. 5–6). It is thus clear that according to Hayek it is permissible to speak of 'cyclical' fluctuations only if and when the automatic and self-regulating mechanism of prices does not follow its natural course – which 'necessarily' leads the economic system towards equilibrium – but is distorted in such a way as to involve the economic system in a *détour* from its equilibrating path.

Hayek's lack of interest in fluctuations due exclusively to changes in real data (because that case 'does not in itself constitute a problem') could appear rather odd on both historical and theoretical grounds. One might find some rationale for such an extreme position in the academic situation then prevailing in Germany. As Hagemann points out (Chapter 6, this volume), when Hayek was writing *Monetary Theory and the Trade Cycle* (which, it will be remembered, was originally addressed to a German audience) European countries were undergoing great fluctuations in prices and money supply and, at the same time, Adolph Löwe and other members of the Kiel school in Germany were launching an attack against the monetary theory of the trade cycle, an attack which Hayek himself regarded as the most serious and theoretically demanding. This might explain why Hayek attached such importance to the monetary causes of trade cycles, why he was determined both to deepen the theoretical and methodological foundations of his theory and to express his position so firmly. Nevertheless, some aspects of his argument may indicate a less rigid position.

There is evidence in *Monetary Theory and the Trade Cycle* that Hayek was not at ease with his narrow definition of the field of trade cycle theory. In Chapter V he took into account explicitly the case of violent fluctuations in voluntary savings, which were regarded as a decisive factor of trade cycles in some of the best known theories in Germany (by Spiethoff and Cassel). While still maintaining that in this case the prerequisite of cyclical fluctuations was not present because 'the passage from boom into depression is not a necessary consequence of the boom itself, but is conditioned by "external circumstances"' (1933, p. 205; cf. also pp. 79–80), at the same time he admitted that those kinds of fluctuation 'act similarly to an artificial lowering of the money rate of interest', that in those cases 'it is permissible to speak of non-monetary cyclical fluctuations', and that they 'present some very important problems in interest theory, the solution of which would be an important aid in estimating the effect of fluctuations conditioned by monetary changes' (1933, pp. 205–6; cf. also 1939c, p. 143).

There is thus a temptation to turn the whole argument presented so far in *Monetary Theory and the Trade Cycle* into a mere problem of definition, and to define monetary changes as the necessary and sufficient cause of trade cycles only if and when the trade cycle phenomenon is as Hayek defined it. Hayek himself seems to share this temptation when he dismisses cyclical fluctuations due to violent fluctuations in savings by asserting that they '[differ], however, from the conception of cyclical fluctuations employed hitherto' (1933, p. 205). This calls for a re-evaluation of Hayek's claim about the 'general validity' of his own monetary approach to trade cycle theory. For now we find that for the appearance of at least some cyclical fluctuations monetary changes are neither necessary nor sufficient.

Moreover Hayek's emphasis on monetary factors did not preclude him from recognizing the importance of real factors from another angle which, once again, seems to throw some doubts on his claim that the monetary factors are both necessary and sufficient causes of the trade cycle. In Chapter V of his *Monetary Theory and the Trade Cycle*, Hayek raises the question whether monetary changes 'would, if not reinforced by other factors, attain the extent and duration which we observe in the historical cycles; or whether in the absence of these supplementary factors they would not be much weaker and less acute than they actually are'. He then answers his own question by stating that

> [p]erhaps the empirically observed strength of the cyclical fluctuations is really only due to periodic changes in external circumstances, such as short-period variations of climate, or changes in subjective data (as e.g., the sudden appearance of entrepreneurs of genius) or perhaps the interval between individual cyclical waves may be due to some natural law. (1933, p. 185)

This means that at best money changes are a necessary cooperating factor in trade cycle phenomena, and entails the recognition by Hayek himself that they are a necessary, but not *sufficient* factor for the emergence of the trade cycle.

Finally, a general understanding of Hayek's trade cycle theory must account for another aspect of his approach which qualifies Hayek's subsequent analysis. Hayek's recognition of the importance of real factors as possible causes of a gap between the market and the natural rate of interest (cf. Hayek, 1933, pp. 182–3) was not only a Wicksellian echo or an acknowledgment to his German colleagues. In the 1920s, in Hayek's agenda the explanation of the harmful effects produced by price stabilization policies was as important as the explanation of how capitalistic economies develop under the spur of progress. In this perspective Hayek's appreciation of credit expansions was very different from that supported in *Prices and Production* and in his subsequent writings:

> [Credit expansions] are, in a sense, the price we pay for a speed of development exceeding that which people would voluntarily make possible through their savings, and which therefore has to be extorted from them. And even if it is a mistake [...] to suppose that we can, in this way, overcome all obstacles standing in the way of progress, it is at least conceivable that the non-economic factors of progress, such as technical and commercial knowledge, are thereby benefited in a way which we should be reluctant to forgo. (1933, pp. 189–90)

Under these conditions, Hayek adds, stabilizing the economic system by way of a stability of the total amount of bank deposits 'would be obtained at the price of curbing economic progress' (1933, pp. 190–91). The reasons why, under dynamic conditions, the ultimate effect of credit expansions and forced saving is *not* nil are to be found in Hayek's essay 'The Present State and Immediate Prospects of the Study of Industrial Fluctuations' (1939a, originally published in Germany in 1933). If the rate of voluntary saving is high, and if the rate of credit expansion is not too fast, 'the result might be that for a time the current voluntary savings will be used to take over, as it were, that capital created by means of forced saving; and current savings would then have to serve [...] merely to maintain capital which has been formed in anticipation of these savings' (1939a, p. 180).

In spite of these promising statements and of the importance ascribed by Hayek to the study of a progressive economy (cf. 1939c, pp. 137–41), it can hardly be overemphasized that such a study was never undertaken by Hayek himself, and that the formal analysis he provided in *Prices and Production* and in subsequent writings on the trade cycle was exclusively concerned with stationary conditions. Hayek himself was extremely clear about this point while constructing his theory, and he also appeared to be awake to the fact that a study of the problem of credit expansions under dynamic conditions would be an altogether different and more difficult matter than the one dealt with in *Prices and Production* (cf. 1935, p. 93, n. 1; 1939b, pp. 47–8, n. 1). Indeed, in 'The Maintenance of Capital' (1935b) Hayek tried to tackle the problem of changes in the stock of capital due to changes in economic data, and this is further evidence of his interest in dynamic analysis. But his inquiry was only a very preliminary step towards the building up of a theoretical apparatus which could account for complex phenomena as trade cycles under dynamic conditions.

Once this is realized, some preliminary questions arise on the significance of Hayek's works in the 1930s. Let us mention just two of them. Firstly, if Hayek's analysis was confined exclusively and consciously to stationary conditions, what is its relevance for an understanding of actual industrial fluctuations which, in Hayek's own words, are mainly due to changes in economic data? In a sense, Hayek himself gave an answer: very little! (see the quotation above, p. 36). This point was understood by some contemporaries, for example, Marget (1932, p. 264), Bresciani-Turroni, (1934, p. 345) and Röpke (1936, p. 117). Secondly, if Hayek's analysis held only in stationary conditions, what was the relevance of Hayek's monetary policy prescriptions which, in turn, were supposed to be grounded on that analysis? The most widespread criticisms of Hayek's theory concentrated on its policy implications. But very few authors, if any, realized its limited field of application. The lack of recognition of this fact by many of Hayek's contemporaries contributed to the muddle which characterized the debate on his trade cycle theory during those years. The clearest examples of such a misunderstanding can be found in Haberler (1937, p. 59) and in Hansen still in 1951 (p. 390). Hayek was responsible for the confusion. For, instead of stressing that his analysis could provide a basis for discussing monetary policy problems only under stationary conditions, he did the opposite. In *Prices and Production* he stated:

> I believe that the conclusion stated above holds here not only for this case of transitions to more capitalistic methods of production but also for an increase of production caused by the absorption of unused resources. Furthermore, by another chain of reasoning – which is too long and complicated to reproduce here, and which I have sketched elsewhere [in 'Intertemporal Price Equilibrium and the Movements in the Value of Money'] – it might be shown to apply *in principle* even to the particularly difficult case of an increase of production caused by the growth of population, the discovery of new natural resources, and the like. (1935, pp. 106–7, emphasis added)

Now, while the case of the absorption of unused resources was studied by Hayek later on in 'Profits, Interest and Investment' under the assumption of stationary conditions (1939b, pp. 38–71), the other cases were not studied at all. In his essay on intertemporal price equilibrium he was *assuming* that a price stabilization policy would force the money prices of a single good at two successive points in time to be equal, then showing that, under dynamic conditions, the 'exchange ratio' thus established between the two money prices differed from the one which would prevail in a barter economy. But contrary to Hayek's belief, this was not an explanation of how relative prices would be distorted by some specific monetary policy. In fact Hayek had no basis for discussing monetary policy problems in a growing economy.

In view of this inconsistency between Hayek's analytical work and his discussion of economic policies, it does not seem fruitful, as many authors did in the 1930s, to reject Hayek's trade cycle theory on the basis of his unacceptable or ill-founded economic policy prescriptions. For this reason in the next section the evaluation of Hayek's work in the 1930s will be limited to his analytical contribution by assuming, as Hayek did, the case of a stationary economy.

Main features of the cycle

Within this perspective, a preliminary remark on the significance of Hayek's contributions in *Prices and Production* and in his subsequent works seems worthwhile. At the time Hayek was writing his book, both in Germany and in the Anglo-Saxon countries, a variety of theories which sometimes have been characterized as theories of the 'productivity' or 'creative power' of credit had established themselves and had already created a large debate. Hayek explicitly referred to that debate (but not to any author in particular) in *Monetary Theory and the Trade Cycle*, when he wrote:

> It has often been argued that the forced saving arising from an artificially lowered interest rate would improve the capital supply of the economy to such an extent that the natural rate of interest would have to fall finally to the level of the money rate of interest, and thus a new state of equilibrium would be created – that is, the crisis could be avoided altogether. This view is closely connected with the thesis, which we have already rejected, that the level of the natural rate of interest depends directly upon the whole existing stock of real capital. Forced saving increases only the existing stock of real capital, but not necessarily the current supply of free capital disposable for investment. (1933, p. 221)

The explanation of Hayek's negative answer is to be found in *Prices and Production* and in subsequent writings and must be evaluated within their analytical context. Even if that context seemes unsuitable to provide a convincing explanation of actual industrial fluctuations, it has the advantage of drawing attention to the more general question of whether, in the neoclassical framework, it is possible to think that monetary factors may permanently change the relative scarcity of capital and the state of full employment equilibrium of an economic system. In *Prices and Production* and after, Hayek's discussion about the formation of saving supply ('the current supply of free capital disposable for investment') in a monetary economy should be considered from this perspective.

In *Prices and Production* Hayek assumed that in a stationary economy with no unused resources the banks extend credit to the entrepreneurs by lowering the money rate of interest below the level of the natural one while, by hypothesis, consumers keep constant their propensity to save and their money expenditure on consumption goods. The lowering of the bank rate of interest acts as an investment incentive for the entrepreneurs in the same way as a lowering of the rate of interest due to an increased supply of saving by the consumers, that is, entrepreneurs will be induced to increase the production of capital goods in order to adapt the 'duration' of the productive process of the whole economy to the new lower level of the rate of interest. A shift towards the build-up of the more 'roundabout', or capital-intensive processes of production begins. But as the economy is already at full employment, entrepreneurs will succeed in their goal only by withdrawing workers from the production of consumption goods, thus causing, after a while, a reduction in their supply and an unexpected and undesired retrenchment of consumption for the society as a whole (this latter being the phenomenon labelled 'forced saving'). In the early stages of the boom, this process will be accompanied and supported by an increase in the prices of capital goods relative to the prices of consumption goods. Nevertheless, towards the end of the boom, according to Hayek, consumers will try to re-establish their desired level of real consumption corresponding to their unchanged time-preference schedules. Once this happens, a reversal movement in relative prices will be set up: the prices of consumption goods will start to increase relative to the prices of capital goods. This change in the price movement will bring with it a corresponding change in the 'duration' of the productive process of the whole economy. Entrepreneurs will find it more profitable to adopt the less roundabout or capital-intensive methods of production they were using before the credit expansion started. The reversal in the profitability of the methods of production corresponds, according to Hayek, to the beginning of the crisis and starts a process which, because of the stationarity assumption, will finally bring the economic system to the 'original' state of equilibrium.

Hayek's theory was based on the assumption that the 'duration' of the period of production was regulated by the level of the bank rate of interest relative to the level of the real wage rate. When the level of the bank rate of interest is low relative to the level of the real wage rate, the upswing of the cycle starts because it becomes profitable to substitute capital for labour (1935, p. 87). This involves an increase in the production of capital goods, which Hayek identified with a lengthening of the time period of the investment structure, which in turn was identified with a lengthening of the production process. When the level of the real wage rate becomes low relative to the bank rate of interest, the turning point of the cycle occurs because it becomes profitable to substitute labour for capital (cf. 1939b, pp. 4–5, for this implicit assumption in *Prices and Production*). This involves a reversal in the above magnitudes. In 1931 Hayek likened these changes in the duration of the production process during the trade cycle to the movements of playing a concertina (*Ziehharmonika*) (1931, p. 92n). Later on, he regarded the explanation of these changes as directly connected with the application of the 'Ricardo proposition' that a general rise (fall) in wages relatively to the prices of the products will reduce (increase) the profitability of the methods employing relatively more (less) capital to a lesser extent than those employing relatively less (more) capital (1942, p. 129).

The crucial point in Hayek's theory was the change from the upswing of the cycle to the crisis. According to Hayek at the latter stages of the boom the fall in real wages due to the reduced supply of consumption goods starts a reaction on the part of the working class which is supposed to become effective because entrepreneurs 'know themselves to be in command – at least nominally – of greater resources and expect greater profits' (1935, pp. 88–9), and thus are ready to meet workers' claims for increased money wages in the face of rising prices of consumption goods (for this last part of the explanation, cf. Hayek, 1931, p. 85). This redistribution of nominal income 'will not change the amount of consumers' goods immediately available, though it may change their distribution between individuals. But [...] it will mean a new and reversed change of the proportion between the demand for consumers' goods and the demand for producers' goods in favour of the former', and thus a rise of the prices of consumers' goods relative to the rise of the prices of producers' goods (1935, pp. 8–9). The results of this reaction could be postponed if the banks are prepared to keep that proportion unchanged by 'progressively increasing their loans' (1935, p. 89; cf. also 1933, p. 215), but they cannot be avoided altogether. This reversal in the movement of the prices of the two sets of producers' and consumers' goods was the pivot upon which Hayek's cycle had to turn. It was the symptom of the scarcity of the supply of voluntary saving.

I have shown elsewhere (1990, pp. xlii–xlvii) that in Hayek's theory the unavoidable occurrence of a shortage of voluntary savings at the latter stages of the boom was not due to his neglect of the possibility of augmented income out of which voluntary saving is made, nor was it due to his neglect of the redistributive effects of money changes. These possibilities were already envisaged in *Monetary Theory and the Trade Cycle*, where Hayek stated that 'the flow of voluntary saving can itself vary as a result of a single change in the proportion of capital formation', though, he added, 'this factor [...] is unlikely to become important enough for its omission to affect the exposition given in the text' (1933, p. 215n). As will be seen later, Hayek tackled this problem explicitly and extensively only in 'Profits, Interest and Investment' (1939b) and in 'The Ricardo Effect' (1942). Here it suffices to recall his explicit contention that

[t]here will, as a rule, be *only one* output stream which in its production will generate an income stream of such size and time shape that the part of that income which at any time will be spent on consumers' goods will just equal the cost of the current output of consumers' goods, inclusive of that rate of return on capital in the expectation of which the method of production actually employed has been decided upon'. (1942, p. 128, n. 6, emphasis added; cf. also 1939b, p. 52)

And for any given state of technical knowledge and amount of resources, that output stream is determined by the rate of saving. Accordingly, any change in the size and timing of that income stream which is generated by changes in monetary factors and which differs from the one determined by real factors must necessarily bring the economy into a cumulative process of disequilibrium (cf. 1942, p. 142).

One of the most common claims about Hayek's trade cycle theory was that he failed to explain why the situation reached by the economic system through forced saving should be more unstable than the same situation reached through a process of voluntary saving. Why, that is, the process of capital formation brought about by credit expansion could not simply stop, but had to reverse itself into a cumulative downswing. Among the authors who made this point were Sraffa (1932, p. 47), Cabiati (1932, pp. 200–201), Hansen and Tout (1933, pp. 139–40), Neisser (1934, pp. 436–9), Haberler (1937, pp. 57–8), and Wilson (1939–40, p. 172).

Some of these authors based their criticism on the capital theory underlying Hayek's trade cycle theory. In the appendix to his review of *Prices and Production* Neisser stated that if Böhm-Bawerk's definition of the average period of production is assumed and applied to stationary conditions '[w]e are [...] justified in identifying a shortening of the period of production, in Hayek's terminology, with a destruction of capital, and vice versa'. But under non-static conditions the use of Böhm-Bawerk's formula is dubious, and the conclusion is no longer justified (1934, pp. 454–5). Along this line of argument, the most critical scrutiny of Hayek's capital theory came from Knight (1935) who rejected the equivalence assumed by Hayek between investment, the lengthening of the time structure of investment, and the lengthening of the production process. Later, Kaldor (1939) based his rejection of Hayek's trade cycle theory on a critique of Hayek's interpretation and use of the Ricardo effect. This kind of critique was used by Wilson in 1939–40, and it was further developed by Kaldor in 1942. Without joining the intricate discussion on pure capital theory, several authors simply regarded Hayek's process of 'capital deepening' as an unrealistic picture of what happens in the real world during a trade cycle (cf. Fanno, 1933; published in 1992, p. 253).

Authors who focused their attention on Hayek's trade cycle theory rather than on his underlying capital theory typically rejected Hayek's thesis that the net result of forced saving is nil, failing to take into account Hayek's assumptions of full employment and stationary conditions. This was the case of Ellis (1934, p. 426), Robertson (1966a, p. 68, n. 4), Haberler (1937, p. 59), and Hansen (1951, pp. 390–91). Nevertheless, two questions raised by Haberler are worth recalling. First, if it were possible, by credit expansion and forced saving, to 'complete' the transition towards more capital-intensive methods of production, would not the economy reach a new and stable equilibrium? The underlying idea was that if the more roundabout methods of production are more productive (as stated by Böhm-Bawerk and assumed by Hayek), then even with a given number of workers there will be an increased real income out of which voluntary saving can increase to sustain the increased amount of capital. The question was justified by the fact that in *Monetary Theory and the Trade Cycle* and in *Prices and Production* Hayek's negative answer rested on the argument that the existing credit institutions could not expand credit 'indefinitely'. This argument gave his readers the opportunity of raising two questions. First, what would happen if the banks continued to expand credit. Secondly, even if the whole process cannot be completed, why could not those capital goods which have already been produced be put into operation instead of going to waste? (Haberler, 1937, p. 58).

In Hayek's theoretical framework the answers to both questions are related to one another, but his arguments, although present in his first two books, came out explicitly only later, in several restatements of his theory. In his reply to Hansen and Tout, Hayek connected the rate of increase of credit expansion with the relation between the rate of increase of money incomes and the rate of increase of the output of consumers' goods (1934, p. 161). The argument was presented again in 'Price Expectations, Monetary Disturbances, and Malinvestment' (1939c, pp. 146–7, originally published in German in 1935) and finally developed in full in 'Profits, Interest and Investment' (1939) and in 'The Ricardo Effect' (1942). In 1939 Hayek, while still retaining the assumptions of stationary conditions and of an elastic supply of credit, conformed to the common usage of starting the analysis of the upswing of the cycle from a situation characterized by high unemployment (mainly concentrated in the sector producing capital goods), and by a fixed distribution of workers between the production of producers' goods and the production of consumers' goods. In addition, he assumed that money wages could not be reduced in the short run.

In Part II of his 1939 essay, Hayek examined how the system approaches full employment. He envisaged three stages 'in the process of investment and saving': a first stage in which 'it will be possible to invest more and at the same time to increase the output of consumers' goods so as to leave the real wages of the increased number employed unchanged'; a second stage in which, while it will still be possible to invest more without decreasing the output of consumers' goods, 'the given (or only slightly enlarged) output of consumers' goods will have to be shared among the larger number of workmen now employed and real wages will fall; and a third stage, only mentioned because it was the one already examined in *Prices and Production*: 'a further increase of investment will be possible only at the price of an actual decrease in the output of consumers' goods' (1939b, p. 44, n. 1).

The 1939 essay, with its new assumptions and its partially new analysis, was a reply to the many criticisms of the kind mentioned above. Here in particular Hayek admitted that in both cases of a growing population and of unused resources, his early conclusion (in *Prices and Production*) was 'erroneous', and that credit expansion could help to increase employment. For, Hayek says:

> capital will now grow in 'height' and 'width' at the same time, [...] There can be little doubt that with much unused equipment in the consumers' goods industries and large surplus stocks in all the late stages of production it will be possible for recovery to proceed a long way before the prices of consumers' goods and profits will rise and real wages fall. [...] [T]his means that total money incomes must increase by exactly the amount by which saving and investment lead to the employment of formerly unemployed resources. [...]The increase of money incomes in this case really means that future savings are anticipated. (1939b, pp. 40, 41, 45, 46)

Nevertheless, as soon as the economy approaches full employment, Hayek comes back again to his main thesis:

> since the amount of unused capacity in the consumers' goods industries is even in the depth of a depression usually fairly limited, [...] the point is bound to come when the demand for consumers' goods will rise more rapidly than the supply of consumers' goods, and profits in the consumers' goods industries will begin to rise. [...] [I]f the rate of interest does not rise [...] [we] get then the anomalous position that [...] the discrepancy between the demand for consumers' goods and the supply of consumers' goods must get larger and larger. It is this anomaly [...], that every further increase in investment will increase profits on consumers' goods still further, that makes the position inherently unstable. (1939b, pp. 54–6)

The argument provided repeatedly by Hayek in support of this thesis was that 'the more "capitalistic" [...] the type of investment undertaken, the slower will be the rate at which after any given interval a given expenditure of investment will contribute to the output of consumers' goods' (1939b, p. 49). This means that, under the assumption of diminishing returns, incomes grow faster than the output of consumers' goods, reaching a point when the output of consumers' goods does not make any further progress. This in turn means that, under the assumption of unchanged time-preference schedules, the more entrepreneurs use their bank loans to increase the production of producers' goods, the more the prices of consumers' goods tend to rise, the more the profits of their producers tend to grow and real wages to fall, and the more the disequilibrium grows. From this argument Hayek deduced that, in order to prevent the prices of consumers' goods from rising faster than the prices of producers' goods, the rate of voluntary saving must progressively increase (1939b, p. 53), or the banks must expand credit at a 'progressively increasing rate'. Although in 1939 Hayek did not discuss explicitly the rate of

credit expansion, that rate seems implicit in his discussion of how to perpetuate the 'cumulative increase of net investment' which characterizes the later
stages of the boom (1939b, p. 54, n. 2). Hayek had, strangely, already defined
such a rate of credit expansion in *Monetary Theory and the Trade Cycle*
(p. 215), much before having provided a clear rationale for it. But if, as
Hayek believed, there is little reason to assume that in these circumstances
the propensity to save of the community will increase, the situation will
remain unstable whatever the banks do. If they maintain an increasing rate of
credit expansion, the unbalanced development of the economy grows wider.
And if they slow down the rate of credit expansion, the prices of consumers'
goods, as well as the profits of their producers, immediately start to rise faster
than the prices of producers' goods, thus initiating the crisis.

Now, in Hayek's theory as presented so far, the occurrence of the crisis is
due to the inevitable shortage of voluntary saving which manifests itself as
soon as credit expansion ceases. But the occurrence of such a 'shortage of
saving' is not self-evident. If the money wages remained constant, and if the
banks continued to expand credit, the prices of the producers' goods would
still increase, and the profits gained by their producers might be voluntarily
saved. It is true, as Hayek asserted, that under the assumption of diminishing
returns the propensity to save should progressively increase, but – as Hicks
pointed out – it is not clear why entrepreneurs should not be interested in
increasing it (Hicks, 1967, p. 209, n. 1). However, in Hayek's theory money
wages do rise. Hayek stated repeatedly that in the latter stages of the boom
incomes of wage earners will be rising because of the amount of money
available to entrepreneurs for investment. In that case it would seem that the
reason why credit creation does not generate sufficient voluntary saving is to
be found in the redistributive effects of changes in monetary factors. The
credit expansion distributes real income in favour of entrepreneurs, in particular to those producing capital goods, as is made clear by the existence of
forced saving.

The effects of the cessation of credit expansion are less clear, for Hayek's
statements on this point – which are scattered here and there in several essays
– appear rather contradictory. In particular, as Sraffa pointed out, it is not
clear which class of people should save or is responsible for not saving
(Sraffa, 1932, p. 45, n. 1). In his reply to Sraffa, Hayek conceded that 'the shift
of incomes from a class less inclined to save to a class [of entrepreneurs]
more so inclined' may ultimately have produced 'some real saving' (Hayek,
1932, p. 242; cf. also 1939c, p. 147). At the same time he insisted that

> as soon as the competition of entrepreneurs for the factors of production has
> driven up wages in proportion to the increase in money, and no additional credits
> are forthcoming, the proportion [of the total real income] which [entrepreneurs]

are able to spend on capital goods must fall. This means [...] that they will be able
to replace their capital only at the same rate as before the forced saving took
place, and their capital will, therefore, be gradually worn down to something
approaching its former state. (1932, p. 243)

In 'The Ricardo Effect' Hayek provided a further clarification of this point.
While *money* wages may have been driven up 'to the discounted value of the
expected price of the marginal product of labour', *real* wages are below 'the
figure corresponding to the low rate of interest' (1942, p. 143). In this
disequilibrium position, neither entrepreneurs nor workers seem responsible
for the shortage of saving: the former because, owing to the fall in their total
profits, they will be unable to maintain and replace all the capital which is the
product of forced saving; the latter because, besides the fact that by definition
their propensity to save is almost zero, they are getting less than their due.
Then the question still remains. Who is consuming too much or is not saving
enough? A possible solution to this puzzle is to be found in a note in Hayek's
essay 'The Ricardo Effect'. Here finally we discover that Hayek assumes that
the *rentiers* are responsible for the actual rate of saving:

> An increase in the sum of money wages will enable labour to encroach on the real
> income of the rentier class. But the rise in money wages necessary to give an
> increased number of people the same real income per head at the expense of the
> people with fixed money incomes would have to be very large indeed – so large
> that it is not likely to be offered by entrepreneurs. (1942, p. 143, n. 2)

The identification of the class of rentiers as 'the consumers' whose unchanged propensity to save prevents the workers from reaching the appropriate level of real wages (i.e. who make the prices of consumers' goods rise
more than money wages, or 'the real wages to fall relatively to the product
prices'), is an important element in explaining why, even if the new more
roundabout processes of production had been completed, as soon as the credit
creation comes to an end the producers of consumers' goods would gain
higher profits in the face of higher money wage bills. Nevertheless, it will be
noted that the conclusion reached by Hayek either in his reply to Sraffa, or in
the case analysed in 'The Ricardo Effect' rests on the assumption, actually
suggested by Sraffa, that entrepreneurs cannot increase their savings because
the fall in the rate of interest has been so large that they are getting not only a
smaller rate of profit, but also a smaller proportion of total real income (cf.
Sraffa, 1932, p. 47, n. 1). Hayek seemed to believe that this was invariably
the case in the later stages of the boom (Hayek, 1942, p. 143).

Hayek's contemporary critics

Hayek's use of the general principles of pure economic theory, including capital theory, may be regarded as the main sources of the difficulties he encountered. But Haberler's critique, as well as the critiques by Hansen, Robertson, and others does not seem very convincing. For example, Haberler's final argument against Hayek's theory was that in a 'progressive economy' (which was excluded in Hayek's analysis) the prices of the final output tend to fall and, consequently, a 'constant rate' of credit expansion would not cause any increase in the prices of the final output (Haberler, 1937, p. 59). Nor does Robertson's argument for the rejection of Hayek's thesis about the inevitable destruction of all capital goods which were the product of forced saving seem appropriate. His claim that 'the railways built in the 'forties are still with us!' (Robertson, 1966a, p. 68, n. 4) introduced an element – invention – which, again, was foreign to Hayek's analysis.

It is difficult to evaluate to what extent the criticisms levelled at Hayek derived from their authors' neglect of Hayek's assumptions, and to what extent those authors would have reached the same conclusion as Hayek had they assumed full employment *and* stationary conditions. Many of them, in their own trade cycle theories, were dealing with credit creation and forced saving within a dynamic context. Changes in real data were usually regarded as the most obvious prerequisite for an analysis of the economic disturbances. In several cases it was because of these changes that some authors could reach the conclusion that not all capital produced by way of forced saving had to go to waste. The general reluctance to accept Hayek's theory was more often due to a failure either to grasp or to keep in mind what – besides the full employment starting-point – was really unique to Hayek's trade cycle theory, namely Hayek's claim that the occurrence of trade cycles could be due to monetary changes alone. Even the case of Robertson's notion of 'induced lacking', which seemed to offer an additional endogenous mechanism in the formation of the supply of saving, does not seem to provide an alternative to Hayek's 'dogmatic' conclusion.

It is well known that Robertson's trade cycle theory was primarily a non-monetary theory: the upswing of the cycle was generated by several possible real causes, all connected with alterations in 'utility and cost', although the occurrence of inventions was repeatedly emphasized. The upper turning point of some 'constructional' cycle was due to an over-estimate of the amount of savings available for taking over the real capital produced or, in Robertson's phraseology, to a deficiency of 'the activity of short lacking'.

Nonetheless, in *Banking Policy and the Price Level* (1926, 1932) Robertson devoted his attention to the understanding of the monetary mechanism and of appropriate policies to reduce industrial fluctuations. It is here that credit expansion (and the connected process of forced saving) comes into play in his analysis as an essential cooperating factor either in the case of economic progress or of cyclical fluctuations. And it is here that Robertson made use of his notion of 'Induced Lacking'.

The origin of the notion of induced lacking, and the possible influence of Keynes on Robertson's use of that concept have already been noted by Presley (1979, pp. 113–16, 227–8), by Bridel (1987, pp. 112–14), and by others. In *Banking Policy and the Price Level* (1932, ch. V; see also 1966b), induced lacking was defined as the activity which may occur when, owing to the increase in the price level, 'people hold money off the market, and refrain from consuming the full value of their current output, in order to bring the real value of their money stocks up again to what they regard as an appropriate level' (1932, p. 49). Robertson saw induced lacking as part of what he named 'imposed lacking' (a combination of induced lacking and automatic lacking), the result of this activity being that the rise in the price level which characterizes the upswing of a constructional cycle financed by credit expansion is restrained, and the same amount of imposed lacking which is needed to build up the new increment of circulating capital now incorporates a voluntary element by way of induced lacking.

In order to see if this new analysis allows Robertson to escape from 'too rigid' and 'dogmatic' results as those of Hayek, let us first consider the role which the notion may play in Robertson's analysis of a constructional cycle (1932, ch. VI). Here Robertson gives several reasons for an acceleration in the rise of the price level necessary to secure correspondence between demand and supply of net saving ('New Lacking'). In the face of rising prices those entrepreneurs who merely desire to keep the real value of their circulating capital intact will be obliged to expend an increased stream of money. Even if it is in their power to provide it because their money receipts are likely to increase in the same proportion, 'it is at least likely that instead of doing so [they] will increase [their] personal consumption or [their] permanent investment, and will apply to the bank for [...] increased money loan[s] to cover their trade expenses'. The same is supposed to happen with those entrepreneurs who, by repaying to the banks an obligation which has remained fixed in terms of money, find themself in possession of a surplus. For, Robertson says, 'it is by no means certain that this surplus will be placed, either directly or through the transformation of Hoarding, at the disposal of the class [of entrepreneurs who are raising fresh loans]: it may be utilized for increased consumption or increased permanent investment' (1932, pp. 72–3). Other reasons for accelerating the rise in the price level come from the 'consuming public'. If prices are expected to go on rising, 'people tend to hurry on with the purchase of goods'. At the same time, those classes of people with fixed money incomes, on whose shoulders the burden of forced saving falls, 'are likely to seek to evade some of the Lacking imposed on them by revising their views as to the appropriate relation between Real Hoarding and expected Real Income. As these classes (consisting largely of *rentiers* and salaried persons) are normally large hoarders, they have a considerable margin available for Dis-hoarding without incurring acute inconvenience' (1932, pp. 75–6).

All the above arguments describe behaviour on the part of both entrepreneurs and the consuming public that seems to go in the opposite direction from that prescribed by an activity – induced lacking – which, by offsetting the effect of increased investment on prices, should diminish the burden of forced saving. On the other hand the cause of the crisis which Robertson saw in the 'inability on the part of the banking-system to extract from the public by any means the Short Lacking required to maintain the current or projected volume of output' (1932, p. 79), or the impossibility of establishing *'any* price-level high enough to elicit the requisite supply of Lacking' (1932, p. 89) seems to confirm that Robertson himself did not regard induced lacking as an activity which might be operative in the later stages of the boom, when the demand for savings is more pressing. Indeed, in a note addressed to Keynes, Robertson made clear that his definition of induced lacking does *not* involve 'attempting to raise the proportion of money-stock/income *above its original level*'. In that note he seemed also ready to agree with Keynes that his treatment of that notion in *Banking Policy and the Price Level* might have given 'an exaggerated idea of the importance of [...] Induced Lacking in practice', and that 'the actual course of prices' may be dominated by the fact that people 'may *not* aim at restoring their balances to the old proportion (1932a, pp. 291, 293).

But the difficulty of dealing with this notion of induced lacking does not stop here. For in a subsequent note addressed to Keynes, Robertson redefined induced lacking by stating that '*Voluntary* Lacking [measured in real terms] or Saving [measured in money terms] may be subdivided into (a) Induced, which is required in order to restore a proportion of money stock to money income which has been infringed [...], (b) other or Spontaneous', and finally that '[t]he fact that Induced Lacking *may* be performed by persons who find the absolute real value of their money stock *increased* makes it [...] inconvenient to try to group together Automatic and Induced Lacking in a supergroup Imposed Lacking, as is done in *BP* p. 49 – "Imposed" is too strong a word to fit this case' (1932b, p. 302, 304n, emphasis added).

Now, the admission that in certain stages of the inflation the activity of induced lacking is not operative does not reduce its conceptual relevance. As pointed out by Presley, in Robertson's analysis the only circumstance in which induced lacking is operative must be found, presumably, in the case of a 'growing economy' with a uniform expansion of circulating capital coupled with a mild inflation (Presley, 1979, pp. 227–8). But in the case considered here – the final stage of a constructional boom – it is difficult to reject Patinkin's claim that 'in [Robertson's] discussion of the real sector of the economy it was assumed that the behaviour was independent of absolute price level and dependent only on relative prices' (letter from D. Patinkin to D.H. Robertson, July 1951; cf. Presley, 1979, pp. 223, 305).

Indeed, it would be difficult to ascribe to Robertson any intention of distinguishing between the final equilibrium of a barter economy and the final equilibrium of a monetary economy if only one remembers that, like Hayek in 1931, in *Banking Policy and the Price Level* Robertson started his inquiry into money, credit and the trade cycle by forewarning the reader that 'while the *results* of the causes of change [...] are correctly expressed by making the hypothesis of direct barter, the chain of motives brought into play by a monetary economy is different, and the results are reached in part by a different route' (1932, p. 23).

As a concluding remark it might be suggested that the source of the critics' confusion and uncertainty is not simply their failure to take proper account of Hayek's assumption of a stationary economy. It was the fact that both Hayek and Robertson, and the other critics were working within the neoclassical framework. In the absence of imperfections or rigidities the only equilibrium of the economy is full employment equilibrium. Any analysis of the changes wrought by the impact of credit, or by any other changes in monetary factors, could be conducted as either comparative static, or as exercises in disequilibrium analysis. In so far as most writers chose the latter then the very indefinite nature of disequilibrium analysis permitted the construction of a variety of competing models – such is the arbitrary element inherent in all disequilibrium analysis. It was then easy to argue at cross purposes.

References

Bresciani-Turroni, C. (1934), '*Monetary Theory and the Trade Cycle. By Friedrich A. Hayek*' (book review), *Economica* (August), 344–7.

Bridel, P. (1987), *Cambridge Monetary Thought. The Development of Saving–Investment Analysis from Marshall to Keynes*, London: Macmillan.

Cabiati, A (1932), 'La moneta "neutrale" in un libro del Dr. Hayek', *La Riforma Sociale*, **XLIII**, 194–204.

Colonna, M. (1990), 'Introduzione' to F.A. Hayek, *Prezzi e produzione. Il dibattito sulla moneta*, ed. by M. Colonna, Napoli: Edizioni Scientifiche Italiane.

Ellis, H.S. (1934), *German Monetary Theory 1905–1933*, Cambridge, Mass.: Harvard University Press.

Fanno, M. (1933), Letter to Prof. F. Vito, dated 10 July 1933, published in Fanno M. (1992), *Teoria del credito e della circolazione*, ed. by A. Graziani and R. Realfonzo, Napoli: Edizioni Scientifiche Italiane, 252–3.

Haberler, G. von (1937), *Prospérité et Dépression. Étude Théorique des Cycles Économiques*, Genève: Société des Nations.

Hansen, A. H. and Tout, H. (1933), 'Annual Survey of Business Cycle Theory: Investment and Saving in Business Cycle Theory', *Econometrica*, **I** (April), 119–47.

Hansen, A.H. (1951), *Business Cycles and National Income*, New York: W.W. Norton.

Hayek, F.A. von (1931) *Preise und Produktion*, Wien: Verlag von Julius Springer.

Hayek, F.A. von (1932), 'Money and Capital. A Reply', *The Economic Journal*, **XLII** (June), 237–49.

Hayek, F.A. von (1933), *Monetary Theory and the Trade Cycle*, trans. by N. Kaldor and H.M. Croome, London: Jonathan Cape. Reprinted by Augustus M. Kelley in 1975. Originally published in German in 1929 as *Geldtheorie und Konjunkturtheorie*, Wien–Leipzig: Hölder–Pichler–Tempsky A.G.

Hayek, F.A. von (1934), 'Capital and Industrial Fluctuations', *Econometrica*, **II** (April), 152–67.

Hayek, F.A. von (1935), *Prices and Production*, 2nd ed., London: George Routledge & Sons. 1st ed., 1931, London: George Routledge & Sons.

Hayek, F.A. von (1935a), *Collectivist Economic Planning*, London: George Routledge & Sons.

Hayek, F.A. von (1935b), 'The Maintenance of Capital', *Economica*, new series, **2** (August). Reprinted in Hayek, F.A. (1939), 83–134.

Hayek, F.A (1937), 'Economics and Knowledge', *Economica*, new series, **4** (February), 33–54.

Hayek, F.A. von (1939), *Profit, Interest and Investment*, London: George Routledge & Sons.

Hayek, F.A. von (1939a), 'The Present State and Immediate Prospects of the Study of Industrial Fluctuations', in Hayek, F.A. (1939), 171–82. Originally published in German in 1933.

Hayek, F.A. von (1939b), 'Profits, Interest and Investment, in Hayek, F.A. (1939), 3–71.

Hayek, F.A. von (1939c), 'Price Expectations, Monetary Disturbances and Malinvestments', in Hayek, F.A. (1939), 135–56. Originally published in German in 1935.

Hayek, F.A. von (1942), 'The Ricardo Effect', *Economica* new series, **9** (May), 127–52.

Hayek, F.A. von (1984), 'Intertemporal Price Equilibrium and Movements in the Value of Money', in Hayek, F.A. (1984), 71–117. Originally published in German in 1928 as 'Das intertemporale Gleichgewichtssystem der Preise und die Bewegungen des "Geldwertes"', *Weltwirtschaftliches Archiv*, **28** (2), 33–76.

Hayek, F.A. von (1984a), *Money, Capital & Fluctuations. Early Essays*, ed. by R. McCloughry, London: Routledge & Kegan Paul.

Hicks, J. (1967), 'The Hayek Story', in J. Hicks, *Critical Essays in Monetary Theory*, Oxford: Clarendon Press.

Kaldor, N. (1939), 'Capital Intensity and the Trade Cycle', *Economica*, **6** (February), 40–66.

Kaldor, N. (1942), 'Professor Hayek and the Concertina-Effect', *Economica*, **9** (November), 359–82.

Keynes, J.M. (1931), 'The Pure Theory of Money. A Reply to Dr. Hayek', *Economica*, **11** (November), 245–56.

Knight, F.H. (1935), 'Professor Hayek and the Theory of Investment', *The Economic Journal*, **XLV** (March), 77–94.

Marget, A.W. (1932), 'Review of *Prices and Production*', *Journal of Political Economy*, **40** (April), 261–6.

Neisser, H. (1934), 'Monetary Expansion and the Structure of Production', *Social Research*, (November), 434–57.

Presley, J.R. (1979), *Robertsonian Economics*, London: Macmillan.

Robertson, D.H. (1932), *Banking Policy and the Price Level*, 2nd ed., London: P.S. King & Son. 1st ed., 1926.

Robertson, D.H. (1932a), 'Notes' (a reply to Keynes's 'Notes on the Definition of Saving'), in Keynes, J.M. (1973), *The Collected Writings of John Maynard Keynes*, ed. by D. Moggridge, London: Macmillan, vol. XIII, 289–94.

Robertson, D.H. (1932b), 'Some Revised Definitions of Saving and Allied Concepts', in: Keynes, J.M. (1973), *The Collected Writings*, cit. vol. XIII, 302–7.

Robertson, D.H. (1966), *Essays in Money and Interest*, London: Fontana Library.

Robertson, D.H. (1966a), 'Industrial Fluctuation and Natural Rate of Interest', in Robertson, D.H. (1966), pp. 64–74. Originally published in 1934 in *The Economic Journal* (December).

Robertson, D.H. (1966b), 'Saving and Hoarding', in Robertson, D.H. (1966), 46–63. Originally published in 1933 in *The Economic Journal*, (September).

Röpke, W. (1936), *Crises and Cycles*, London: William Hodge & Company.

Sraffa, P. (1932), 'Dr. Hayek on Money and Capital', *The Economic Journal*, **XLII** (March), 42–53.
Wilson, T. (1939–40), 'Capital Theory and the Trade Cycle', *The Review of Economic Studies*, **VII**, 169–79.

3 Credit money and cyclical crises: the views of Hayek and Fisher compared*

Mario Seccareccia

Much has been written about the fundamental debate between Hayek and Keynes during the 1930s.[1] The critical issues involved are, perhaps, too well known to necessitate much further discussion, except to say that they pertain to the significance of scarcity, especially with regard to the capital market. Indeed, in an attempt to dramatize the importance of the neoclassical concept of scarcity and to draw a sharp division between their two methods, Hayek (1941, p. 373) provokingly described Keynes's supposed vision of the unbounded productive capacity of the economic system as the 'economics of abundance'. As is all too well known, Hayek continued to hold this hostile position towards Keynesian economics and to characterize the postwar inflationary environment as the result of the implementation of misguided Keynesian policies.

The purpose of this paper is to provide a comparison of the ideas of Hayek and another celebrated economist whose views are not so diametrically opposed and whose position would undoubtedly qualify him as being member of the same opposing camp: Irving Fisher. Both Hayek and Fisher explained the Depression of the 1930s as the result of excessive credit creation and overindebtedness, and both proposed unique policy options to deal with the crisis that entailed large-scale institutional changes within the monetary system. Yet, while Fisher opted in favour of the 'nationalization' of money – a policy proposal which was to remain for some time the hallmark of the Chicago school – Hayek was ultimately to support the 'denationalization' of money. These fundamental policy differences were the logical denouement of developments within deeply-rooted traditions in monetary theory going back to medieval times. These respective currents of thought, to which these two economists individually subscribed, generally viewed with distrust the role played by money in disturbing the underlying economic order, especially when the monetary decision-making process is left to the sole discretion of the state, through its central bank, or to commercial banking institutions, through their interaction with the public.

*Special thanks must go to D. Laidler of the University of Western Ontario and to H.-M. Trautwein of Universität Hohenheim for the very helpful written comments. The author also benefited from the useful discussions with A. Cohen and J.N. Smithin of York University. The usual disclaimer applies.

Credit money and overinvestment: Hayek's explanation of cyclical crises

As a preamble to a discussion of Hayek's theory of cyclical crises, it would perhaps be worthwhile to note that his early theory was conceptually inter-woven with his general philosophical viewpoint regarding the nature of social order. Hayek had been strongly influenced by eighteenth-century think-ers such as Smith and Mandeville who portrayed social coordination as an evolutionary process resulting from the spontaneous actions of individuals (cf. Barry 1979, pp. 6–7). From this general philosophical outlook, Hayek conceives the history of market economies as tracing a long process of evolution and adaptation, periodically interrupted by the actions of govern-ment (Hayek 1988, chs 1 and 2).

As pointed out by Tomlinson (1990, p. 50), for Hayek this government abuse has been especially noteworthy in the monetary domain. The state's exclusive right to issue and regulate money, its so-called right of seigniorage, has made it possible for governments to wield enormous powers historically and to acquire real resources at the expense of the community. Monetary controversies during the middle ages over the state's privilege to issue money, regardless of its commodity value, present for Hayek a striking example of how governments have exploited and defrauded the public (Hayek 1976b, p. 27). As illustrated by the work of such early scholastic writers as Oresme (1355) and then subsequently reiterated by nineteenth-century currency theo-rists, such as Ricardo, the fundamental issue was about how to establish rules or standards of conduct that would prevent the state from unduly appropriat-ing the community's real resources and disrupting individual exchanges. This is why such early writers favoured a metallic standard that would somehow tie the hands of the monetary authorities to a set rule.

While sympathizing with the Ricardian position, Hayek rejected the frame-work of the quantity theory that underlay these earlier approaches. This was so primarily for methodological reasons having to do with the use of aggre-gates (cf. Dow 1985, p. 170). The quantity theory rested on such questionable aggregative concepts as the 'price level' and the 'quantity of money', that can neither be identified unambiguously in the actual world nor serve any purpose in explaining the behaviour of specific causal processes (Hayek 1931, pp. 4–5; 1928, p. 90). Hayek's ideas, as they emerged during the late 1920s, appear to be much more closely connected with those of the nine-teenth-century loanable funds theorists such as Henry Thornton and Thomas Joplin who had directed their attention to the saving–investment mechanism in generating monetary disturbances. However, their analysis was not rigor-ously formalized before the turn of the century when, first through the work of Knut Wicksell (1898), and then as elaborated by Hayek's mentor in eco-nomics, Ludwig von Mises (1912), it found its clearest expression.

In its simplest form, the Wicksellian system can be dichotomized into a real sector from which there emerges a set of expected 'real' or 'natural' rates materializing in the productive sphere that are captured by a specific variable – the natural rate of interest – determined principally by technical progress. There exists, in addition, a sophisticated monetary or financial sector that is capable of supplying credit *ex nihilo* without the savings constraint and which can fix a 'money' rate of interest exogenously by the decisions of a monetary authority. Any discrepancy between these two autonomously-given rates, leading to a divergence between the flows of saving and investment, brings about a cumulative expansion or contraction of the key endogenous variable in the system, the price level of consumption goods. In particular, an increase in the natural rate, unaccompanied by an equivalent rise in the money rate, would activate a process of expansion of the flow of investment and, with it, result in the general lengthening of the time-structure of production in accordance with Austrian theory. As Wicksell (1898, p. 133) put it:

> ... those processes which for technical reasons involve a long period of production will become relatively more profitable, while those processes where the period of production is short will become relatively less profitable. There will ensue an expansion in the one and a contraction in the other.

Associated with this general restructuring of the temporal profile of production in favour of more time-intensive activities is a rise in the prices of consumption goods or, as Wicksell (1906, p. 14) described it: '... the enforced general reduction of consumption which results from the creation of credit constitutes just that accumulation of real capital which is the indispensable preliminary to a higher degree of capitalistic production.' This 'enforced real saving' becomes the necessary concomitant of a disequilibrium in the capital market due to a discrepancy between the money rate and the natural rate of interest. Only through an explicit central bank policy that would tie the value of the bank rate to the level of the natural rate could overall price fluctuations be prevented.

The Austrian theory of the trade cycle, especially as developed by Hayek during the late 1920s, is a mere extension of this Wicksellian monetary analysis. In three important books written on the topic – *Monetary Theory and the Trade Cycle* (1933a), which was the English publication of an original set of articles first published in German during 1928–29; *Prices and Production* (1931), which reproduced a series of four lectures delivered at the University of London during the 1930–31 session; and *Profits, Interest and Investment, and Other Essays on the Theory of Industrial Fluctuations* (1939), which was a collection of articles written between 1929 and 1939 – Hayek spelled out the essentials of his theory. As pointed out in the preface to his

1933 book, while in that publication he emphasized 'the *monetary causes* which *start* the cyclical fluctuations', in his 1931 work he concentrated on the *'successive changes in the real structure of production*, which *constitute* those fluctuations' (emphasis in original) (1933a, p. 17).

In accordance with Austrian marginalist principles, Hayek proceeds in these volumes by using an analysis that is not unlike that of Wicksell and von Mises before him. Following the Jevons–Böhm-Bawerkian theory of capital, a community's resources devoted to the process of production can be theoretically organized in time-specific stages (Hayek 1931, Lecture II). The higher the stage of production, the more temporally remote the stage is from the ultimate consumer and, therefore, the more the economy is geared towards producing intermediate goods or, simply, investment goods. The lower the stage of production, instead, the less roundabout is the process and, hence, the more the economy is involved in the production of consumers' goods. In a stationary environment, the aggregate shape of this time-structure of production is not, however, arbitrary or determined exogenously. It depends, rather, on the public's time-preference which regulates the community's decision to allocate its income between consumption and saving. Through the mechanism of saving, in particular, individuals communicate their desire that factor resources be placed in the higher stages of producing investment goods. Through their consumption spending, instead, individuals express their preference that factor resources be withdrawn from the more roundabout activities and shifted to the lower stages of producing consumers' goods. It is, however, through the ubiquitous capital market, whose role is to permit the smooth transfer of the pool of savings to entrepreneurs wanting to invest in lengthier or more roundabout methods of production, that these signals or desires on the part of the public are formally transmitted. Unless there are institutional obstacles to the proper clearing of the capital market, a natural or equilibrium rate of interest emerges. This rate then equates the real savings of the community to a desired level of accumulation on the part of firms, with whose activities is associated an equilibrium time-structure of production over time.

How then can an economy be dislodged from this equilibrium time path with its underlying real saving–investment relations disturbed? For Hayek (1933a, ch. IV), the culprit is bank credit which arises from a discrepancy between the natural rate and the money rate of interest along Wicksellian lines. In a monetary system in which commercial banks behave as neutral intermediaries, instability leading to structural maladjustment can never arise since the aggregate flow of investment would be limited by the available savings fund as in a barter or real-exchange economy. However, as soon as this constraint on the capacity of the banking system to create credit money is lifted, the money rate of interest can be set independently of the natural rate and thus result in cyclical problems of overinvestment. It is, for Hayek (1933a, p. 87), the highly elastic nature of credit money which constitutes the perturbing factor in what is perceived as an intrinsically self-regulating productive system.

As in Wicksell before him and in the modern writings on the theory of the real business cycle, let us suppose that a discrepancy between the natural and money rates occurs, say, because of supply shocks pushing upwards the natural rate. If the banking system does not adjust proportionally the money rate of interest, it becomes profitable for enterprises to obtain loans, and thus the flow of bank credit rises. This credit expansion induces firms to adopt methods of production which are more roundabout. The swelling of demand for investment goods pushes upwards the relative price of these goods of higher order (cf. Mises, 1928, p. 120) and brings about a slow transfer of resources away from the lower stages of producing consumption goods. As the switching towards more capitalistic production progresses, consumer goods become increasingly scarce, and thus, as had also been argued by Spiethoff (1923, p. 123), a shortage of circulating capital appears. If the economic expansion had taken place by a voluntary cut in household consumption, the fall in demand for consumption goods would have made available the circulating capital necessary for the expanding investment goods industries. In this case, however, no such voluntary releasing of resources has taken place, since the additional investment is financed by bank credit in excess of household saving. In accordance with Wicksellian theory, therefore, consumption good prices must rise in such a way as to realize a 'forced saving' equal to the proportion of total investment expenditures financed by the endogenous flow of credit money.

This cumulative process of expansion in favour of the more roundabout processes of production can only be sustained by a continued infusion of newly-created credit money. Since the consuming public has not voluntarily endorsed the modification in the time-structure of production engendered by the existence of an artificially low money rate of interest, the forced saving connected with the rising prices of consumption goods will ultimately bring the pendulum to swing in the opposite direction by rendering production in the consumer goods industries more profitable for entrepreneurs. Once the credit expansion ceases, entrepreneurs are thus induced to return to less capitalistic methods involving a painful process of sectoral restructuring. In this way, it is the shortage of voluntary savings that triggers a renewed transfer of resources from the higher to the lower stages of production, a reduction of output in the investment goods sector relative to the consumption goods sector, and a large-scale abandonment of projects having longer gestation periods. The business cycle is thus viewed largely as an endogenous see-saw movement that 'consists essentially in alternating expansions and contractions of the structure of capital equipment.' (Hayek 1931, p. 101). In this respect, there is embedded an underlying general pattern of economic behaviour which '*must* always recur under the existing credit organization, and that it thus represents a tendency inherent in the economic system ...' (Hayek 1933a, pp. 146–7).

By the early 1930s, Hayek had thus advanced a comprehensive theory of the genesis and recurrence of the trade cycle in which excessive bank credit, made possible by the historical development of the fractional reserve system of banking, was seen as '*the* decisive factor determining the course and extent of the cyclical movement.' (Hayek 1933a, p. 170). This is why he had described his approach as the 'Additional Credit Theory of the Trade Cycle' (Hayek 1933a, p. 177), later to be dubbed the monetary overinvestment theory of cyclical fluctuations (cf. Haberler 1941, p. 33). The proximate cause of the crisis is the malinvestment of capital undertaken during the boom phase, which in turn has been brought about by the original misalignment of interest rates in the capital market that occasion an excessive expansion of bank credit and affect relative prices (cf. Steele, 1992).

During the 1930s and 1940s, however, his theory brought sharp criticism. Economists such as Sraffa (1932), Kaldor (1937), Wilson (1940), and even those more sympathetic to his theories, such as Phillips, McManus and Nelson (1937, p. 132) questioned the logical coherence of some of the theoretical constructs employed by Hayek, such as the 'natural rate of interest' and 'time-structure of production', while others, such as Hansen and Tout (1933), and Kaldor (1939, 1942) also questioned the empirical relevance of much of his analysis.[2] For instance, only under the questionable assumptions of full employment and price flexibility can an increase in employment in the investment goods sector, due to an extension of bank credit, be effected at the expense of employment in the consumption goods sector and result in a rise in prices of consumer goods. For Hayek, the overinvestment crisis comes about because the general rise in the price of consumer goods that precedes it eventually brings upward pressures on interest rates, makes production of investment goods less attractive, and precipitates the downturn. In the world of the 1930s, then characterized by massive unemployment, continued low interest rates and sticky prices, such a theory appeared to have extremely limited applicability. This is why he was to propose a competing mechanism of the downswing that no longer relied on the original Wicksellian analysis whereby ensuing changes in interest rates play the main disrupting role.

In the first article of his 1939 book *Profits, Interest and Investment*, Hayek sought to provide an alternative explanation of the overinvestment crisis in terms of the so-called 'Ricardo effect'. As in his previous works, Hayek remains a determined opponent of the general application of the acceleration principle that points to growth in consumption spending as a stimulus to investment. Near the peak of the boom where prices of consumer goods are quickly rising and real wages are falling, the investment goods sector becomes relatively less profitable. This is because firms in the consumption goods sector (now beginning to face lower relative labour costs) reduce their demand for labour saving machinery and eventually bring about a decline of overall production in the investment goods sector. This 'deceleration principle', as Hayek (1939, p. 33) described it, acts in the same way as would a rise in interest costs and brings about a decline in investment. In either case, however, the argument is the same: 'the turn of affairs will be brought about in the end by a "scarcity of capital" independently of whether the money rate of interest rises or not.' (1939, p. 32). Yet, in both the former and latter scenarios, the ultimate cause is the existence of excessive credit money propelling forward the cyclical process (cf. Moss and Vaughn, 1986, p. 555).

Debt money and overinvestment: Fisher's explanation of cyclical crises
In conformity with the basic Wicksellian model, Hayek's analysis relied on the explicit assumption of the money supply as an endogenous variable. Bank credit fills the gap between investment and saving, thereby enabling prices to vary; but the supply of this credit money is not exogenous as it is postulated within the framework of the quantity theory. The modern reader would be surprised to find, however, that while espousing the strict logic of the quantity theory as it had been handed down from Jean Bodin, through John Locke, David Hume, David Ricardo and the currency school, Irving Fisher defended a theory of cyclical crises substantively similar to that of Hayek.

In his *Purchasing Power of Money*, which was perhaps the most widely-accepted pre-Friedmanite statement of the quantity theory, Fisher asserted:

> Since ...a doubling in the quantity of money ... will not appreciably affect either the velocity of circulation of money or of deposits or the volume of trade, it follows necessarily and mathematically that the level of prices must double. ... there is no possible escape from the conclusion that a change in the quantity of money (M) must normally cause a proportional change in the price level (the p's). (1911, pp. 156–7)

This proportionality and unidirectional causality was *ultimately* true, however, only if one were to abstract from what Fisher described as 'the temporary effects during the period of transition' (1911, pp. 55–6). During transition periods, characterized by price fluctuations, none of the parameters of the quantity equation could be taken as given. In particular, not only would nominal interest rates be moving in the same direction as prices, but so would velocity and the ratio of deposits to currency in circulation. In this regard, the supply of money (widely defined) is very elastic in the short run and, as in the Wicksell–Hayek model, depends on the movement in the rate of interest.

Indeed, he argued that one of the chief objects of *The Purchasing Power of Money* was 'to show that the peculiar behaviour of the rate of interest during transition periods is largely responsible for the crises and depressions in which price movements end.' (1911, p. 56).

To understand Fisher's original explanation of the key short-run role played by interest rates, let us briefly describe the sequence of events depicting the upswing of his typical credit cycle. Following Fisher, we shall first suppose that some exogenous monetary factor disturbs the original state of equilibrium so that aggregate prices are displaced upwards. This initial rise in prices drags with it the nominal interest rate, but not sufficiently to neutralize its disequilibrating effect in the capital market where demand for loans increases due to higher expected profits. As bank loans rise, the ratio of deposits to currency also moves endogenously upwards to fuel still further the inflationary process. This upward price spiral continues as long as 'the interest rate lags behind its normal figure' (Fisher 1911, p. 60). One may be tempted to presume that Fisher's so-called 'normal figure' would coincide with the magnitude of Wicksell's 'natural' or 'normal' rate of interest but, unfortunately, he remained terribly vague on this question. Sooner or later, however, this maladjustment in the rate of interest is rectified, with the result being a collapse in investment which now initiates the downward spiral of the price level. The downward process is analogous to the upward movement, and taken together they constitute the credit cycle. On this basis, Fisher blames the banking system for not adjusting the interest rate quickly enough to avert booms and depressions. Hence, to prevent abnormal oscillations in prices: 'The rate of interest ... ought to be high when the prices are rising; and, reversely, ... ought to be low while prices are falling' (Fisher, 1914, p. 84).

Though never accepting the notion of a business *cycle* in the sense of *regular* oscillations in economic activity, from his early analysis of transition periods Fisher began to take an increased interest in explaining aggregate fluctuations. Two articles published in the *Journal of the American Statistical Association* (1923, 1925) and another in the *International Labour Review* (1926) are of particular importance, especially the latter, in making him progenitor of the first empirical 'Phillips curve'. For instance, in referring to his graphical exposition of the relation between unemployment and the percentage rate of change in prices, Fisher (1926) reached the following conclusion about the causal forces at work:

> ... as the economic analysis ... certainly indicates a causal relationship between inflation and employment or deflation and unemployment, it seems reasonable to conclude that what the charts show is largely, if not mostly, a genuine and straightforward causal relationship; that the ups and downs of employment are the effects, in large measure, of the rises and falls of prices, due in turn to the inflation and deflation of money and credit. (1926, p. 792)

Hence, consistent with his previous analysis of the 'transition periods', it is the excessive credit expansion which first creates the upward price spiral and, in turn, alters the level of employment and unemployment as overall demand expands.

It is, however, Fisher's impression of the 1929 panic which definitively placed him within the camp of the overinvestment theorists. In his *Stock Market Crash and After* (1930a), Fisher points his finger to the inordinate credit expansion that propelled upwards stock prices, led to overconfidence and excessive speculation, and eventually culminated in the crash. In *Booms and Depressions* (1932a), he was to articulate further this position in favour of the monetary overinvestment theory of the crisis.[3] Fisher began by pointing out that debts are not only essential to both production and distribution but, in essence, a monetary economy may actually be ruled by little else. He pointed out that 'what is called the "money market" is really the debt market' (1932a, p. 8); and he accused previous analysts of cyclical fluctuations, such as W.C. Mitchell and A.H. Hansen, for having made 'no specific mention of a debt cycle' (1932a, p. 61).

In accordance with the Wicksell–Hayek analysis, the process of overindebtedness begins with some exogenous event:

> ... of which the most common appears to be new opportunities to invest at a big prospective profit, ... such as through new inventions, new industries, development of new resources, opening of new lands or new markets. Easy money is the great cause of over-borrowing. (1932a, p. 11)

It is thus the gap between expected profit and borrowing costs which triggers the credit expansion. A vicious spiral of growth in debts and prices takes hold that is fuelled by declining real interest rates and the falling real value of these contracted debts. This upward spiral, however, cannot continue indefinitely. Although Fisher does not furnish the more complete account of the cyclical turning point found in Hayek, innumerable shocks to confidence, such as a dramatic rise in interest rates, may first slow down the cyclical expansion and then ultimately push the pendulum to swing in the opposite direction. Once the psychosis of expansion is broken, certain individuals now begin to seek the liquidation of some of their financial claims. The huge burden of the previously-accumulated financial debt serves only to magnify any initial downswing, as its real value starts to rise with the decline of some security prices. With confidence waning, the downward spiral intensifies and leads to what Fisher describes as *stampede liquidation* involving distress selling. This process of falling commodity prices and debt deflation continues as the money stock shrinks and ultimately brings the economy to the trough of a depression. With the burden of the debt largely eliminated through distress selling and widespread bankruptcies, a dynamic capitalist economy cannot for very long remain stuck in the trough. Once again some exogenous event finally initiates a new recovery with the pendulum repeating its upward climb.

Instead of Hayek's *credit cycle*, we have a periodic swinging back and forth constituting Fisher's *debt cycle*. Yet it would be hard not to notice the obvious similarities between the two views. In a sense, they are merely two sides of the same coin. A state of overindebtedness, when studied from the angle of individual economic agents, would be a situation of excessive credit when looked at from the angle of the banking and financial system. Moreover, both view the cyclical instabilities as a problem of maladjustment in the capital market. For Fisher, the overindebtedness occurs because the rate of interest lags behind the rate of return on investment. For Hayek, it is because the money rate fails to adjust to the natural rate, thus causing a disequilibrium between investment and saving. While packaged differently with, for instance, the emphasis on aggregate prices rather than relative prices, the core of their analysis is the same.[4]

Except for a few historians of economic thought, such as Schumpeter (1954, p. 1122) and Pribram (1983, pp. 350, 480), who have at least recognized the strong affinity between these two strands of thought on the business cycle, Fisher has been almost entirely eclipsed by Hayek in the literature on the overinvestment theory of the trade cycle. Perhaps one reason, emphasized by Schumpeter (1954), has to do with the very different styles of their written works. Hayek attempted meticulously to situate his research within the broad currents of thought which preceded him and to address the economics profession. Fisher, on the other hand, was somewhat of a propagandist whose more descriptive research effort was directed at convincing the informed public about the nature of the crisis. Hence, as Schumpeter (1954, p. 1122) put it: '... the true dimensions of what is really a great performance [by Fisher] are so completely hidden from the reader's view that they have to be dug out laboriously and in fact never impressed the profession as they should have done.' A possible second reason may have to do with the more glaring contradictions evident in Fisher's analysis. Of these, the most conspicuous is his continued belief in the quantity theory when, in fact, his implicit assumption of an endogenous debt money seemed completely to deny the former theory's usefulness in explaining cyclical fluctuations. Finally, a third reason why Fisher's theory did not take over the driver's seat in the continued discussions over the business cycle may have to do with the simple fact that it was Hayek who found himself at the centre of the theoretical debates, especially with Keynes, during the 1930s. Despite its more limited success *vis-à-vis* Hayek's work, Fisher's analysis still retains some influence among modern students of financial crises (cf. Wolfson 1986, p. 25) and continues to form the backbone of theoretical research on financial instability by such contemporary heterodox economists as Hyman Minsky (1982).

Proposals for monetary stabilization: nationalization versus denationalization of money

The common thread that binds together the views of Hayek, Fisher and other monetary overinvestment theorists of the period, including such disparate writers as Ludwig von Mises and Frederick Soddy, is the belief that cyclical crises are the essential feature of a highly elastic monetary system. If only one could guarantee the degree of discipline within the monetary and financial system that would least disturb the all-important capital market in which savers and investors transact, such dramatic swings in economic activity would have become a thing of the past.

Two distinct policy views had surfaced during the 1930s around which these various monetary overinvestment writers rallied. The most well known, to which Fisher subscribed and became one of its leading advocates, is the '100 per cent money' plan for monetary stabilization. This specific proposal is also sometimes described as the 'Chicago plan', since a group at the University of Chicago led by Henry Simons (1934) had already formulated it much before Fisher (1935), and it had widespread support in numerous intellectual circles at the time. Paradoxically, Fisher (1932b) had already shown interest in the 'stamped money' proposal for stabilizing velocity and eliminating widespread hoarding – a proposal first advanced by Silvio Gesell.[5] The Gesell plan, however, did not directly address the problem of overindebtedness which was seen by Fisher as the central problem of the Depression, but, rather, it tackled the problem of excessive hoarding or underconsumption – as was highlighted, for instance, by Keynes in the *General Theory*. The 100 per cent money plan, instead, pointed directly to the problem of excessive debt and offered what appeared to be an easy and direct solution.

The essence of Fisher's plan was to break the link between money and bank credit, which was the by-product of fractional reserve banking, and hence 'to divorce the process of creating and destroying money from the business of banking' (1935, p. xvii). Through the creation of a currency commission, the government would transform into cash a large fraction of the assets of commercial banks up to 100 per cent reserves without, however, changing the total volume of the circulating medium during the interim process. Only the composition of the money supply would necessarily change. As in the Chicago plan, Fisher proposed to set up two types (or branches) of financial institutions. There would be the 'check' or 'deposit' banks (or departments) that would be mere 'storage warehouses' in which deposits would be covered by 100 per cent reserves, and 'investment' banks (or departments) that would acquire their capital through security issue and would perform the pure intermediary function of lending institutions intervening in the capital market. In this way, he argued: 'the banks could no longer *over*lend by manufacturing money out of thin air so as to cause inflation and a boom' (1935, p. 17). With the proper working of the capital market, money and real rates of interest would move *pari passu* with the profitability of the real economy and would no longer deviate as with an elastic monetary system, i.e. 'interest rates would seek their level in a natural way according to the supply and demand for loans, and real rates would not be perverted by misbehaviour of money' (1935, p. 140).

Debt money is thus a *false* money that inevitably distorts the interest rate structure in the capital market and results in overinvestment. His plan for 100 per cent money would thus force the monetary system to behave as a commodity money economy of the type founded on the basic principles of the original Peel Act of 1844 in Britain, but without the troubles associated with convertibility (1935, pp. 191–2). The restoration of a properly working capital market, that would function in accordance with the neoclassical principles of supply and demand, was thus of overriding concern to Fisher. To quote him again *in extenso:*

> Normally, be it repeated, investments come out of savings. If investments are made out of borrowed money, they should at least come out of somebody else's savings. But, under the 10% system, they may, for an ominous period, seem to come out of thin air, that is, out of inflation. ... [or] out of the forced savings, *i.e.* reduced consumption, of the public from the resulting higher cost of living.
>
> This sort of false investment and shifted sacrifice is exactly what happens under the 10% system, ... Under the 100% system, not only will savings and investments go hand in hand, as they should, but real and nominal interest will also go hand in hand, as they should. Both investment and interest will follow supply and demand normally, unperverted by changes in the value of the dollar.
>
> In short, to restore to the rate of interest its proper significance and its function of clearing the loan market would be one of the merits of the proposed 100% system. (1935, pp. 144–6)

Moreover, as had been emphasized by Simons (1934, 1936), it would reduce the discretionary powers of the monetary authorities and would further transfer economic decision making within the framework of the market. Indeed, Fisher's proposal for nationalizing money was seen as a way to return to a world first idealized by Oresme and Ricardo in which a *quasi*-commodity money was supreme and to restore 'the conservative safety-deposit system of the old goldsmiths, before they began lending out improperly what was entrusted to them for safekeeping.' (1935, p. 18).[6]

Given the similar concerns about forced saving and the need to restore a smooth functioning capital market, one would expect that Hayek would have been more supportive of those numerous economists, in Chicago and elsewhere, pushing for the 100 per cent money plan during the 1930s. This however did not happen. For one thing, the plan still entrusted the currency commission, the sole monopolist, with too much discretionary power in effectuating changes in the money supply. Yet, of even greater importance, a crucial question (that others were also raising at that time [cf. Lin 1937, pp. 76–86]) was left unanswered about the endogenous nature of monetary creation. Hayek wrote:

> The most serious question which it raises ... is whether by abolishing deposit banking as we know it we would effectively prevent the principle on which it rests from manifesting itself in other forms. ... the question is whether, when we prevent it from appearing in its traditional form, we will not just drive it into other and less easily controllable forms. Historical precedent rather suggests that we must be wary in this respect. The Act of 1844 was designed to control what then seemed to be the only important substitute for gold as a widely used medium of exchange and yet failed completely in its intention because of the rapid growth of bank deposits. Is it not possible that if similar restrictions to those placed on bank notes were now placed on the expansion of bank deposits, new forms of money substitutes would rapidly spring up or existing ones would assume increasing importance? And can we even to-day draw a sharp line between what is money and what is not? Are there not already all sorts of 'near-moneys' like saving deposits, overdraft facilities, bills of exchange, etc., which satisfy at any rate the demand for liquid reserves nearly as well as money?' (1937, pp. 82–3)

Reiterating the same type of arguments that banking theorists had used against the Peel Act (and the currency school that was behind it) in the nineteenth century, and in a style that predates the famous Radcliffe Report in Britain, Hayek contended that money is a sort of will-o'-the wisp that cannot be so rigidly controlled by merely regulating one bank liability – the demand deposits of commercial banks. In fact, writers such as Simons (1936, p. 17), had recognized this problem now described as bank liability management, but no satisfactory answer was forthcoming from them.[7]

Given his rejection of the quantity theory framework and his preoccupation with relative price effects, Hayek first opted in favour of a less direct approach to dealing with the problem of monetary overinvestment that still accorded importance to central bank interest rate policy. The only effective check against cyclical maladjustments is a Wicksellian policy of raising interest costs whenever inflation occurs so as to abort the boom that must inevitably lead to a severe retrenchment in demand for investment goods. In order to minimize the damages that credit money can inflict on the real economy, Hayek proposed a policy of 'neutral money'. However, Hayek's policy of neutral money was, for practical purposes, nothing more than a slightly modified version of the original Wicksellian norm for the stabilization of the price level. For Hayek, this meant 'the stabilization of some average prices of the original factors of production' (1933b, p. 161), since these factor prices would provide the early warnings of the coming structural maladjustment and crisis. From this, there later came the view that the monetary authorities should take aim at a precise composition of a standard basket of commodities whose price they should try to keep constant in terms of their domestic currency (cf. Hayek, 1943). However, recognizing the possible inefficacy of an interest rate policy, by the late 1930s he reverts to a more nebulous policy of linking the volume of notes and deposits to changes in their reserves within the framework of some revitalized international gold standard (1937, pp. 84–94).[8] Unfortunately, this proposal was never very clear and, during the postwar period, it was finally abandoned in favour of a purely private institutional structure of the monetary and banking system.

Instead of moving in the direction of Fisher, Simons and Allais, later followed by Friedman (1960, 1967), who more quietly also gave his support to the 100 per cent money scheme, during the 1960s and 1970s Hayek was to follow a path largely inspired by nineteenth-century advocates of the banking school. It is well known that both Tooke and Fullarton, through their famous law of reflux, had argued that competitively-issued currency could never be overissued by private banks as to generate inflation.[9] In this endogenous money world in which there exists 'free trade' in banking, competitive pressures are brought to bear on each individual unit not to endanger their respective position in the credit market by bringing about the depreciation of their private bank notes through overissuing. Hayek, who had never felt comfortable with either the older or modern quantity theorists, was to develop this position, especially in an important work published in 1976 on the denationalization of money. Much like the nineteenth-century banking theorists, Hayek argued that there exists no sharp distinction between money and non-money. Hence, a programme for 'nationalizing' money *à la* Fisher–Simons or, for that matter, a policy of targeting any precise monetary aggregate, would be completely misdirected and futile. He explained:

> ... although we usually assume there is a sharp line of distinction between what is money and what is not ... so far as the causal effects of monetary events are concerned, there is no such clear difference. What we find is rather a continuum in which objects of various degrees of liquidity, or with values which can fluctuate independently of each other, shade into each other in the degree to which they function as money.
>
> I have always found it useful to explain to students that it has been rather a misfortune that we describe money by a noun, and that it would be more helpful for the explanation of monetary phenomenon if 'money' were an adjective describing a property which different things could possess to varying *degrees*. (1976b, p. 47)

Since money represents a complete array of different objects of liquidity, it becomes desirable for a community to be given the choice as to which object(s) should 'have currency' in the marketplace. The government's exclusive right to issue money and to bestow on its own currency the status of legal tender has been a method adopted historically not to secure benefits to the community at large but rather, as was understood by medieval theorists, to assert and strengthen the coercive powers of the state. Being subject to persistent political pressure from interest groups, the State must constantly use its prerogative to finance government expenditures. One of the unfortunate consequences of this abusive activity by the state is therefore the recurring cycle in economic life (Hayek 1979, pp. 7–8).

How then can this abuse, and its accompanying cyclical instabilities, be eliminated? Hayek's answer is that the public should be given the choice of currency in a market setting, i.e. the freedom 'to refuse any money they distrusted and to prefer money in which they had confidence' (1976a, p. 18). Following a deeply-rooted tradition in Austrian monetary theory that could be traced to Menger (1871, p. 261) and Mises (1912, pp. 69–71), for Hayek money should be the result of market interaction and not a creature of the state. With the abolition of the state's monopoly of money and the current legal restrictions on the production of competitive currencies lifted, private banks would finally be on an equal level in being able to create circulating media and compete for consumer confidence. From this, Hayek is able to show that contrary to public belief, the result would be the application of a Gresham's law *in reverse.* This is because the original law applied '*only* to different kinds of money between which a fixed rate of exchange is enforced *by law*' (Hayek 1976b, p. 35). As soon as such a legal equivalence is broken, then the opposite would be true. The public would choose to hold that currency with the least probability of depreciation and, thus, select the currency that would be the least prone to overissuing. The role of the state in this context is solely to provide the legal framework within which individuals can effectively carry out their market activities and banks produce the desired constant purchasing-power monies. Free competition in currencies would thus be left to resolve the endemic problem of booms and depressions.[10]

Just as with the 100 per cent money plan, numerous objections have been raised against Hayek's proposal, especially from those strong defenders of what may be described as the 'hard money' view. In addition to the traditional arguments about economies of scale in producing fiduciary money and in acquiring and disseminating information about the relative exchange rates of the existing currencies (as referred to by 'free banking' theorists such as Glasner, 1989, p. 176), Friedman and Schwartz (1986, p. 54) point to the importance of the lender-of-last-resort function which has kept the modern economies from facing generalized liquidity crises. Of greater theoretical importance, there is the problem of logical coherence in Hayek's analysis. We have seen that while Hayek's explanation of cyclical crises has changed very little since the 1930s regarding the distorting effect an elastic credit money has on the structure of relative prices and production (Hayek 1984, p. 34), his policy position evolved a great deal. From a hybrid Wicksellian interest-rate policy of economic stabilization, Hayek jumped to a policy of competing currencies. In his early days he was describing the dangers of an excessive flow of credit money in stretching the gap between investment and saving. This overinvestment process was propelled forward by firms' demand for credit. The later Hayek, instead, tended to emphasize the inherent instabilities arising from the existence of a given *stock* of state-produced outside money. Indeed, all his examples of competing currencies and the desirability of constant purchasing-power money pertain to some form of outside money. As soon as inside money enters the picture, Hayek's argument that the market will necessarily favour the more stable bank liabilities becomes less obvious. After all, while his argument would probably apply to the behaviour of creditors (households) in the financial market who would have a clear preference for price stability, the opposite would be true with regard to debtors (firms) who would justifiably have a stake in a depreciating liability. The stabilizing effect of Hayek's scheme thus becomes less certain in a world in which credit money is dominant. Nevertheless, Hayek did provide an alternative policy for those monetary overinvestment writers dissatisfied with either the 'hard money' Fisher plan or with the modern Friedmanite policy of 'controlling' a predefined monetary aggregate.

Concluding remarks
The object of this paper has been to review two competing versions of what has commonly been described as the monetary overinvestment theory. Both the Hayek model and the Fisher version are substantively the same in providing a particular explanation of what they had dubbed respectively the *credit* or *debt* cycle. Given the two-sided nature of the cyclical phenomenon, each author highlighted different characteristics of the monetary process. Hayek pointed to the endogenous nature of the excessive credit creation while Fisher identified the endogenous process of debt expansion made possible by the existence of an elastic monetary system. Given the different emphasis, from otherwise similar explanations of the cyclical phenomenon, Hayek and Fisher derived policy conclusions that can best be characterized as polar opposites.

Though both advocated institutional frameworks that would somehow discipline the financial markets, Hayek's libertarian position in favour of free markets encouraged practically a complete disengagement of the state in money matters. Money would still be created endogenously through the mechanism of competitive banking, but the state would wield no special monopoly powers. In contrast, Fisher's different conception of the role of the state brought him to contrive an alternative scheme. For Fisher, it was not so much the abuse of the monetary authorities as the abuse of the loan and deposit functions of private banking. In this light, the government's prerogative to control the creation of money should be maintained, but strict control should be exercised over the capability of banks to create excessive debt. As in the textbook analogy of the vertical money supply curve, private banks would be restricted to a role of pure financial intermediation and the money stock would become an exogenous variable as in a pure commodity money world!

It is an ironic twist of fate that, in modern discussions of money matters, it has been post-Keynesian writers, the closest disciples of the dreaded inflationist and interventionist Keynes (cf. Hayek 1972, Part III), who have championed the cause of endogenous money by using arguments against Friedmanite monetarism that, in essence, differ little from those of Hayek (cf. Moore, 1988).[11] Yet, perhaps, still more ironic, in this broad Post-Keynesian family, the ideas of Fisher, whose plan was to render the money supply purely exogenous, have also gained credence. Not only have Fisher's ideas on debt deflation been married to those of Keynes to constitute a peculiar brand of business cycle theory *à la* Minsky but, of still greater interest, Fisher's proposal for 100 per cent money has been revived as a possible formula for eliminating the burden of overhanging debt and for dealing with contemporary financial crises just as in the 1930s (cf. Hotson, 1987; and Kregel, 1990). Moreover, others, such as Tobin (1985) and Litan (1987), have rekindled a variant of the Fisher plan that would establish a set of so-called 'narrow banks' (or deposit banks) according to the 100 per cent proposal so as to deal more effectively with the rising cost of deposit insurance in a currently deregulated financial system. Given the problems correctly referred to by Hayek long ago and the implications of such a policy in relying exclusively on the accommodating role of the monetary authorities in directly financing economic growth, some of the current scepticism about the efficacy of such 'new' proposals is understandable. As the old dictum goes: *plus ça change, et plus c'est la même chose!*

Notes

1. Cf. Hudson (1988), Parguez (1988) and, among others, Dostaler (1990).
2. His original assumptions of full employment and price flexibility in *Prices and Production* were by far the major irritants for any economist looking at the realities of the Great Depression. In addition, the phenomenon of production periods becoming longer or shorter during the successive phases of the business cycle (the so-called *concertina effect*) was for numerous authors, such as Kaldor (1939, p. 40; 1942, p. 363), practically non-existent or, at best, insignificant in the real world. For an excellent summary of some of the issues, see Moss and Vaughn (1986, pp. 545–65).

3. In his *Booms and Depressions, Some First Principles* (1932a), he writes: 'The theory which, perhaps, comes nearest to covering the same ground as the one set forth in this book is the overinvestment theory. But, if overinvestment be accomplished without borrowing, there would seem to be no reason to imagine that it would be followed by anything so severe as a stock market crash, or an epidemic of bankruptcies, or vast unemployment' (1932a, pp. 63–4). Other writers of the period also noticed the substantive similarity between his views and that of other overinvestment writers; see Haberler (1941, p. 115).

4. It is surprising and, indeed, perplexing that in Fisher's biography, written by his son Irving N. Fisher (1956), there is no mention of any possible correspondence with Hayek and other overinvestment theorists. In fact, only in Fisher's *100% Money* (published in 1935, *i.e.* after *Booms and Depressions*) is there a reference in the bibliography to Hayek's German edition of *Prices and Production* (1931).

5. For details of the original proposal, see Gesell (1929), and Seccareccia (1988).

6. Fisher also points out that '... in fact, under the 100% system, there would be a much better chance that the old-style gold standard, if restored, would operate as it was intended' (1935, p. 17).

7. As is well known, during the early 1980s this problem of liability management was also a significant factor in discrediting the monetarist targeting of monetary aggregates. However, some modern advocates of 100 per cent money have recognized this problem and have sought alternatives. For instance, Maurice Allais, who subscribed to the Fisher plan as early as in 1947, points out: 'Despite its many interesting features, the Chicago school's proposal completely neglects the monetisation of banks' and financial intermediaries' assets other than those corresponding to demand deposits, and it cannot be considered as an adequate remedy for the major blemishes afflicting the credit system today' (1984, p. 524). While accepting the Fisher proposal of separating banking institutions into *deposit banks* and *lending banks*, Allais argues that the monetary authorities should at the same time also control the asset/liability structures of the *lending banks* (1984, p. 525).

8. Later on, for instance, Hayek writes: 'Although I have myself given currency to the expression 'neutral money' (which, as I discovered later, I had unconsciously borrowed from Wicksell), it was intended to describe this almost universally made assumption of theoretical analysis and to raise the question whether any real money could ever possess this property, and not as a model to be aimed at by monetary policy. I have long since come to the conclusion that no real money can ever be neutral in this sense, and that we must be content with a system that rapidly corrects the inevitable errors' (1976b, p. 69)

9. See, for instance, the recent studies by Arnon (1991, pp. 166 et seq.) and Skaggs (1991, pp. 457–80).

10. Free competition in currencies should not, however, be confused with 'free banking' as it was originally understood in the nineteenth century. For instance, Hayek points out that 'the demand for free banking at the time was wholly a demand that the commercial banks should be allowed to issue notes in terms of the single established national currency. So far as I am aware, the possibility of competing banks issuing *different* currencies was never contemplated' (1976b, p. 71). For further discussion, see Glasner (1989, pp. 175 et seq.)

11. Contrary to Moore (1988) who has argued that it is money-supply endogeneity which fundamentally distinguishes the neoclassical from the post-Keynesian conception of money, one would like to think that there is something substantially more than merely the endogeneity/exogeneity issue that separates them. After all, in addition to Hayek and other Austrian writers, modern neoclassical theorists of the real business cycle, as well as contemporary 'free banking' advocates, also rely on a specific endogeneity of the money supply and, in that sense, are indirectly espousing a view of the monetary system that is not monetarist and is more like that of Hayek.

References

Allais, M. (1947), *Économie et intérêt*, Paris: Imprimerie nationale et Librairie des publications officielles, English trans. 1984.

Allais, M. (1987), 'The Credit Mechanism and Its Implications', in G. R. Feiwel (ed.) *Arrow and the Foundations of the Theory of Economic Policy*, New York: New York University Press.

Arnon, A. (1991), *Thomas Tooke, Pioneer of Monetary Theory*, Aldershot, England: Edward Elgar.

Barry, N.P. (1979), *Hayek's Social and Economic Philosophy*, London: Macmillan.

Dostaler, G. (1990), 'Aperçus sur la controverse entre Keynes et Hayek', *Économies et sociétés*, **24**, (6) juin, 135–62.

Dow, S.C. (1985), *Macroeconomic Thought, A Methodological Approach*, Oxford: Basil Blackwell.

Fisher, I. (1911), *The Purchasing Power of Money, Its Determination and Relation to Credit, Interest and Crises*, New York: Macmillan.

Fisher, I. (1914), *Why is the Dollar Shrinking? A Study in the High Cost of Living*, New York: Macmillan.

Fisher, I. (1923), 'The Business Cycle Largely a Dance of the Dollar', *Journal of the American Statistical Association*, **18**, (144) December, 1024–28.

Fisher, I. (1925), 'Our Unstable Dollar and the So-called Business Cycle', *Journal of the American Statistical Association*, **20**, (149) June, 179–202.

Fisher, I. (1926), 'A Statistical Relation between Unemployment and Price Changes', *International Labour Review*, **12**, (6) June, 785–92.

Fisher, I. (1928), *The Money Illusion*, New York: Adelphi.

Fisher, I. (1930a), *The Stock Market Crash and After*, New York: Macmillan.

Fisher, I. (1930b), *The Theory of Interest*, New York: Macmillan.

Fisher, I. (1932a), *Booms and Depressions, Some First Principles*, New York: Adelphi.

Fisher, I. (1932b), *Stamp Scrip*, New York: Adelphi.

Fisher, I. (1933), 'The Debt-Deflation Theory of Great Depressions', *Econometrica*, **1**, 337–57.

Fisher, I. (1935), *100% Money*, New York: Adelphi.

Fisher, I.N. (1956), *My Father Irving Fisher*, New York: Comet Press Books.

Friedman, M. (1960), *A Program for Monetary Stability*, New York: Fordham University Press.

Friedman, M. (1967), 'The Monetary Theory and Policy of Henry Simons', *Journal of Law and Economics*, **10** (October), 1–13.

Friedman, M. and A.J. Schwartz (1986), 'Has Government Any Role in Money?' *Journal of Monetary Economics*, **17**, (1) January, 37–62.

Gesell, S. (1929), *The Natural Economic Order*, Berlin-Frohnau: Neo-Verlag.

Glasner, D. (1989), *Free Banking and Monetary Reform*, Cambridge: Cambridge University Press.

Haberler, G. von (1941), *Prosperity and Depression, A Theoretical Analysis of Cyclical Movements* (3rd ed.), Geneva: League of Nations.

Hansen, A.H. and H. Tout (1933), 'Annual Survey of Business Cycle Theory: Investment and Saving in Business Cycle Theory', *Econometrica*, **1**, 119–47.

Hayek, F.A. von (1928), 'Intertemporal Price Equilibrium and Movements in the Value of Money', *Money, Capital & Fluctuations, Early Essays*, London: Routledge & Kegan Paul, 1984.

Hayek, F.A. von (1931), *Prices and Production*, London: George Routledge & Sons.

Hayek, F.A. von (1933a), *Monetary Theory and the Trade Cycle*, London: Jonathan Cape.

Hayek, F.A. von (1933b), 'On "Neutral Money"', *Money, Capital & Fluctuations, Early Essays*, London: Routledge & Kegan Paul, 1984.

Hayek, F.A. von (1937), *Monetary Nationalism and International Stability*, London: Longmans, Green & Co.

Hayek, F.A. von (1939), *Profits, Interest and Investment, and Other Essays on the Theory of Industrial Fluctuations*, London: George Routledge & Sons.

Hayek, F.A. von (1941), *The Pure Theory of Capital*, Chicago: University of Chicago Press.

Hayek, F.A. von (1942), 'The Ricardo Effect', *Economica*, **9**, (34) May, 127–52.
Hayek, F.A. von (1943), 'A Commodity Reserve Currency', *Economic Journal*, **53**, (210) June–September, 176–84.
Hayek, F.A. von (1972), *A Tiger by the Tail*, London: Institute of Economic Affairs.
Hayek, F.A. von (1976a), *Choice in Currency: A Way to Stop Inflation*, London: Institute of Economic Affairs.
Hayek, F.A. von (1976b), *Denationalisation of Money, An Analysis of the Theory and Practice of Concurrent Currencies*, London: Institute of Economic Affairs.
Hayek, F.A. von (1979), 'Toward a Free Market Monetary System', *Journal of Libertarian Studies*, **3**, (1) Spring, 1–8.
Hayek, F.A. von (1984), 'The Future Unit of Value', in P. Salin (ed.), *Currency Competition and Monetary Union*, Boston: Martinus Nijhoff.
Hayek, F.A. von (1988), *The Fatal Conceit: The Errors of Socialism*, Chicago: University of Chicago Press.
Hixson, W.F. (1991), *A Matter of Interest: Re-examining Money, Debt and Real Economic Growth*, New York: Praeger.
Hotson, J.H. (1987), 'The Keynesian Revolution and the Aborted Fisher-Simons Revolution or the Road Not Taken', *Économies et sociétés*, **21**, (9) septembre, 185–219.
Hudson, M. (1988), 'Keynes, Hayek and the Monetary Economy', in J. Hillard (ed.), *J.M. Keynes in Retrospect: the Legacy of the Keynesian Revolution*, Aldershot: Edward Elgar.
Kaldor, N. (1937), 'Annual Survey of Economic Theory: The Recent Controversy on the Theory of Capital', *Econometrica*, **5**, 201–33.
Kaldor, N. (1939), 'Capital Intensity and the Trade Cycle', *Economica*, **6**, (21) February, 40–66.
Kaldor, N. (1942), 'Professor Hayek and the Concertina-Effect', *Economica*, **9**, (36) November, 359–82.
Kregel, J.A. (1990), 'The Policy Implications of the Current Bank Crisis, or Is Free Market Capitalism Compatible with Endogenous Money', Paper presented at Conference on Monetary Theory and Policy, Jerome Levy Institute, Bard College, November.
Lin, L. (1937), 'Are Deposits Money?', *American Economic Review*, **27**, (1) March, 76–86.
Litan, R. (1987), *What Should Banks Do?*, Washington, D.C.: The Brookings Institution.
Machlup, F. (ed.) (1976), *Essays on Hayek*, New York: New York University Press.
Menger, C. (1871), *Principles of Economics*, Glencoe, Ill.: The Free Press, 1950.
Minsky, H.P. (1982), *Can 'It' Happen Again? Essays on Instability and Finance*, Armonk, N.Y.: M.E. Sharpe.
Mises, L. von (1912), *The Theory of Money and Credit*, London: Jonathan Cape, 1934.
Mises, L. von (1928), 'Monetary Stabilization and Cyclical Policy', *On the Manipulation of Money and Credit*, New York: Free Market Books, 1978.
Moore, B.J. (1988), *Horizontalists and Verticalists, The Macroeconomics of Credit Money*, Cambridge: Cambridge University Press.
Moss, L.S. and K.I. Vaughn (1986), 'Hayek's Ricardo Effect: A Second Look', *History of Political Economy*, **18**, (4) Winter, 545–65.
O'Driscoll, G.P. (1977), *Economics as a Coordination Problem, The Contributions of Friedrich A. Hayek*, Kansas City: Sheed Andrews & McMeel.
Oresme, N. (1355), 'A Treatise on the Origin, Nature, Law and Alterations of Money', in C. Johnson (ed.), *The De Moneta of Nicholas Oresme and English Mint Documents*, London: Thomas Nelson & Sons, 1956.
Parguez, A. (1988), 'Hayek et Keynes face à l'austérité,' in G. Dostaler and D. Éthier (eds), *Friedrich Hayek, Philosophie, Économie et Politique*, Montréal: ACFAS.
Phillips, C.A., T.F. McManus and R.W. Nelson (1937), *Banking and the Business Cycle, A Study of the Great Depression in the United States*, New York: Macmillan.
Pribram, K. (1983), *A History of Economic Reasoning*, Baltimore: Johns Hopkins University Press.
Schumpeter, J.A. (1954), *History of Economic Analysis*, New York: Oxford University Press.
Seccareccia, M. (1988), 'Système monétaire et loi d'entropie: la notion gesellienne de préférence pour la liquidité', *Économies et sociétés*, **22**, (9) septembre, 57–71.

Seccareccia, M. (1990), 'The Two Faces of Neo-Wicksellianism during the 1930s: The Austrians and the Swedes', in D.E. Moggridge (ed.), *Perspectives on the History of Economic Thought*, Vol. 4, Aldershot: Edward Elgar.

Simons, H.C. (1934), A *Positive Program for Laissez Faire: Some Proposals for a Liberal Economic Policy*, Chicago: University of Chicago Press.

Simons, H.C. (1936), 'Rule versus Authority in Monetary Policy', *Journal of Political Economy*, **44**, (1) February, 1–30.

Skaggs, N.T. (1991), 'John Fullarton's Law of Reflux and Central Bank Policy', *History of Political Economy*, **23**, (3) Fall, 457–8.

Soddy, F. (1934), *The Role of Money*, London: George Routledge & Sons.

Spiethoff, A. (1923), 'Business Cycles', *International Economic Papers*, no. 3, 1953, 75–171.

Sraffa, P. (1932), 'Dr. Hayek on Money and Capital', *Economic Journal*, **42**, (165) March, 42–53.

Steele, G.R., (1992), 'Hayek's Contribution to Business Cycle Theory: A Modern Assessment', *History of Political Economy*, **24**, (2) Summer, 477–91.

Tobin, J. (1985), 'Financial Innovation and Deregulation in Perspective', *Bank of Japan Monetary and Economic Studies*, **3**, (2), 19–29.

Tomlinson, J. (1990), *Hayek and the Market*, London: Pluto Press.

Wicksell, K. (1898), *Interest and Prices*, London: Macmillan, 1936.

Wicksell, K. (1906), *Lectures on Political Economy*, London: George Routledge & Sons, 1935.

Wilson, T. (1940), 'Capital Theory and the Trade Cycle', *Review of Economic Studies*, **7** (June), 169–79.

Wolfson, M.H. (1986), *Financial Crises, Understanding the Postwar U.S. Experience*, Armonk, N.Y.: M.E. Sharpe.

4 Hayek's double failure in business cycle theory: a note

Hans-Michael Trautwein

Throughout his life, Friedrich August von Hayek firmly held the view that voluntary real saving is the prerequisite of undisturbed growth, whereas the creation of credit money in national banking systems causes inflation, forced saving and crises. Accordingly, Hayek's early contributions to economics, which lay in the field of business cycle theory, all circled around the proposition that monetary expansion is *the* endogenous cause of cyclical fluctuations.[1] In order to prove this point, Hayek used the notion of *intertemporal equilibrium*, in which money is neutral, as benchmark for the disequilibrium phenomena of the credit cycle. Extending the equilibrium reference to an interequilibrium growth path, he also used a *savings traverse*, on which additional voluntary savings finance a sustainable increase of output – contrary to the crisis in the wake of credit expansion and forced saving.

In the following it is argued that Hayek's monetary theory of the business cycle fails to support his well-known stand against 'easy money' policy and other anticyclical government action, because his theory has two crucial defects:

1. There is no link between equilibrium and disequilibrium. Intertemporal equilibrium and the business cycle are logically disparate states of economic systems that cannot be connected by transitions from neutrality to non-neutrality of money. Hence, the 'real savings/investment' mechanism provides no viable reference base for the analysis of a monetary economy. In terms of his own economics of credit creation, Hayek's distinction between voluntary and forced saving becomes irrelevant.
2. There are no inevitable turning points. Hayek's account of the business cycle gives no endogenous explanations of the changes from boom to crisis and from crisis to boom (or back into equilibrium).

Before these critical arguments can be spelt out, a summary of Hayek's concepts of intertemporal equilibrium, the credit cycle and the savings traverse is in place.

Intertemporal equilibrium

Hayek's concept of *intertemporal price equilibrium* explicitly includes changes in data, provided 'that no deviation from the expected cause of events takes place during the period' (1984a p. 85). The equilibrium of price movements is thus characterized by compatibility of all individual plans for present and future production and consumption. Although Hayek develops this equilibrium concept in a hypothetical barter system, he insists that this is only done to bring out the neutrality assumptions customarily employed in static equilibrium theory: '... that, while money is indeed present to facilitate indirect exchange, it can be neglected as a factor influencing the relative level of prices' (1984b p. 159). This means that business cycle theory should start with the classical monetary science fiction that, while money is not *qualitatively* neutral (as it makes the exchange of goods more efficient), it is *quantitatively* neutral in the sense of not affecting the price structure (cf. Samuelson, 1968 pp. 2ff).

Hayek moves on to explain that this equivalence of barter and neutral money is a purely analytical construct. In the real course of time, money is bound to be quantitatively non-neutral, since practically any change in the circulating volume of money represents a one-sided change in demand which is not counterbalanced by an equivalent change in supply. Money, therefore, breaks Say's law in its narrow sense because its quantitative fluctuations bring about a 'falsification of the pricing process, and thus a misdirection of production' (1933, p. 140).

Nevertheless, the intertemporal price equilibrium fulfils three central functions in Hayek's analysis of the business cycle. It serves:

- as *reference base* for the assessment of disequilibria in changes of prices and production (1984a, p. 75ff);
- as *point of departure*, from which any endogenous explanation of business cycles has to start (1935, p. 34); and
- as real-resource determined gravitation centre, from which the capital structure cannot escape by way of monetary credit expansion (1933, pp. 212ff, 1935, pp. 95ff and 1984a, pp. 75ff).

The credit cycle

In Hayek's view, 'the primary cause of *cyclical fluctuations* must be sought in changes in the volume of money' (1933, p. 140), which mislead investment decisions by distorting the intertemporal price signals of consumer preferences and resource availabilities. The primary cause of such changes in the volume of money must, in turn, be sought in the elasticity of credit supply. Due to the money multiplier inherent in the banking business, Hayek (1933, ch. IV) assumes this elasticity to be very high.

The price of credit is the money rate of interest. If, for some reason,[2] this rate comes to be lower than the equilibrium rate (i.e. the rate of return on capital, at which investments equal the supply of savings), credit demand will rise and additional credit money will be injected into the economy by lengthening the banks' balance sheets. Since the relatively interest-elastic production projects tend to be longer and more capital-intensive, the lengthening of banks' balance sheets triggers a lengthening of the processes of production. Thus 'the *monetary causes* which *start* the cyclical fluctuations...' are followed by '*successive changes in the real structure of production*, which *constitute* these fluctuations' (Hayek 1933, p. 17 – italics in original).

Starting from the full-employment equilibrium assumption, a credit expansion implies that producers of capital goods in the 'new' processes bid away resources from 'older' processes of production. As prices of capital goods and labour rise relatively to the prices of consumer goods, and as the rates of return on capital in the 'older' processes fall, a self-reinforcing redirection of capital towards the 'new', more capital-intensive processes begins (1935, Lectures II and III).

Sooner or later, however, the tide begins to turn. The output of consumption goods declines, whereas consumer preferences have not changed and money incomes have risen. Shortages of consumer goods thus drive up their prices. On one hand, this process constitutes the mechanism of 'forced saving'. On the other hand, it makes the redirection of resources back into shorter processes of consumer goods production profitable. But so long as the credit *expansion* continues to inject additional purchasing power into the more capital-intensive projects, money incomes lag behind, while the supply of consumer goods lags even further behind. 'Forced saving' continues to feed the boom.

This cannot go on forever since, at some point, the credit expansion must stop. In different writings, Hayek has offered three different reasons for a change in the elasticity of credit supply:

- The money rate of interest is a function of the default risk which, in turn, increases with the debt–equity ratio (1942, pp. 138ff and 1969, p. 283).
- In the course of a credit boom, the need of cash will increase along with money incomes and prices. The ensuing cash drain will force the banks to restrict credit supply (1933, p. 175).
- Even though there may be no reserve restrictions in terms of outside money, a credit expansion must stop before an accelerating rate of inflation makes money lose its function as the unit of account (1935, p. 151f and 1969, p. 282).

When the credit expansion stops, the completion of various 'new', capital-intensive projects will become unprofitable. The specific resources employed in these processes of production, both capital and labour, will become redundant, and even the unspecific resources may not be integrated into the remaining profitable processes without frictions. The credit boom is thus inevitably followed by unemployment and depreciation of capital, and the crisis is nothing but a cure of the price mechanism:

> The market process triggered by the injection of money... is a self-reversing process... Economic recovery must consist of liquidating the 'malinvestments' and reallocating resources in accordance with actual intertemporal preferences and resource availabilities (Garrison and Kirzner, 1989, p. 127)

The savings traverse

Hayek contrasts the self-reversing, futile process of 'forced saving' with an increase in *voluntary savings* that pushes the economy on to a *traverse* to a new equilibrium on a higher level of output (1935, Lectures II and III). If consumers change their time-preference such that they are willing to sacrifice an additional part of their claims to current output in exchange for more consumption in the future, the supply of savings in the loan markets rises, whereas the demand for consumer goods declines.

Hayek (1935, p. 84) admits that even this process may cause temporary discrepancies of supply and demand. But there is no need for cyclical adjustments since both the interest-rate mechanism and the price mechanism set the right signals for sustainable growth. The increase in voluntary savings reduces the market rate of interest which makes investment projects profitable that are both more capital-intensive and more productive. On the savings traverse even a temporary excess supply of consumer goods is functional: it serves as buffer stock against shortages before the restructuring is completed (1935, p. 88). Thus, Hayek does not trace out the traverse as a sequence of *dis*equilibria, as he does with the credit cycle. In his eyes, the traverse is a straight passage *inter equilibria*.

Equilibrium gap

In Hayek's concepts of intertemporal equilibrium and the savings traverse, money is *functional* and – by definition – *not dysfunctional*: it reduces transaction costs without distorting the price structure. Implicitly, the same applies to banks in equilibrium and on the traverse: they mediate payments and transfers of capital without creating excess demand by producing additional claims to output. A closer look at essential intertemporal aspects of money and banking reveals, however, that both are *neither functional nor dysfunctional* in the Hayekian equilibrium. The set of functions fulfilled by money and banking in the equilibrium is not identical with the set of their functions in the business cycle. Both 'states' are not just different episodes of the same economic process; they require logically disparate assumptions about expectations of future price movements. Hence, Hayek's equilibrium concept cannot serve as point of departure for the analysis of disequilibria in the cycle.

Where exactly is the gap? Hayek (1984a, p. 75) assumes both equilibrium and cyclical fluctuations to be results of utility maximization. Including the use of money and credit, his definition of equilibrium is one of rational behaviour under the restrictive assumption of 'a correct anticipation of future price movements' (1935, p. 131). As Hicks demonstrated, the implicit 'condition for equilibrium, in this widest sense, is Perfect Foresight. Disequilibrium is the Disappointment of Expectations' (1982, p. 32 [1933]).

With perfect foresight, money is – at best – the unit of account and medium of exchange. It is no store of value, because it would be irrational to hold non-interest bearing liquid assets if there is no disappointment of expectations. All stocks of money would be lent out until payments have to be made (cf. Hicks, 1982, p. 34). Similarly there is no credit demand in excess of savings (including 'inventories' of exchange media), since investors will identify and shun the traps of malinvestment.

As soon as the perfect-foresight assumption is dropped, and *before* taking the banks' credit *creation* into consideration, the supply and demand for credit is differently determined. With imperfect foresight, rational behaviour implies situations of excess demands for money and excess supplies of goods, which arise from divergent expectations, from uniform expectations of a fall in (some) prices or simply from uncertainty. Money is clearly not neutral, then, if one does not assume away distributional effects – as is frequently done in the post-Patinkin literature, but certainly not by Hayek, who took great pains to bring out the Cantillon-effect in the case of an 'excess supply' of money (1935, p. 8f; cf. also Lutz, 1969). In Hayek's own terms of a scarcity of free, circulating capital, excess demands for money are the complementary phenomenon of the dark side of the cycle. There, money suddenly has the function of a store of value, which Hayek otherwise ignores (see also Sraffa, 1932, p. 43f). Thus there is a substantial difference between money *in* equilibrium and money *out* of equilibrium.

This difference poses a dilemma: either there is a logical gap between perfect-foresight equilibrium and the imperfect-foresight business cycle, in which case intertemporal equilibrium is no appropriate starting point for the analysis of the cycle, or equilibrium is stochastic (cf. Desai 1982, p. 165), i.e. a transitory state of the 'industrial fluctuations', at which all plans *accidentally* mesh in a price structure identical with prices at perfect foresight. In the latter case, the use of the equilibrium as gravitation centre and the savings traverse as equilibrium growth-path reference is in serious doubt.

Endogenous explanations

The liquidity preference of banks plays, according to Hayek's *stylization of facts*, a crucial role in the cycle (1933, p. 169ff): In the boom, lender risks seem low; deposits grow with turnover, and the banks start to decrease the ratio of reserves to deposits by an increase in lending, which both offsets and increases their liabilities. By creating credit money, they reinforce the boom. Then, at some point, they stop it by increasing their liquidity preference, i.e. the reserve ratio.

The double trouble with Hayek's story is that it inadvertently refutes his interequilibrium concept of the savings traverse; and is not convincing when it comes to the upper turning points of the cycle. In the type of monetary economy sketched out by Hayek (1933, ch. IV), an increase of voluntary savings would result in a growth of bank deposits, which triggers exactly the kind of credit expansion that Hayek assumes to cause cyclical fluctuations. His distinction between voluntary and forced saving is blurred: they are complements rather than opposites, if rational behaviour on behalf of the banks is taken into account. As with neutral money in intertemporal equilibrium, the savings traverse can only serve as equilibrium reference at the cost of a logical gap between an essentially non-monetary and a monetary economy. As Desai has pointed out, Hayek (1933, p. 189ff) is well aware of the virtual impossibility of ever attaining intertemporal equilibrium:

> But he cannot admit of disequilibrium as a persistent tendency. Thus an institutional factor – elasticity of currency – keeps the monetary economy permanently out of equilibrium. (Desai, 1982, p. 163f)

Hence, Hayek's dilemma evolves into a schizophrenic treatment of the institutional factor – the banking system – as endogenous and exogenous cause of cyclical fluctuations. In order to establish an equilibrium tendency, by which the structural effects of forced saving are reversed, he needs to rely on *ad hoc* assumptions about bank behaviour that run counter to his analytical intentions. This is evident from his explanations of the critical changes in credit supply (see above):

1. Even *if* the money rate of interest is a function of the default risk, it is not clear why banks – in the boom! – should raise interest rates to such an extent that default risks drastically increase. The debt–equity ratio cannot suffice as an explanation for the turning point as it increases right from the outset of the boom. Hayek needs an additional argument about a change in the banks' risk assessment. Such an argument could possibly be derived from a disappointment of producers' price expectations in a glut resulting from the credit-induced growth of production. It would,

however, turn Hayek's overinvestment theory on its head – into a theory of underconsumption.

2.   A credit squeeze in the wake of a drain from the banks' liquidity reserves may be plausible under a strict gold standard. But where the volume of money consists of liabilities of the central bank (cash) and other banks (deposits), a rise of prices in the boom does not automatically result in a decrease of the banks' liquidity. Inflation is a strong incentive to econo-mize on cash holdings through cashless payments and interest-bearing 'cash management'. Furthermore, the money supply grows endogenously with the amount of rediscountable bills. For an explanation of the critical change in the rate of credit expansion, Hayek would need to resort to *restrictive monetary policy*. But then the cause of crisis would be pre-cisely the kind of policy that Hayek advocates for its avoidance.

3.   Even the hyperinflation argument is weak. It relies on the implicit as-sumption that the longer, more productive processes never yield results *before* the credit expansion is stopped. Once they bring about an in-creased output of consumption goods, the inflationary pressure decreases, and with it the *necessity* of a further credit expansion. On the other hand, '[t]here is no reason whatever why the volume of bank credit might not *steadily* continue to rise indefinitely' (Hansen and Tout, 1933, p. 140).[3] A turning point into crisis could be found only by making a choice between Hayek's dilemma of the first and second arguments: either the crisis results endogenously from excess supplies of consumption goods, entailing the disappointment of creditors' expectations; or it is brought about by exogenous restrictions of the money supply, by deliberate gov-ernment action to stave off inflation.

Hayek's theory does not, in any case, underpin his views on monetary policy.

Conclusion
All in all, Hayek's reference to intertemporal equilibrium as starting-point and gravity centre of business cycles is flawed. From his own stylization of facts, he cannot exclude that increases in voluntary saving trigger credit cycles, whereas forced saving may finance traverses to (stochastic) higher-output equilibria. Hence his use of the savings traverse as equilibrium growth-path reference is irrelevant. The concept of equilibrium is, at best, reduced to a notional reference to a state in which the price system fully reflects intertemporal preferences and resource availabilities. Yet that notion has no relevance to industrial fluctuations as it is no part of the disequilibrium dynamics Hayek had set out to explain. The equilibrium tendency remains a mere assertion.

Possibly, these fundamental deficits – among other reasons – have led Hayek to leave the field of business cycle theory and drop the explicit reference to equilibrium concepts in his later works. They did not, however, lead him to change his basic views on monetary policy.

Notes

1. This view was successively developed in Hayek (1984a[1928]), (1933[1929]) and (1935[1931]). The dates in square brackets refer to the year of the original edition.
2. Hayek was ambivalent about the causes of deviations of the market rate from the equilibrium rate. In *Monetary Theory and the Trade Cycle* (1933, pp. 147f and 182f), he supported Wicksell's view of fluctuations in the equilibrium rate, which the banks do not immediately perceive and follow. From 1935 onwards he rather followed Mises in presupposing a deliberate 'easy money' policy on behalf of the (central) banks.
3. See also Laidler's contribution to this volume (chapter 1).

References

Desai, M. (1982), 'The Task of Monetary Theory. The Hayek–Sraffa Debate in a Modern Perspective' in M. Baranzini (ed.), *Advances in Economic Theory*, Oxford: Blackwell.

Garrison, R.W. and I.M. Kirzner (1989), 'Friedrich August von Hayek', in *The New Palgrave – Invisible Hand*, London/Basingstoke: Macmillan.

Hansen, A. and H. Tout (1933), 'Annual Survey of Business Cycle Theory: Investment and Saving in Business Cycle Theory', *Economica*, **1**, 119–47.

Hayek, F.A. von (1933), *Monetary Theory and the Trade Cycle* (reprint), New York: Kelley (*Geldtheorie und Konjunkturtheorie*, 1929).

Hayek, F.A. von (1935), *Prices and Production* (2nd ed., reprint), New York: Kelley.

Hayek, F.A. von (1942), 'The Ricardo Effect', *Economica*, **9**, 127–52.

Hayek, F.A. von (1969), 'Three Elucidations of the Ricardo Effect', *Journal of Political Economy*, **77**, 274–85.

Hayek, F.A. von (1984a), 'Intertemporal Price Equilibrium and Movements in the Value of Money', in R. McCloughry (ed.), *Money, Capital and Fluctuations. Early Essays*, London: Routledge & Kegan Paul. ('Das intertemporale Gleichgewichtssystem der Preise und die Bewegungen des "Geldwertes"', 1928.)

Hayek, F.A. von (1984b), 'On "Neutral Money"', in R. McCloughry (ed.), *Money, Capital and Fluctuations. Early Essays*, London: Routledge & Kegan Paul. (Über "neutrales Geld"', 1933.)

Hicks, J. (1982), 'Equilibrium and the Cycle', in *Money, Interest and Wages. Collected Essays on Economic Theory*, vol. II. Oxford: Blackwell. ('Gleichgewicht und Konjunktur', 1933.)

Lutz, F.A. (1969), 'On Neutral Money', in E. Streissler, G. von Haberler, F.A. Lutz and F. Machlup (eds), *Roads to Freedom. Essays in Honour of F.A. Hayek*, London: Routledge.

Samuelson, P.A. (1968), 'What Classical and Neoclassical Monetary Theory Really Was', *Canadian Journal of Economics*, **1**, 1–15.

Sraffa, P. (1932), 'Dr. Hayek on Money and Capital', *Economic Journal*, **42**, 42–53.

5   Competition, prices and market order

John Eatwell and Murray Milgate

...only through the principle of competition has political economy any pretension to the character of a science. So far as rents, profits, wages, prices, are determined by competition, laws may be assigned for them. Assume competition to be their exclusive regulator, and principles of broad generality and scientific precision may be laid down, according to which they will be regulated.

(John Stuart Mill, 1848, p. 242)

In an economy operating according to a generalized process of market exchange, prices are the fundamental parameters of economic activity. The calculation of profit and loss, whether individual or corporate, is the stimulus to consumption and to production. Understanding how prices are determined, and what their role might be in all aspects of economic behaviour, is therefore the key to understanding how the economy works. A satisfactory explanation of any economic phenomenon, whether, for example, the demand for individual commodities, the overall level of employment, or the rate of technological change, must include an examination of the role of prices – even if only to demonstrate that prices have no role.

An adequate theory of what determines relative prices is, therefore, the foundation upon which an understanding of the working of the market mechanism is based.

But an 'adequate' model is far more than a set of abstract, formal relationships, however prettily put together. If it is to be useful it must bear some relationship to the empirical phenomena it purports to explain. Even at the most general level there must be some sort of link between the construction of the model, and the 'real-world' quantities and relationships which the model is supposed to portray. The primary link is provided by the idea that economic relations are systematic, and that the variables of economic life – prices and quantities – do display a sufficient regularity and consistency to permit statements of theoretical generality to be made about them. Competition is the key. As John Stuart Mill pointed out, it is competition which endows variables in a market economy with the necessary regularity and consistency which permits the formulation of the 'principles of broad generality and scientific precision ... according to which they will be regulated'.

Competition creates an environment in which 'price' is, at once, an empirical fact and an analytical category. An empirical fact because competition defines the common economic characteristics of objects (commodities) and

82

an analytic category because competition validates the idea of the natural or normal price as a 'centre of gravitation' and hence the legitimate object for the study of the general characteristics and role of prices in a market economy. It is the persistent assertion of competitive forces which allows economics to move from description to analysis, by creating the general category: price. It was Adam Smith's remarkable insight in defining the analytic concept of natural price as 'the central price, to which the prices of all commodities are continually gravitating' (Smith, 1776, p. 65) which first linked the empirical characteristics of competition to the abstractions of deductive theorizing.

The exact definition of 'competition' is therefore an essential part of any analysis of price determination. For the classical economists the notion of competition was essentially one of capital mobility and the openness of markets. Competition was the motive force behind the flows of resources between alternative uses which determine the gravitation of market prices. This process leads, in turn, to the characterization of the general rate of profit and of natural prices. For neoclassical economists competition would also involve the idea of price-taking behaviour by an infinity of infinitesimally small actors – the idea of 'perfect competition' (see Eatwell, 1982).

Hayek sharply distinguishes his characterization of competition from neoclassical perfect competition. Both the presentation of his theory of competition and his complementary attack on the orthodox neoclassical concept of perfect competition (Hayek, 1946 and 1978a) are attractive and persuasive. Not only did Hayek seem to capture within his portrayal of competition many of the fundamental characteristics of a capitalist market economy, including the process of competitive change (in this his formula is similar to that of the classical economists and of Marx), but he also exposed some of the analytical sterility of perfect competition. It would be difficult not to agree, for instance, that 'the theoretical picture of perfect competition' is 'entirely remote from all that is relevant to an understanding of the process of competition' (1946, p. 102).

Yet Hayek's arguments, both positive and negative, contain an important internal contradiction. Despite his rejection of perfect competition, he claims virtues for the price mechanism which can only be proved by assuming perfect competition. Hayek never appears to have paused to ask himself the rather obvious question: 'What is perfect competition *for*?' Had he done so, he would have been led to consider the relationship between perfect competition and the foundations of the neoclassical theory of value. This would, in turn, have led him to consider the relationship between the determination of relative prices and any claims which might be made for the efficiency of markets. It is these links – between perfect competition and the determination of prices, and between perfect competition and market efficiency – and their implications for the viability of Hayek's arguments, that we propose to explore in this paper.

Hayek's theory of competition

Hayek asserts persistently that his idea of competition is 'dynamic'. 'Competition is by its nature a dynamic process', he claims, one whose 'essential characteristics are assumed away by the assumptions underlying static analysis' (1946, p. 94). Thus, according to Hayek, competition is a 'process of discovery'; 'a procedure for the discovery of such facts as, without resort to it, would not be known to anyone, or at least would not be utilised' (1978a, p. 179).

With the introduction of the concept of 'discovery' Hayek takes the idea of competition as a dynamic process beyond the coordinating role of the invisible hand and the higgling of the market. Competition is no longer just a means of ensuring that whilst pursuing his or her own interest every individual is led, as Adam Smith put it, to promote an end which was no part of their intention. Competition is more than the process by which 'the law of supply and demand' adjusts the composition of production (and hence the allocation of resources) to the composition of demand. As Hayek would have it, 'competition is valuable only because, and so far as, its results are unpredictable and on the whole different from those which anyone has, or could have, deliberately aimed at' (1978a, p. 180). He provides an illustration of the kind of thing he has in mind: 'in sports or in examinations', he says, 'no less than in the award of government contracts or of prizes for poetry, it would clearly be pointless to arrange for competition, if we were certain beforehand who would do best' (1978a, p. 179).

The idea of competition as dynamic, as a persistent force for change and as a process of discovery, is reminiscent of Marx's linkage between competition and technological change as the underlying dynamic of the capitalist economy – with the added ingredient that Hayek's 'process of discovery' is entirely endogenous.

This portrayal of the dynamics of competition as a process of discovery has an important methodological consequence which Hayek himself noticed. On this line of reasoning, 'the validity of the theory cannot be tested empirically', because if 'we do not know the facts we hope to discover by means of competition, we can never ascertain how effective it has been in discovering those facts that might be discovered' (1978a, p. 180). Furthermore, he concedes that this means that it is impossible to argue for the superiority of competitive markets from the characteristics of competition alone. He therefore concludes, rather weakly:

All we can hope to find out is that, on the whole, societies which rely for this purpose on competition have achieved their aims more successfully than others. This is a conclusion which the history of civilisation seems eminently to have confirmed. (1978a, p. 180)

History has, of course, confirmed nothing of the kind. Whilst it might be argued with some hope of success that competition has played a vital role in the process of accumulation, it would be far more difficult to find historical evidence for Hayek's fundamental hypothesis that there is a positive monotonic relationship between the 'degree' of competition (whatever that might mean) and material prosperity.

Contrasting his idea of competition as a 'process of discovery' with the neoclassical definition of perfect competition, Hayek contemptuously dismisses the entire orthodox apparatus:

[W]hat the theory of perfect competition discusses has little claim to be called 'competition' at all ... if the state of affairs assumed by the theory of perfect competition ever existed, it would not only deprive of all their scope all the activities which the verb 'to compete' describes but would make them virtually impossible. (1946, p. 92)

Hayek derides the view that a situation in which individuals are price takers accords in any way with a *process* of competition – a point which was made later in more formal and more measured terms by Kenneth Arrow. Arrow points out that 'perfect competition can prevail only at equilibrium' so that 'each individual participant in the economy is supposed to take prices as given and determines his choices and purchases and sales accordingly; there is no one left over whose job it is to make a decision on price' (Arrow, 1959, pp. 41–3). Arrow goes on to argue that out-of-equilibrium behaviour is necessarily imperfectly competitive, with firms, for example, facing downward-sloping demand curves and hence having scope for actions which affect prices.

Hayek, however, also rejects the orthodox formulation of the theory of imperfect competition as being no less static and sterile than that of perfect competition. Both perfect and imperfect competition presume known 'data', such as the production function, rather than a process of competitive discovery. As Hayek put it: 'If anyone really knew all about what economic theory calls data, competition would indeed be a very wasteful method of securing adjustment to these facts' (1978a, p. 179).

Unfortunately, Hayek's case for competitive discovery goes somewhat awry when he confuses the data of the theory of price determination with the conclusions of that theory:

> [E]conomic theory sometimes appears at the outset to bar its way to a true
> appreciation of the character of the process of competition, because it starts from
> the assumption of a 'given' supply of scarce goods. But which goods are scarce
> goods, or which things are goods, and how scarce or valuable they are – these are
> precisely the things which competition has to discover, (1978a, p. 181).

These assertions suggest not only ignorance of Abraham Wald's discussion of
the determination of free goods (1936), but also a significant failure to
understand what Walrasian general equilibrium theory is all about.

Hayek's apparent failure to understand the structure and conclusions of
neoclassical price theory is compounded in his discussion of the relationship
between competition and 'market order'. Hayek argues that not only must
competition be a process of 'discovery', but that competition would also
establish a 'market order' which 'produces in some sense a maximum or
optimum' (1978a, p. 183).

It is very important to realize that Hayek defines this 'maximum or optimum' in the traditional terms of productive efficiency and allocative efficiency. For productive efficiency:

> [T]he market ... secures that whatever is being produced will be produced by
> people who can do so more cheaply than (or at least as cheaply as) anybody who
> does not produce it ... and that each product is sold at a price lower than that at
> which anybody who in fact does not produce it could supply it. (Hayek, 1978a, p.
> 185).

For allocative efficiency:

> [T]he expectations of transactions to be effected with other members of society ...
> can mostly be realised. This mutual adjustment of plans is brought about by
> what, since the physical sciences have also begun to concern themselves with
> spontaneous orders, or 'self-organising systems', we have learnt to call 'nega-
> tive feedback'. [...] [T]he market ... brings about an approach towards some
> point on that n-dimensional surface, by which pure economic theory represents
> the horizon of all possibilities to which the production of any one proportional
> combination of commodities and services could conceivably be carried. (Hayek,
> 1978a, pp. 184–5).

Hayek does not appear to appreciate that in advancing these claims for the
allocative efficiency of competitive markets he goes beyond a general characterization of the dynamic process of competition and advances very specific propositions about its outcomes – propositions which can be sustained
only by a *theory* of price determination, not just the process of competition.

As far as productive efficiency is concerned, the efficiency of the competitive process may, of course, be related to any arbitrary set of prices. Given
prices, entrepreneurs minimize costs. In such circumstances, however, noth-

ing at all can be said about the efficiency of the resource allocation associated with those arbitrary prices. It is quite possible, for example, for the cost-minimizing production associated with an arbitrary set of prices to be combined with underutilization of all factor services.

Allocative efficiency, on the other hand, attaining the 'horizon of all possibilities', as Hayek put it, involves propositions about the relationship between prices and quantities – propositions which are the stuff of Walrasian general equilibrium theory, and of the fundamental theorem of welfare economics. As is well known, the first part of that fundamental theorem states that a perfectly competitive equilibrium is Pareto optimal; that is, it has the properties of allocative efficiency which Hayek is claiming. Moreover, it is not possible to sustain even this limited proposition on allocative efficiency once the assumption of perfect competition is dropped.

It is not just the normative gloss Hayek wishes to give to the 'market order' which is jeopardized by his rejection of perfect competition. The very proposition that prices are determined by the interaction of the forces of supply and demand upon which Hayek rests his analysis of the 'market order' can no longer be logically maintained without the assumption of perfect competition.

As Hayek himself makes clear, perfect competition was not formulated as even an ideal type of the competition manifest in observable markets. Regrettably, what Hayek does not appear to appreciate is that the modern concept of 'perfect' competition was developed in response to the formal mathematical requirements of the proof that prices are determined by the mutual interaction of demand and supply. Without the assumption of perfect competition, that proposition cannot, in general, be sustained.

In *Economica* for 1945, Hayek published an edited version of John Stuart Mill's notes on Senior's *Political Economy*. In those notes Mill had argued that it seemed to him to be necessary 'when we speak of the ratio between the demand for a commodity and the supply of it, that the two quantities should be, in the mathematical sense, homogeneous – that both of them should be estimated in numbers of the same unit' (Mill, 1945, p. 134). Mill concluded that the heterogeneity of the determinants of cost (subsistence wages, profits as surplus, and rent as the return to a limited supply of land) meant that the requisite homogeneity between demand and supply was absent, and that it could not therefore be shown (as Senior had tried to do) that prices are determined by the balance of demand and supply.

The necessary homogeneity was created, of course, by Jevons, Menger and Walras. They constructed a unified theory of cost, in which cost as disutility could be balanced against the utility of demand. The logical starting-point of this unified theory is the theory of individual constrained utility maximization. But in moving from the individual to the social determination of prices in the economy as a whole, whilst preserving the functional relationships between price and quantity defined by individual behaviour, it is necessary to assume that all agents are price takers. This assumption permits the continuity of individual demand and offer functions (that continuity being attained by the assumed quasi-concavity of the utility function) to be translated into the continuity of the excess demand functions – an essential condition for the proof of the existence of equilibrium.

The assumption of price taking would appear unreasonable if it were not related to some sort of behavioural characterization about the organization of a market economy. What the content of such a characterization might be was investigated by Cournot and Edgeworth, both of whom suggested that price taking would rule in an economy composed of an infinite number of agents. In recent years these conjectures of Cournot and Edgeworth have been formally proved. The basic result, expressed in terms of the limit theorem on the core of a competitive economy, is nicely summarized by Robert Aumann:

> The notion of perfect competition is fundamental in the treatment of economic equilibrium. The essential idea or notion is that the economy under consideration has a 'very large' number of participants, and that the influence of each individual participant is 'negligible'. [...] [T]he influence of an individual participant on the economy cannot be mathematically negligible, as long as there are only finitely many participants. Thus a mathematical model appropriate to the intuitive notion of perfect competition must contain infinitely many participants. (Aumann, 1964, p. 39)

The assumption of an infinity of infinitesimally small traders (a continuum) permits the construction of continuous excess demand functions even in cases in which non-convexities result in discontinuities in certain individual demand and offer functions.

Dropping the assumption of perfect competition has very destructive consequences for neoclassical price theory. While a number of attempts have been made to construct general equilibrium models in which price taking is not assumed, beginning with Negishi's (1961) celebrated paper on monopolistic competition and general equilibrium, Roberts and Sonnenschein (1977) have since demonstrated that models of this class rest on mathematical assumptions which have no economic rationale:

> Despite these important contributions, the problem of such mixed Cournot–Chamberlain–Walras equilibria is not yet adequately resolved, since each of the above mentioned theorems employs assumptions made directly on the constructs to be used in the proofs, and the properties thus assumed are not derived from hypotheses on the fundamental data of preferences, endowments and technology. This is, of course, in sharp contrast with the theorems for the purely competitive case, in which, for example, all the properties of the excess demand correspondence used

in the proofs are derived from conditions on the individual agents' characteristics ... the properties of reaction curves used in the existing theories of imperfectly competitive equilibrium have not been derived from the technological conditions and the behaviour these theories claim to address. (Roberts and Sonnenschein, 1977, pp. 101–4; see also Roberts, 1987).

Therefore, it is not just the fundamental theorem of welfare economics which rests on the assumption of perfect competition, but also the very proposition that prices are determined by the relationship between demand and supply. Without perfect competition, Hayek is left with only the proposition that competition will tend to establish some set of prices. But how the magnitudes of those prices are determined, and how they interact with the determination of quantities, cannot be deduced from the process of competition described by Hayek. To suppose that competition alone could determine prices was, of course, the error of the 'vulgar' economists (Marx, 1867, p. 146n).

Competition as selection
The internal contradictions in Hayek's analysis of competition and market order are also to be found in the portrayal of market competition as a process of selection.

Hayek was not the first to propose the idea that market competition was akin to a process of selection. The notion dates back (at least) to sociologists like Spencer and Weber – and it found its most enthusiastic exponent in Schumpeter. The work of Alchian (1950) and more recently that of Nelson and Winter (1982) are leading species of the same genus. The relevance of these developments to the present discussion is that they allow us to view the fundamental inadequacy of Hayek's theory of competition from another angle. For it turns out that even if one chooses to think of competition as selection, it is nonetheless the case that the only context in which it is possible to show that a selection process will render individual production and consumption plans 'mutually compatible' and establish an 'optimum' is one which essentially replicates the perfectly competitive conditions of Walrasian price theory. In short, if one wishes to contemplate the process of competition as securing these beneficent ends, as Hayek manifestly wishes to do, then perfect competition must be assumed.

The conditions for any portrayal of competition as selection involve specifying a range of possible behaviours for competitors (call them firms rather than species, so as to make the story sound like economics rather than biology) and a dynamic process whereby success involves survival and expansion, while failure involves decline and contraction. The simplest forms of competitive selection processes in economic theory specify profit maximization as one of a range of possible behaviours and equate profitability with success and lack of profitability with failure.

The behavioural rules and the selection criteria, once specified, constitute the data of the model. These data replace the data of orthodox neoclassical price theory (preferences, technology and endowments). The solution concept is customarily a stationary position of the dynamic process. In the absence of any further elaboration of the precise restrictions (assumptions) to be applied to the data, models of competition as selection may have just one solution, many solutions, or none at all. In Hayek's terminology, that solution (if it exists) is the 'market order'.

As we have already seen Hayek makes strong claims about this 'market order'. It is not just that competition produces order (i.e. determinate outcomes), but that that order has two important properties: (1) it is characterized by the mutual adjustment of individual plans; and (2) it is efficient in (at least) the Paretian sense (1978a, pp. 184–5).

To establish just how far these claims are consistent with Hayek's rejection of perfect competition, the questions to be asked are: first, under what restrictions on the data will a model of competition as selection yield a solution in which prices and quantities are such that individual production and consumption plans cohere; and, second, do all configurations in the solution set display an efficient allocation of resources?

There are several results available in the economic literature on selection processes which bear directly upon these questions. They are sometimes called 'mimicry theorems' since the subject really being addressed is the conditions under which an orthodox neoclassical equilibrium of prices and quantities would be the outcome of a selection process.

Though the available theorems differ in small details, that advanced by Nelson and Winter (1982, pp. 144–54) is fairly typical and has the virtue of being the least complicated. As it happens, the conditions which satisfy properties (1) and (2) above are rather strong.

Take a selection process of the simplest kind. 'Mimicry' requires (Winter, 1987, pp. 545–6) first, a guarantee that there will be no 'entrepreneurial rents' in equilibrium which could be used to weaken or eliminate the threat of failure and so create 'safe' departures from cost minimization. For this it is necessary to assume constant returns to scale. Second, it requires a guarantee that scale (output) increases and decreases directly with conditions of profitability. For this it is necessary either simply to assert that existing firms themselves expand as profitability increases, and/or (since there is no convincing intuitive reason why they should do this rather than simply enjoy windfall gains) to assume that in such cases the market is joined by firms which are able to imitate the processes of existing firms perfectly. Third, there must be a guarantee that the solution is stationary. For this it is necessary to assume that firms just breaking even (average cost equal to average revenue) make no alterations in their output decisions and that no new firms enter the market at the break-even point. Lastly, it must be assumed that some firms are actually profit maximizers.

These conditions may be summarized as follows:

1. Technological condition: constant returns to scale.
2. Survival condition: free entry by perfect imitators.
3. Break-even condition: no behavioural changes or entry/exit when price equals marginal cost.
4. Profit maximization.

It may be shown that a selection process where the range of behavioural possibilities includes profit maximization, and whose dynamic process involves the survival of profitable and the extinction of unprofitable firms, has a solution which precisely mimics the properties of an orthodox neoclassical competitive equilibrium. For the usual reasons, that solution will also be Pareto optimal. It should be fairly evident, however, that the restrictions applied to the model (1–4 above) also 'mimic' the prescribed conditions of perfect competition (in fact, they do a little more than replicate them). The coexistence of constant returns to scale and the absence of any 'entrepreneurial rents' must mean that the demand curve faced by the individual firm is horizontal; that is, the firm is a price taker. The conditions required for mimicry therefore reproduce the characteristics of perfect competition.

So even when the competitive process is modelled as being akin to the process of natural selection (a favourite analogy deployed by Hayek), it is impossible, without invoking assumptions broadly in line with those of perfect competition, to accept his idea that the operation of the market mechanism can be consistently thought of as involving the mutual interaction of the forces of demand and supply (activated by the utility and profit-maximizing behaviour of individual agents) or to subscribe to his assertion that the 'market order' is optimal.

Thus we reach by a different route the conclusion of the previous section of this paper: that if we wish to exorcise the extraordinary assumption of perfect competition from the theory of price determination then it is necessary to think again about the adequacy of the demand-and-supply model of the market mechanism. It is also necessary to abandon the proposition that the market order achieves an efficient allocation of resources – where the efficiency is defined as the social expression of individual utility maximization.

Conclusion

The contradictions in Hayek's arguments on competition and market order could be resolved in two ways: by abandoning his characterization of competition altogether and accepting perfect competition as an integral part of the theory of price determination: or by preserving the insights he has into the nature of capitalistic competition and seeking some replacement for the neo-classical theory of price determination.

There are clear similarities between Hayek's discussion of competition as a process and classical discussions of competition, similarities which find even stronger echoes in Schumpeter's analysis of competition as 'creative destruction' (Schumpeter, 1942), the importance of which for economic welfare is far greater that the allocative efficiency of orthodox theory. It is therefore not surprising to find that the classical approach to the analysis of value and distribution is entirely compatible with Hayek's characterization of competition as a process of 'discovery'.

References

Alchian, A. A. (1950), 'Uncertainty, evolution and economic theory', *Journal of Political Economy*, **58** (3), June, 211–21. Reprinted in A.A. Alchian, *Economic Forces at Work*, (1977, 15–35).

Alchian, A.A. (1977), *Economic Forces at Work*, Indianapolis: Liberty Press.

Arrow, K.J. (1959), 'Toward a Theory of Price Adjustment', in: M. Abramovitz et al., *The Allocation of Economic Resources: Essays in Honor of Bernard Francis Haley*, Stanford: Stanford University Press.

Aumann, R.J. (1964), 'Markets with a continuum of traders', *Econometrica*, **32**, (1–2), 39–50.

Eatwell, J. (1982), 'Competition', in: I. Bradley and M. Howard (eds.), *Classical and Marxian Political Economy*, London: Macmillan.

Hayek, F.A. von (1925), 'Review of *Grenznutzen und Wirtschaftsrechnung* by Leo Schönfeld', *Archiv für Sozialwissenschaft und Sozialpolitik*, **54** (2), 547–52. Translated as 'Marginal utility and economic calculation: a review, and reprinted in Hayek (1984).

Hayek, F.A. von (ed), (1935), *Collectivist Economic Planning: Critical Studies on the Possibilities of Socialism*, London: George Routledge & Sons.

Hayek, F.A. von (1936), 'Technischer Fortschritt und Überkapazität', *Österreichische Zeitschrift für Bankwesen*, **1**, 9–23. Translated as 'Technical progress and excess capacity', and reprinted in Hayek (1984).

Hayek, F.A. von (1937), 'Economics and knowledge', *Economica*, new series, **4** (13), February, 33–54. Reprinted in Hayek (1949).

Hayek, F.A. von (1945a), 'The use of knowledge in society', *American Economic Review*, **35** (4), September, 519–30. Reprinted in Hayek (1949).

Hayek, F.A. von (1945b), 'Individualism: true and false', in Hayek (1949).

Hayek, F.A. von (1946), 'The meaning of competition', in Hayek (1949).

Hayek, F.A. von (1949), *Individualism and the Economic Order: An Inquiry into the Foundations of Theoretical Psychology*, London: Routledge and Kegan Paul; Chicago: University of Chicago Press.

Hayek, F.A. von (1952), *The Counter-Revolution of Science*, Glencoe, Illinois: The Free Press. Reprinted Indianapolis: Liberty Press, 1979.

Hayek, F.A. von (1978a), 'Competition as a discovery procedure', in Hayek (1978c).

Hayek, F.A. von (1978b), 'Dr Bernard Mandeville', in Hayek (1978c).

Hayek, F.A. von (1978c), *New Studies in Philosophy, Politics, Economics and the History of Ideas*, London: Routledge & Kegan Paul.

Hayek, F.A. von (1984), *Money, Capital and Fluctuations: Early Essays*, ed. by R. McCloughry, London: Routledge & Kegan Paul.

Marx, K. H. (1867), *Capital*, Vol. 1. Edited with an Introduction by Ernest Mandel. New York: Vintage, 1977.

Mill, J.S. (1848), *Principles of Political Economy*, London: Parker.

Mill, J.S. (1945), 'Notes on N.W. Senior's *Political Economy*, ed. by F.A. Hayek', *Economica*, new series **12** (47), 134–9.

Negishi, T. (1961), 'Monopolistic competition and general equilibrium', *Review of Economic Studies*, **28** (77), June, 196–201.

Nelson, R.R. and S.G. Winter (1982), *An Evolutionary Theory of Economic Change*, Cambridge, Mass.: Harvard University Press.

Roberts, J. and H. Sonnenschein (1977), 'On the foundations of the theory of monopolistic competition', *Econometrica*, **45** (1), January, 101–13.

Roberts, J. (1987), 'Perfectly and imperfectly competitive markets', in *The New Palgrave: A Dictionary of Economics*, Vol. 3.

Schumpeter, J. A. (1942), *Capitalism, Socialism and Democracy*, New York: Harper and Row.

Smith, A. (1776), *An Inquiry into the Nature and Causes of the Wealth of Nations;* London: Methuen, 1961.

Wald, A. (1936), 'Über einige Gleichungssysteme der mathematischen Ökonomie', *Zeitschrift für Nationalökonomie*, **7**, 637–70. Translated by Otto Eckstein as 'On some systems of equations in mathematical economics', and reprinted in *Econometrica*, **19** (4), October 1951, 368–403.

Winter, S. G. (1987), 'Competition and selection', *The New Palgrave: A Dictionary of Economics*, Vol. 1.

Comment

Giancarlo de Vivo

I think I am broadly in agreement with what seems to me the main thrust of Professor Laidler's paper: that however much one may like (or dislike) Hayek's conclusions on monetary theory and policy, it is difficult to see how these conclusions can be sustained by his analysis.

Hayek's purported objective was to integrate the theory of money and the theory of capital. I should like to make some brief comments on both sides, starting with capital.

Hayek of course came from Austria, the homeland of capital theory, and used to make the most of his country's reputation on this subject, rebuking his opponents, specifically John Maynard Keynes, for not having taken the trouble of adequately studying Böhm-Bawerk and Wicksell (Hayek, 1931a, pp. 401–2). But if we look at what is the main text of interest to us for Hayek's attempts to integrate money and capital theory – *Prices and Production* – we find it quite disappointing. Professor Laidler does not really discuss the grave problems which beset the capital theory of *Prices and Production*, but I think one ought to go a little into them.

In *Prices and Production* there is heterogeneous capital – but only in the sense in which there is heterogeneous capital in theories using the average period of production, in that capital is reduced to a single quantity. Everybody will be familiar with the critique of the average period of production, for instance that it requires (as a necessary hypothesis) that profits be reckoned at simple rate. Wicksell himself became aware of these difficulties, and accordingly produced his *Lectures*, taking a significant step forward from the average period. Hayek, writing 30 years after Wicksell's *Lectures*, seems unaware of it, at least as far as this important point is concerned. And Hayek not only does not follow Wicksell in taking a step forward from Böhm-Bawerk's average period – he actually takes a step backwards from it.

It seems to me that the great importance of the conception of the average period of production in the theory of capital was that it tried to solve the problem of the heterogeneity of capital by reducing it to a single quantity – but not in the obvious, trivial way, that is in value. This single 'quantity of capital', which could be used to measure capital intensity, was reckoned in terms of a 'technical unit', to use Wicksell's words (Wicksell, 1929, p. 149), that is a unit which (if the necessary assumptions are granted) is independent of value and distribution. I say that *Prices and Production* is a retrogression

94

with respect to Böhm-Bawerk (not to mention Wicksell), because all Hayek's reasonings are essentially conducted in terms of value. His triangles, rectangles, etc., at difference from the similar ones used by Wicksell, are in terms of value. Thus their whole point is missed. Owing to this, it is virtually impossible to discuss the path through which Hayek, allegedly basing himself on them, arrives at his results. Although Hayek's intention in *Prices and Production* might have been, as Hagemann writes in his paper (Chapter 6), to emphasize 'changes in the real structure of production' brought about by monetary changes, he completely failed to analyse them, given that his discussion of these alleged 'changes in the real structure of production' is essentially conducted in value terms. Basically, his 'theory' amounts to wishful thinking.

Hayek's numerical examples in *Prices and Production* (which play an important role in his arguments) are not only arbitrary in their *starting*-point – which of course is always the case in numerical examples – but also in their *final* point – which again appears as a set of arbitrary figures, whose relation with the initial ones is wholly unexplained. An illustration of this we find in the well known example of forced saving, that Hayek discusses in the second lecture of *Prices and Production*. Hayek assumes that, no increase in voluntary saving having taken place, the banks increase the credit granted to producers, and a process of forced saving is put in motion, which temporarily ends in a situation similar to that of an increase in voluntary saving, but with prices higher than in that case. The process by means of which this is achieved is thus described by Hayek:

> in the case we are now considering ... [the result] can only be brought about by a retrenchment of consumption. But now this sacrifice is not voluntary ... consumers ... are forced to forego part of what they used to consume ... because they get less goods for their money income. (Hayek, 1931b, pp. 52–3).

And yet, as Sraffa pointed out, the diagram which describes the situation at the end of this 'first round' entails money prices of consumers' goods which are actually *lower* than the prices ruling at the moment when the process of forced saving started (Hayek, 1931b, p. 50, fig. 4). The only way of reconciling Hayek's own account of the forced saving process with this astonishing implication of his diagram, would be in my judgement to acknowledge the fanciful nature of the diagram. I should therefore think that Professor Laidler is a little overgenerous to Hayek, when he writes in his paper that Hayek's analysis of the first round of the process of forced saving is 'impeccable' in logic.

I should like to stress that I am not criticizing Hayek's theory of capital simply for its being subject to the so-called Cambridge critique, to which of course also Böhm-Bawerk's and Wicksell's theories are subject. This would have been idle. My point is rather that Hayek failed to see the *strong* points of Böhm-Bawerk's and Wicksell's theories, and took a significant step backwards with respect to them. In other words, Hayek was guilty of the same sin of which he accused Keynes: that of not having adequately studied Böhm-Bawerk and Wicksell.

I should like to mention another important example of confusion in Hayek's *Prices and Production*, also linked to the confusion between value and quantity, which can be found in his discussion of the rectangles in the diagrams of Lecture II. Hayek writes that

> as the figure represents values and not physical production, the surplus return obtained by the roundabout methods of production is not represented in the diagram. In this lecture I have intentionally neglected interest. (1931b, p. 38)

It is difficult to make sense of this statement. Whether one looks at things in value or in physical terms, if there is a surplus it will show itself. And in any case, Hayek's statement would seem to imply that in this, the central lecture of *Prices and Production*, the one where we find the discussion of forced saving etc., Hayek would be 'neglecting' interest. I think one must strongly sympathize with Keynes, who defined *Prices and Production* as 'one of the most frightful muddles ... ever read' (Keynes, 1931, p. 252).

It is clear that to discuss the integration of monetary theory with such a real theory as the one I have just outlined would be useless. But I should like to add one point with respect to Hayek's monetary theory.

I am surprised to see that writers on Hayek's monetary theory normally fail to comment on what Hayek himself stressed as a very important point of his own theory, i.e. the conception that the primary task of monetary theory is that of studying the effects of money on *relative* prices. It would appear to me that it is very difficult to reconcile this with the orthodox real theory which Hayek espouses (say Wicksell's real theory), and with those parts of traditional monetary theory that he retains. A theory of money which claims that money affects relative prices in an essential, persistent, way must also allow that money determines (or at least codetermines) the rate of interest. Put in another way, the problem would appear to be the consistency between Hayek's view that money determines (or codetermines) relative prices, and the generally accepted view that it is the rate of profits that determines the rate of interest, and not the other way around. I do not think that Hayek would have been prepared to turn orthodox theory upside down, to allow his ideas on money and relative prices to run their full course, and therefore one could see this as another source of inconsistency in Hayek's thought. I should have liked to see this problem dealt with in the papers on Hayek's monetary theory, which instead follow the common practice of not really discussing this issue.

References

Hayek, F.A. von (1931a), 'The pure theory of money: A rejoinder to Mr. Keynes', *Economica*, November.

Hayek, F.A. von (1931b), *Prices and Production*, London: Routledge.

Keynes, J.M. (1931), 'The pure theory of money. A reply to Dr Hayek', reprinted in *The Collected Writings of John Maynard Keynes*, vol. XIII, ed. by D. Moggridge, London: Macmillan, 1973.

Wicksell, K. (1929), *Lectures on Political Economy* (3rd ed.), vol. 1, ed by L. Robbins, London: Routledge, 1934.

PART II

HAYEK AND STRUCTURAL THEORIES OF THE BUSINESS CYCLE

6 Hayek and the Kiel school: some reflections on the German debate on business cycles in the late 1920s and early 1930s*

Harald Hagemann

Hayek's business cycle theory consists of integrating monetary theory and capital theory. In the latter the structure of production and the system of relative prices play an important role. It is a central characteristic of Hayek's theory that monetary factors cause the business cycle but real phenomena constitute it. While in *Prices and Production* (1931) emphasis is on changes in the real structure of production, in *Monetary Theory and the Trade Cycle* (1933) Hayek stresses the monetary causes starting the cycle.

It is important to notice that the latter work was published in German as early as 1929 under the title *Geldtheorie und Konjunkturtheorie*, two years before *Prices and Production*, which was based on Hayek's four influential and controversial LSE lectures, made him known to a wider English audience. The historical order matters not just for chronological reasons but even more so for significant shifts of emphasis. In the new foreword to the 1976 German reprint of *Preise und Produktion* Hayek points to an important difference between the two works. In the late 1920s and early 1930s there existed the strange situation that English economists were inclined to a monetary explanation of the business cycle based on an oversimplified quantity theory whereas in the German language area he had to fight to establish that changes on the monetary side were attached any importance at all in the context of trade cycle theory (see Hayek, 1976, p. 11).

A closer look into *Geldtheorie und Konjunkturtheorie* which emerged from Hayek's contributions to the meeting of the Verein für Sozialpolitik held in Zürich in 1928 (see Hayek, 1928b and 1929b) and which also was the *Habilitationsschrift* he submitted to the University of Vienna in 1929, reveals very soon that it is characterized by the challenge arising from the attack which had been launched by Adolph Löwe[1] and other members of the Kiel school,[2] like Fritz Burchardt[3] and Hans Neisser,[4] against monetary theories of the business cycle. Moreover, Hayek not only regarded the arguments made by these scholars as the most serious contemporary critique against monetary

*I should like to thank Christian Gehrke and Gary Mongiovi for valuable comments on an earlier draft of this paper.

theories of the business cycle but also explicitly accepted Lowe's methodological thesis 'that the incorporation of cyclical phenomena into the system of economic equilibrium theory, with which they are in apparent contradiction, remains the crucial problem of Trade Cycle theory' (Hayek, 1933, p. 33). Hayek and Lowe both insisted that the theory of cyclical fluctuations must present a causal factor immanent to the economic system itself and which dissolves the set of equilibrium interrelationships, thus allowing a theoretical explanation of the business cycle. Moreover, both authors agreed on the importance of the underlying real structure of production and of changes in that structure over time. However, the decisive difference lies in the basic causal factor identified by Hayek on the one hand and the Kiel economists on the other. Although he dissociated himself from oversimplified versions of the quantity theory and accepted most of Lowe's criticism of existing monetary theories of the business cycle, Hayek nevertheless resorted to money and credit as the factor whose introduction broke the equilibrium system and made endogenous fluctuations both possible and necessary. Lowe (1928), on the other hand, in his critical evaluation of monetary explanations of the business cycle, came to the conclusion that nobody had succeeded in demonstrating the systematic nature of the monetary fluctuations themselves. He regarded monetary factors as playing, at best, an intermediate causal role and as being likely to intensify any disequilibrium induced by non-monetary causes. Lowe thus saw the decisive endogenous disturbing factor in the era of progressive industrialization to be technological change.

Adolph Lowe's contribution to the study of business cycles, to which the economics profession in Germany had turned in the 1920s, can hardly be overemphasized. With his seminal works, especially his article on 'The current state of research on business cycles in Germany' (1925) and his 1926 paper 'How is business-cycle theory possible at all?' he became the *spiritus rector* of the debates on business cycle theory in the Weimar Republic.[5] Lowe's leading role in these debates is reflected in Hayek's *Monetary Theory and the Trade Cycle*, in which the dispute with Lowe, Burchardt and Neisser plays a most fruitful role. It is widely overlooked that for the developing and sharpening of his own theory of the business cycle at this early stage the dispute with the critics from Kiel had an importance on Hayek's thinking which is only matched by the influence exerted by Mises's theory of money and credit, Wicksell's distinction between the natural and the market rate of interest and Böhm-Bawerk's theory of capital.[6]

Hayek and Lowe were among the most impressive representatives of a new generation of young researchers appearing on the economic scene in Germany and Austria in the 1920s. Through their theoretical work, and by the development of original and innovative ideas and a much more international extension of the discussion, they contributed to the decline of the hitherto dominating influence of the Historical school. Thus the debates on monetary theories of the business cycle taking place in Germany and Austria ran parallel to and reacted to what was happening in Great Britain, the United States and Sweden, where Hawtrey, Keynes, Robertson, Fisher, Wicksell and others were working on the same subject. While enormous fluctuations in prices and the money supply were a common characteristic of most European countries during World War I and after, the experience with hyperinflation in the early 1920s gave the German debate its particular historical background. It is therefore not surprising that the role of money and credit in cyclical fluctuations and questions whether it would be justifiable to expect the disappearance of the cycle to accompany a stable price level were central issues. The *Verein für Sozialpolitik*, the German Society for Economic and Social Sciences, had chosen the explanation of business cycles as the main topic for its annual meeting in 1928. During the Zürich conference, and among the group of economists who wrote special reports for the preparation of the conference, both Hayek and Lowe played a most active role.[7]

In the following I shall first examine the methodological requirements a theory of the business cycle has to fulfil according to the views of Lowe and Hayek. The following section examines the different basic causal factor endogenous to the system itself which distorts the rigid interrelations implied in the system of static equilibrium, namely money and credit versus technological change. The importance of the underlying structure of production is taken up in the third section. Hayek's 'vertical' treatment of economic structure in the Austrian tradition focuses on the relationships between the fund of productive resources and the production of final output in which the time dimension of production matters. The 'horizontal' approach, on the other hand, is characterized by a completely different treatment of the durable means of production.[8] Sectoral models of the Quesnay–Marx–Leontief–Sraffa type concentrate on the circular character of economic relationships. Intertemporal complementarities in the productive process are put into sharp focus in traverse analysis, i.e. the study of the macroeconomic consequences of disturbances, such as technological change or a change in the supply of labour or natural resources, in an economy which originally has been in a steady state equilibrium. The two pioneers in the field of traverse analysis are Hicks (1973) and Lowe (1976). Differences and similarities will be discussed with regard to their special 'Hayek connection' in the concluding section. Emphasis will be laid in particular on the underlying concept of the structure of production and on the factor which is believed to cause cyclical fluctuations.

The problem of the business cycle: methodological reflections

In his 'brilliant article'[9] Lowe (1926) emphasized not only the relevance of the departmental scheme to the analysis of the business cycle but also that the concept of equilibrium that has been central in all systems of economics since the Physiocrats is logically bound up with a closed interdependent, and therefore a static, system. Lowe's critical analysis of the existing literature on business cycle theories led him to the following conclusion:

> The business cycle problem is no reproach *for* but a reproach *against* a static system, since it is an *antinomic* problem in it. It is soluble only in a system in which the polarity of upswing and crisis arises analytically from the conditions of the system just as the undisturbed adjustment derives from the conditions of the static system. Whoever wants to solve the business cycle problem must sacrifice the static system. Whoever adheres to the static system must abandon the business cycle problem. J. B. Say who consciously took this step, however, vis-à-vis reality got into the logical neighbourhood of Palmström who concludes with shrewdness, '*daß nicht sein kann, was nicht sein darf.*' (Lowe, 1926, p. 193)

Lowe stated the problem clearly: if economic theory is satisfactorily to explain the business cycle, it cannot do so simply by outlining the consequences of a disturbing factor exogenously imposed upon an otherwise static economy. Rather, it must seek for some causal factor endogenous to the system itself which can distort the rigid interrelations implied in the system of static equilibrium.

How did Hayek react to Lowe's claim for a fundamental revision of the methodological foundations of business cycle theory? First, there are important elements common to both Hayek's and Lowe's positions. Hayek (1933, p. 28) explicitly agreed with Lowe's view on the relation between *empirical* observation and *theoretical* explanation:

> Our insight into the *theoretical* interconnections of economic cycles, and into the structural laws of circulation, has not been enriched at all by descriptive work or calculations of correlations. ... To expect an immediate furtherance of *theory* from an increase in *empirical* insight is to misunderstand the logical relationship between theory and empirical research. (Lowe, 1926, p. 166)

Furthermore, Hayek accepted Lowe's seminal argument that all existing theories of the business cycle suffer from the fundamental weakness that they rely on *exogenous* shocks or disturbances and adjustments to such shocks in an equilibrium framework. Such a procedure could hardly result in a satisfactory theory to explain economic fluctuations which occur in a somewhat regular fashion. The logic of equilibrium theory

properly followed through, can do no more than demonstrate that such disturbances of equilibrium can come only from outside – i.e. that they represent a
change in the economic data – and that the economic system always reacts to such
changes by its well-known methods of adaptation, i.e. by the formation of a new
equilibrium. (Hayek, 1933, pp. 42–3)

Trade cycle theory, like any other economic theory, must fulfil two criteria of
correctness to avoid the pitfalls of creating cyclical fluctuations via the introduction of exogenous shocks into an otherwise static system.

Firstly, it must be deduced with unexceptionable logic from the fundamental
notions of the theoretical system; and secondly, it must explain by a purely
deductive method those phenomena with all their peculiarities which we observe
in the actual cycles. Such a theory could only be 'false' either through an inadequacy in its logic or because the phenomena which it explains do not correspond
with the observed facts. (Hayek, 1933, pp. 32–3)

Hayek explicitly points to the parallels of his argument with the views expressed by Lowe (1928). Most important, however, is his making common
cause with Lowe in identifying the incorporation of cyclical phenomena into
equilibrium theory as the crucial problem of business cycle theory and in the
demand for an endogenous factor causing the cycle.

Nevertheless, the two authors differ fundamentally in the conclusions drawn
from their methodological reflections. This holds in particular for the role of
the concept of equilibrium. While Lowe claims that the traditional concept of
a static equilibrium has to be replaced by a new concept of a dynamic system
in which the polarity of upswing and crisis takes the same position as the
equilibrium in a static system (see, e.g., Lowe, 1926, pp. 194–5), Hayek
adheres to the concept of equilibrium as an indispensable tool for economic
theory in general and the understanding of intertemporal price relationships
in particular.[10] To start from the assumption of equilibrium therefore is essential for Hayek's explanation of cyclical fluctuations. *Prices and Production* is
characterized by Hayek's 'conviction that if we want to explain economic
phenomena at all, we have no means available but to build on the foundations
given by the concept of a tendency towards an equilibrium' (Hayek, 1935,
p. 34). For the analysis of dynamic questions it is essential to incorporate the
element of time into the notion of equilibrium and to take into consideration
differences in the prices of the same goods at different points in time.

Hayek's adherence to the concept of equilibrium in his business cycle
analysis has theoretical as well as empirical reasons. While he regards the
free market economy as inherently stable so that all movements can essentially be regarded as equilibrating adjustment processes, Lowe is convinced
of disorderly tendencies in uncontrolled industrial markets in which profit
maximization has lost its classical determinacy. Hence his later plea for

interventionism in order to combine political and economic freedom with the goal of collective rationality (see Lowe, 1965).

Hayek's business cycle theory rests on the idea that prices determine the direction of production. The function of prices as an intertemporal coordination mechanism is to give entrepreneurs the required information for their investment and allocation decisions. If in an equilibrium framework supply and demand are equilibrated via the price mechanism, how is it possible that cyclical fluctuations are a regular phenomenon, since no change *within* the system can give rise to it?

> The obvious, and the only possible way out of this dilemma, is to explain the difference between the course of events described by static theory ... and the actual course of events, by the fact that, with the introduction of money ..., a new determining cause is introduced. Money being a commodity which, unlike all others, is incapable of finally satisfying demand, its introduction does away with the rigid interdependence and self-sufficiency of the 'closed' system of equilibrium, and makes possible movements which would be excluded from the latter. Here we have a starting point which fulfils the essential conditions for any satisfactory theory of the Trade Cycle. (Hayek, 1933, pp. 44–5)

Identifying the endogenous factor: money and credit versus technological change

It was Lowe's closest collaborator, Fritz Burchardt, who in his outstanding 1928 paper on the history of monetary trade cycle theory, which even his main opponent Hayek (1929a, p. 57) praised as 'very valuable in its historical part', showed how structural changes in economic history alter the character of theory. During the nineteenth century crisis theory evolved into trade cycle theory. Credit expansion and interest-rate movements became more important as symptoms of the cycle. Recognizing monetary influences in particular manifesting themselves through changes in the price level, Burchardt concluded that monetary factors alone cannot explain cyclical phenomena. In his view non-monetary factors have to play an important role. This holds especially for technical progress which is recognized as the central determinant of the cycle. With reference to Wicksell's influential theory, for example, Burchardt emphasized that, although changes in the market rate of interest are important for movements of the price level, the real impulse for the disturbance of equilibrium of an economy is given by technical progress which leads to an increase of the natural rate (see Burchardt, 1928, p. 119).

Hayek, on the other hand, pointed out that any theory of business cycles must take the influences arising from money (and credit) as its starting point. A theory of the monetary economy therefore could explain processes like cyclical fluctuations characterized by disproportionate developments that are unthinkable in the equilibrium system of a barter economy. The starting-point for the explanation of crises has to be a change in the money supply automatically occurring in the normal course of events, and not evoked by any forcible interventions (see Hayek, 1928b, pp. 285–6).

Hayek not only regarded his trade cycle theory most decisively as a monetary one but also emphasized that a theory of cyclical fluctuations other than a monetary one is hardly conceivable. Accordingly, he saw the main division in trade cycle theory to be that between monetary and non-monetary theories. However, in a new footnote to the English translation of *Geldtheorie und Konjunkturtheorie*, Hayek made an important qualification:

> Since the publication of the German edition of the book, I have become less convinced that the difference between monetary and non-monetary explanations is *the most important* point of disagreement between the various Trade Cycle theories. On the one hand, it seems to me that within the monetary group of explanations the difference between those theorists who regard the superficial phenomena of changes in the value of money as decisive factors in determining cyclical fluctuations, and those who lay emphasis on the real changes in the structure of production brought about by monetary causes, is much greater than the difference between the latter group and such so-called non-monetary theorists as Prof. Spiethoff and Prof. Cassel. On the other hand, it seems to me that the difference between these explanations, which seek the cause of the crisis in the scarcity of capital, and the so-called 'under-consumption' theories, is theoretically as well as practically of much more far-reaching importance than the difference between monetary and non-monetary theories. (Hayek, 1933, p. 41)

This change of emphasis is not surprising since Hayek from the beginning stressed two arguments:

1. His trade cycle theory essentially is a monetary one. But while *monetary* factors *cause* the cycle, *real* phenomena *constitute* it. Although cyclical fluctuations caused by monetary factors, in particular credit expansion, are unavoidable in modern industrial economies, it is the impact on the real structure of production which is most important.
2. Monetary theory has by no means accomplished its task when it has explained the absolute level of prices. Thus he argued against simplified quantity theories which focus exclusively on the relationship between the quantity of money and the general level of prices. The classical dichotomy has to be seen as a cardinal error of economic theory. A far more important task of monetary theory is to explain changes in the structure of relative prices caused by monetary 'injections' and the consequential disproportionalities in the structure of production which arise because the price system communicates false information about consumer preferences and resource availabilities. Misallocation of resources due to credit expansion may even occur despite price level stability, i.e.

constant prices cannot automatically be regarded as a sign of monetary stability, as Hayek (1925) has pointed out with reference to US monetary policy during the prosperous 1920s.

These arguments also form the basis for Hayek's reaction against the criticism which has been raised by Burchardt and Lowe against monetary theories of the trade cycle. On the one hand, Hayek explicitly agrees to several points of criticism. In particular he views Lowe's most important argument against contemporary monetary theories of the cycle as unquestionably valid, even with reference to the theory as it has been developed earlier by his admired tutor Mises. The argument concerns the *exogenous* character of the theory as it comes in by taking arbitrary interferences on the part of the banks as the starting point. Hayek thus dedicates the whole Chapter IV of *Monetary Theory and the Trade Cycle* to the issue raised by Lowe and to show that he neither has to rely on arbitrary interferences on the part of the banks nor on the general tendency of central banks to depress the money rate of interest below the natural rate but that the fundamental cause of cyclical fluctuations is of an *endogenous* nature.

> The situation in which the money rate of interest is below the natural rate need not, by any means, originate in a *deliberate lowering* of the rate of interest by the banks. The same effect can be obviously produced by an improvement in the expectations of profit or by a diminution in the rate of saving, which may drive the 'natural rate' (at which the demand for and the supply of savings are equal) above its previous level; while the banks refrain from raising their rate of interest to a proportionate extent, but continue to lend at the previous rate, and thus enable a greater demand for loans to be satisfied than would be possible by the exclusive use of the available supply of savings. The decisive significance of the case quoted is not, in my view, due to the fact that it is probably the commonest in practice, but to the fact that it *must inevitably recur* under the existing credit organization.' (Hayek, 1933, pp. 147–8)

The most important reason for an improvement in the expectations of profit which leads to an increase of the natural rate is the occurrence of technical progress, an argument which exactly had been made before by Wicksell and was repeated by Burchardt. However, when Hayek maintains that a discrepancy between the natural and the money rate of interest does not presuppose any deliberate action by the monetary authorities, and that technical progress may cause an increase in the natural rate which is not matched by an immediate adjustment of the money rate, the important question then is whether this discrepancy, and hence money and credit, is or is not *essential* for the emergence of cyclical fluctuations. Lowe would argue that it is not, i.e. that, although the fluctuations may be intensified if excessive credit is given to innovators, the latter would also occur in the absence of additional credit money. Hayek, on the other hand, insists that a satisfactory model of business cycles must be a monetary one. Whereas he recognizes the importance of non-monetary factors, such as technical progress, as a propagation mechanism for cyclical fluctuations, he nevertheless views monetary factors as the ultimate cause.[11]

We can identify here Hayek's most innovative achievement. While Wicksell in his cumulative process analysis concentrated on changes in the purchasing power of money and never developed his monetary theory into a business cycle theory, Hayek accomplished precisely that task. He combined Wicksell's analysis of the cumulative process with the classical concept of forced saving to produce a monetary theory of cyclical fluctuations (especially in the production of capital goods) in which the expansion of bank credit leads to disturbances in the system of relative prices and distortions in the time-structure of production via discrepancies between the natural (equilibrium) rate and the market rate of interest.

The main point of criticism levelled by Hayek against Burchardt and Lowe is that they follow Wicksell supposing

> that only general price changes can be recognized as monetary effects. But general price changes are no essential feature of a monetary theory of the Trade Cycle; *they are not only unessential, but they would be completely irrelevant if only they were completely 'general' – that is, if they affected all prices at the same time and in the same proportion.* (Hayek, 1933, p. 123, original italics)

In contrast to economists like Hayek who regarded the cycle as caused by monetary factors, Lowe emphasized the role of *technical progress*. Indeed, technical progress was seen by him as the central determinant of both the cycle and the long-run growth trend, i.e. he denied the possibility of separating these two aspects from each other. The research programme of the Kiel school consisted in the attempt to develop a theory of accumulation, technical progress and structural change. Against the background of the current microelectronics revolution it turns out that the programme as well as the methods used are pronouncedly up-to-date in many respects. The main research interest of the group was on the construction of a theoretical model of cyclical growth with the basic working hypothesis that a satisfactory explanation of industrial fluctuations must fit into the general framework of an economic theory of the circular flow as it was developed by Quesnay and Marx. The first step consisted in the construction of a model that incorporated both the physical and the value dimensions and that could be made amenable to dynamic transformation. For Lowe and the other members of the Kiel school the physical and technical aspects represent a fundamental determinant of an economic system, especially as important constraints on structural change and behaviour during transition processes. This structural dimension could only be neglected if the production factors were perfectly flexible, mobile and adaptable in the face of change. In order to develop a frame of reference for a sectoral study of economic growth the attention of the Kiel group was directed back to classical and Marxian analysis, since neither the Lausanne nor the Cambridge school, with their emphasis on price variables and the far-reaching exclusion of the physiotechnical structures, offered a fruitful starting-point.

Lowe's attempt to develop a theory of accumulation, technical progress and structural change culminated more than 40 years later in *The Path of Economic Growth* (1976). It shows Lowe as the second pioneer, after John Hicks, in the field of traverse analysis, i.e. in studying the conditions that have to be fulfilled in order to bring the economy back to an equilibrium growth path after a change in one of the determinants of growth, such as the supply of labour or natural resources or technical progress.

One of the most challenging tasks for economic analysis concerns the problems of structural change and technological unemployment. The main message of Lowe's traverse analysis is that capital formation is a prime condition for a successful compensation of technological unemployment. The derivation of possible adjustment paths based on structural requirements is a necessary first step in Lowe's instrumental approach to political economics which is an attempt to formulate an economic policy designed to achieve the macro goal of balanced growth. Structural analysis has to be supplemented by force analysis, i.e. the study of the behavioural and motivational patterns which will put the economy on a goal-adequate traverse. It is force analysis which has a special significance for the analysis of adjustment processes in market systems. Lowe's force analysis reveals the crucial role of expectations and the significance of a functioning price mechanism.

The importance of the structure of production

As is well known, Hayek's theory of the business cycle is built on the twin pillars of Wicksell's interest rate theory and Böhm-Bawerk's theory of capital. Deviations of the money rate of interest, the price of credit, from the equilibrium rate (a term Hayek prefers to the Wicksellian term 'natural rate') have identifiable effects on the capital structure (as conceived by Böhm-Bawerk), i.e. they are the main cause of the cyclical disproportionalities in the structure of production. It was one of Hayek's greatest contributions to have shown the importance of the temporal structure of production processes for industrial fluctuations.

While Hayek in *Monetary Theory and the Trade Cycle* concentrated on the monetary causes which start the cyclical fluctuations, in *Prices and Production* he elaborated the changes in the real structure of production over time which constitute those fluctuations. Consumption goods are produced with the aid of capital goods in processes which for technological and economic reasons take some definite period of time. Capital goods, however, are no original factors of production. The longer the process needed to produce a certain amount of consumer goods, the greater is the stock of capital involved and the more productive is the process itself. The relevant characteristics of the structure of production are shown by Hayek's famous triangles. While the ordinate represents the time dimension of the structure of production, i.e. the degree of roundaboutness, the abscissa measures the money value of the output of consumption goods. Slices of the triangle perpendicular to the time axis indicate the different *stages* of production among which the resources are allocated. The supplies and demands for resources at the various stages differ in their sensitivity to changes in the interest rate because of their different temporal dimension. Changes in the rate of interest therefore will have a systematic effect on the structure of relative prices that allocates resources among the different stages of production. The lower the interest rate the longer are the production processes that a rational capitalist would adopt, thus drawing more resources into the early stages of production. This case is represented by a relative lengthening of the time axis of the Hayekian triangle.

Hayek starts by assuming the system to be in equilibrium initially, i.e. the market and the natural rates of interest coincide and the degree of roundaboutness corresponds to consumers' time-preference, i.e. the demand for capital is matched by an equivalent amount of voluntary savings. Hayek makes a crucial distinction between interest-rate changes which occur because of changes in the intertemporal preferences of consumers and interest-rate changes attributable to monetary injections by the banks. In the latter case, in contrast to the former, monetary factors cause false price signals which result in a misallocation of resources among the different stages of production. Investors are encouraged to spend the additional money in the earlier stages thereby bidding up the prices of capital goods specific to these stages and reallocating unspecific resources away from later to these earlier stages of production. Sooner or later a shortage of consumption goods and later-stage capital goods will emerge. As long as money wages lag behind the increase in prices of these goods, forced saving will be imposed on consumers. 'Yet as soon as the competition of entrepreneurs for the factors of production has driven up wages in proportion to the increase in money, and no additional credits are forthcoming, the proportion which they are able to spend on capital goods must fall' (Hayek, 1932, p. 243). As a consequence, the market rate of interest will start to rise again and the new roundaboutness of production will then turn out to be too lengthy. This will bring about losses and curtailments of production in the earlier stages thus causing a collapse of the boom. The results will be, among other things, excess capacities in early-stage industries producing capital goods and unemployment.

Now let us have a closer look at what the members of the Kiel school thought of the Austrian model of production at the time when it was used by Hayek. In two influential papers Fritz Burchardt (1931–32) set out to compare, contrast and combine the two most important alternative ways of conceiving the production system, the schemes of the stationary circular flow in Böhm-Bawerk and Marx, and thus undertook the first synthesis of the vertical integration approach and the interindustry approach. Together with Lowe's suggestions that the key investment sector I of Marx's reproduction scheme should be divided into two subsectors, Burchardt's seminal synthesis of the sector model and the stage model, which Lowe later applied to the analysis of real capital formation and transition processes between equilibrium growth paths, was a profound contribution to the progress of the Kiel school's research. Though for the most part concerned with the static aspects of a scheme of reproduction, Burchardt left no doubt about its relevance as an instrument for dynamic analysis.

Burchardt's main point of critique in his attack on the linear model of production originally devised by Böhm-Bawerk and picked up by Hayek in his *Prices and Production* was the unsatisfactory treatment of fixed capital goods in the 'Austrian' representation of the structure of production in which a sequence of original inputs is transformed into a single output of consumable commodities. No distinction is made between fixed and circulating capital; both types of capital are 'intermediate products' or 'working capital', i.e. goods in process that sooner or later will be turned into consumers' goods. The production process is thought of as being *unidirectional*, i.e. causal, rather than *circular*. Each stage or circle of Böhm-Bawerk's *'Ringschema'* represents intermediate products, with the highest stage or innermost circle where original factors (labour and natural resources) continuously produce the first intermediate products of the synchronized production process without the aid of intermediate products (capital goods), and the lowest stage or outermost circle passing each year into consumption. This way of tracing back the production process to some original combination of labour (and land) leaves unexplained the reproduction and expansion requirements of the stock of fixed capital goods. Böhm-Bawerk's scheme of production thus proves deficient mainly in two respects. First, Burchardt criticized Böhm-Bawerk for mixing up two entirely different problems, namely the *historical* conditions of the original building up of a capital stock and the *present* conditions of reproduction of the existing capital stock. Second, in an industrial system the physical *self-reproduction* of some fixed capital goods is an important technological characteristic, i.e. a particular group of fixed capital goods, which Lowe later called 'machine tools', can be maintained and increased only with the help of a circular process in which these machine tools also act as inputs. The role which these goods play in industrial production is thus analogous to the role of seed-corn in agricultural production. Therefore it is not possible to trace all finished goods technically back to nothing but labour and land and to treat fixed capital goods as the output of some intermediate stages in the vertical model, as Böhm-Bawerk and his 'Austrian' followers have suggested. However, it has to be remembered that the vertical model was not developed for its own sake, but as a basis for a theory of capital, and that there is a certain justification for the Böhm-Bawerkian view of capital as intermediate products because capital goods are incapable of serving human wants directly and thus have no intrinsic utility. Neither Burchardt nor Lowe questioned the ability of Austrian analysis to deal with the problem of working capital. They have both emphasized that the downward flow to the lowest or final stage of finished output properly describes the structure of working capital if on the highest stage a stock of fixed capital goods is added to the original inputs of labour and natural resources. That is, in order to account for the reproduction, expansion and structural change of an industrial economy the vertical model must be supplemented by a classical model of the circular flow which clearly depicts the self-reproduction of certain fixed capital goods. 'It is the failure of most models based on the Austrian concept of the structure of production that they disregard the circular flows, concentrating rather on the linear ones' (Lowe, 1952, pp. 154–5).[12]

Sraffa's well known demonstration that fixed capital generally cannot be reduced to dated quantities of labour and his showing the impossibility of Böhm-Bawerk's concept of the 'period of production' to function as an adequate measure of the quantity of capital may be considered as a continuation and elaboration of the critique raised by Burchardt and Lowe about the problematical role of fixed capital in Austrian theory. In striking contrast to the circular vision of the productive process, the vertical vision of the Austrian approach turns out to be a further variant of neoclassical analysis, which conceives of the production process as 'a one-way avenue that leads from "Factors of production" to "Consumption goods"' (Sraffa, 1960, p. 93).

Interestingly, although Hayek's vertical treatment of economic structure stays firmly within the Austrian tradition and Lowe is a representative of the opposing horizontal or interindustry approach, both authors give some hints for a necessary complementary perspective combining the advantages of the two approaches. Whereas Hayek had overlooked the importance of the durability of existing capital as a constraint on investment in his use of Austrian capital theory as a basis for his trade cycle analysis, the critique of Burchardt, 'which, although I cannot agree with all of it, still appears to me not only as the first but also as the most fruitful of all the recent criticisms of the

"Austrian" theory of capital' (Hayek, 1939, p. 23), had some impact on his thinking. This becomes especially clear if one looks into the section on '[t]he structure of capitalistic production' in his *Profits, Interest and Investment* where Hayek concedes that the concept of the 'stages of production', which he had used in *Prices and Production* 'gives the impression of a simple linearity of the dependency of the various stages of production which does not apply in a world where durable goods are the most important form of capital' (Hayek, 1939, pp. 21–2). The stages concept may give an undue impression of linearity while in fact production relationships may in many respects be rather circular in character. On the other hand, Hayek views the 'crude dichotomy of industry into consumers' goods industries and capital good industries' as 'certainly wholly insufficient to reproduce the essential features of the complicated interdependencies between industries in actual life' since the 'capital goods industries are ... further organised in a sort of vertical hierarchy' (p. 21).

The latter argument had been the reason for Lowe to split up the key sector I of Marx's reproduction scheme, in which capital goods are produced, into two subsectors: sector Ia producing the equipment for the replacement and expansion of both capital goods sectors, and sector Ib producing the equipment for the consumer-good group. Moreover, Lowe's scheme of industrial production comprises not only three sectors but also four successive stages within each sector that lead up to the finished goods. Thus Lowe's category of equipment-good industries includes not only the production of the final fixed capital goods but also the preceding stages of mining and the production of pig iron and steel. Similarly, the consumer-good industries include not only the making of the finished dress ready for sale to the individual consumer but also the preceding stages of cultivating cotton, spinning yarn and weaving clothes. The fact that all sectors are divided into stages representing the successive maturing of natural resources into final goods with the help of labour and fixed capital goods brings into light the often neglected role of working capital goods as goods in process. Lowe introduces this 'Austrian' element into his model to make possible the analysis of adjustment processes in historical time when intertemporal complementarities play an important role in processes of structural change, an intention which comes rather close to Hayek's. However, one important difference should not be overlooked. Whereas the output of working capital or intermediate goods of the preceding stage serves as an input in the subsequent stage from the second stage onwards, in the Lowe model it is already the very first stage in which fixed capital goods are to be applied in the production process.

The Hayek–Hicks–Lowe connection

Lowe's attention in more than 60 years of research has been focused upon technological change as the mainspring of destabilizing tendencies in industrial economies. One of the reasons for this is that innovations are an ever-present feature of capitalist economies and are endogenously generated by the competitive process. In his last work Lowe is particularly concerned with the present dominant form of technological change, the so-called microelectronic revolution, because displacement of labour is no longer confined to the production of goods but nowadays also affects services (see Lowe, 1988, ch. 6). The spectre of technological unemployment is on the stage again. Lowe emphasizes that, in principle, compensation is possible. The main issue, however, 'is the question of whether the market system of late capitalism is endowed with a *self-regulating mechanism* capable of achieving compensation by the uncontrolled actions of private consumers and producers, or whether *public intervention* is necessary in order to counter destabilizing tendencies that an uncontrolled market is likely to create' (Lowe, 1988, p. 99). Although both Hayek and Lowe have addressed the relevance of the time-structure of production to economic fluctuations, the last statement points to a significant difference in their positions. There is no money in Lowe's model, nevertheless the adjustment process is full of difficulties. Lowe's work, as that of Hicks (1973), the other pioneer of traverse analysis, shows that by getting rid of money, the economy is not automatically in equilibrium, neither in a stationary one nor on a steady state growth path.

Hicks repeatedly pointed out how he had been influenced in his economic thinking by Hayek during the LSE years in the early 1930s.[13] In particular Hayek had introduced him to the work of Wicksell and had made him think of the productive process as a process in time. However, Hicks always had been sceptical about Hayek's claim that the economy would be in equilibrium if there were no monetary disturbances. This is already manifest in his early essay on equilibrium and the trade cycle which essentially is the result of Hicks's grappling with Hayek's *Prices and Production* and Hayek's 1928 concept of intertemporal equilibrium. Here we find Hicks arguing against Hayek's statement 'that a change in the effective volume of monetary circulation is to be regarded as an independent cause of disequilibrium. I cannot accept this in its literal sense, though I am prepared to agree that in a world of imperfect foresight monetary changes are very likely to lead to acute disequilibrium' (Hicks, 1933, p. 445). Hicks realized that to analyse money one must consider uncertainty and expectations. He had a long struggle to present an inherently dynamic vision of the economy in which agents' present decisions represent attempts to cope with an uncertain future in view of monetary and real constraints imposed upon them by past actions. But although Hicks made important contributions to monetary theory over a period of almost six decades,[14] he did not become too tired to emphasize 'the *real* (non-monetary) character of the cyclical process' (Hicks, 1950, p. 136). Indeed it had been one of the main objectives of his *Contribution to the Theory of the Trade Cycle* 'to show that the main features of the cycle can be adequately explained in real terms' (ibid).

In *Capital and Time* Hicks (1973) presented a 'neo-Austrian' approach to capital theory in order to study the employment consequences of technological change. Like Lowe, Hicks started his investigation from Ricardo's analysis of the machinery problem. But they have used alternative notions of economic activities, namely *horizontally* integrated versus *vertically* integrated models of economic structure. Hicks based his traverse analysis on the concept of a neo-Austrian, vertically integrated production process, in which a stream of labour inputs is transformed into a stream of consumption-good outputs. In contrast to Böhm-Bawerk and the early Hayek,[15] Hicks gave up the notion of the degree of roundaboutness or the period of production. Furthermore, Hicks saw the decisive advantage of his approach over that of the 'old Austrians' as lying in the possibility of incorporating fixed capital into his approach, which had been the Achilles' heel of the Austrian model.[16]

It is precisely the focus on innovations that take the form of new methods of production for making the same final product (consumption good) that has led Hicks to the vertical integration approach of his neo-Austrian theory in which intersectoral transactions are dispensed with in order to avoid having to deal with the physical transmutation of the capital stock under the influence of innovations. With reference to Hayek and the early debate between Hayek and Lowe on the endogenous factor causing the cycle, it is very illuminating to look at Hicks's final conclusion:

> Where ... I do not go along with him [Hayek] is in the view that the disturbances in question have a monetary origin. He had not emancipated himself from the delusion ... that with money removed 'in a state of barter' everything would somehow fit. One of my objects in writing this book has been to kill that delusion. It could only arise because the theory of the barter economy had been insufficiently worked out. There has been no money in my model; yet it has plenty of adjustment difficulties. It is not true that by getting rid of money, one is automatically in 'equilibrium' – whether that equilibrium is conceived of as a stationary state (Wicksell), a perfect foresight economy (Hayek) or any kind of steady state. Monetary disorders may indeed be superimposed upon other disorders; but the other disorders are more fundamental. (Hicks, 1973, pp. 133–4)

However, the non-neutrality of money in Hayek's theory only holds for the cycle. In the long run, an increase in the volume of money will not have any positive real effects. The income allocation between saving and investment will return to its previous equilibrium level because in Hayek's opinion the income mechanism, whereby savings would equal credit-financed investment *ex post*, is doomed to failure.[17] Thus the classical dichotomy is on the stage again.

Notes

1. Adolph Löwe (from September 1939 Lowe), born 1893 in Stuttgart, received the Dr. Juris from the University of Tübingen in 1918. From 1919 to 1924 he served as section head in the Ministries of Labour and Economics in Berlin. In the period 1924 to 1926 he was head of the international division of the Federal Bureau of Statistics and a close cooperator of Ernst Wagemann who founded the Deutsches Institut für Konjunkturforschung, the first German institute for the study of business cycles, in 1925. In 1926 Lowe became director of research at the Institute of World Economics in Kiel, where he was also appointed Professor of Economic Theory and Sociology at the university in 1929. In 1931 he accepted an offer from the University of Frankfurt where in Spring 1933 he was among the first professors to be fired by the Nazis. Lowe emigrated immediately to England, where he was appointed special honorary lecturer in economics and political philosophy at the University of Manchester. In Summer 1940 he moved to the New School for Social Research in New York, where he became professor of economics at the Graduate Faculty which had been founded by Alvin Johnson as the 'University in Exile' in 1933. After his retirement in 1963 Lowe remained active as Emeritus Professor in the department of economics at the New School until his return to Germany in 1983. Lowe also received the Veblen-Commons Award in 1979.

2. The term 'Kiel school' refers to the most important section of the Institut für Weltwirtschaft und Seeverkehr in Kiel in the years 1926–33. The new department of statistical international economics and research on international trade cycles was founded and led by Adolph Lowe (1926–31) who had managed to bring together a group of extremely talented young economists. Besides Lowe and Gerhard Colm, who served as chairman (1931–33) after Lowe's departure to the University of Frankfurt, such distinguished scholars as Hans Neisser, Fritz Burchardt, Alfred Kähler and, for a period of time, Wassily Leontief (1927–28) and Jacob Marschak (1928–30) were also members of this scientific community.

   The work on cyclical growth being done in Kiel was supported by the Rockefeller Foundation as the research on trade cycles in Vienna (under the direction of Hayek and Morgenstern) or, e.g., the business cycle studies in Berlin (Wagemann), Bonn (Spiethoff), Oslo (Frisch), Rotterdam (Tinbergen) and Stockholm (Ohlin) (see Craver, 1986). The members of the Kiel group, who fought against wage cuts in the debates at the end of the Weimar Republic and later, like Colm, made important contributions as policy advisers within the Roosevelt and Truman administrations, are internationally recognized among the most important precursors of the theory of employment (Garvy, 1975) and in the development of modern non-neoclassical capital and growth theory (Clark, 1984, who has also compared the Kiel group with Keynes's Political Economy group in Cambridge operating at the same time.)

3. Fritz (later Frank) Burchardt (1902–58) took his Ph.D. degree at the University of Kiel (1925) with a dissertation on Schumpeter's contributions to the problem of statics in which he called into question Schumpeter's assertion that dynamics, understood as a theory of development, was necessarily less precise than, and unrelated to, the theory of stationary equilibrium. Burchardt became the closest collaborator of Lowe in Kiel and Frankfurt between 1926 and 1933. He had already submitted his habilitation thesis at the University of Frankfurt when the Nazis came to power and stopped his university career. Burchardt emigrated to England in 1935 where he was closely associated with the Oxford Institute of Statistics and was appointed its director in 1949. There he built up the Institut's *Bulletin* and was also the editor of the famous cooperative 1944 study on *The Economics of Full Employment*. For a more detailed evaluation of Burchardt's contributions to economics see Lowe (1959).

4. Hans Neisser (1895–1975) had already achieved a considerable reputation as a young economist in the Weimar Republic. In the years from 1927 to 1933 he acted as a deputy director of research in the Institute of World Economics. While at Kiel he published his first major work, *Der Tauschwert des Geldes* (*The Exchange Value of Money*, 1928), an important contribution to monetary theory. The book was not only esteemed highly by Hayek but also evoked international response and was one of the very few books outside the Anglo-Saxon world that Keynes quoted with full approval in his *Treatise on Money* (Keynes, *Collected Writings* V, p. 178). It was on the basis of that reputation that after emigrating from Germany in 1933 Neisser entered the second stage of his career as a professor of monetary theory at the University of Pennsylvania. During World War II he worked in the Office of Price Administration in Washington, before he finally joined the Graduate Faculty of the New School for Social Research in New York (1943) where he remained as professor until his retirement in 1965.

    For a more detailed discussion of Neisser's contributions to economic theory see Hagemann (1990b) who especially comments on Neisser's seminal contribution to the theory of general equilibrium in which the author showed that the existence of a Walrasian equilibrium required more than the counting of equations and that the mere equality of equations and unknowns is not sufficient for a meaningful solution. His genuine contribution is his pointing out that equilibrium prices might be negative (see Neisser 1932, 1990).

5. For a retrospective view see Lowe (1989). The impact of Lowe's contribution was also recognized outside Germany, as is shown, for example, by the two articles written by Kuznets (1930a and 1930b), and, more recently, by Hudson (1988).

6. For a more detailed analysis of these three pillars of Hayek's theory of the business cycle as well as of the innovative elements see the contribution of Laidler to this conference (Chapter 1).

7. See Lowe (1929), Hayek (1929b) and Hayek (1928b), Lowe (1928). Interestingly, Lowe's 1928 article is based on a lecture he presented under the title '*Gibt es eine monetäre Konjunkturtheorie?*' to the Nationalökonomische Gesellschaft in Vienna on 26 March 1928. In a letter to Oskar Morgenstern in Paris, dated 16 March 1928, Hayek reports on long discussions he had with Löwe and Neisser in Kiel during a visit to Germany and is looking ahead to Löwe's visit to Vienna. Hayek's expectations are that Löwe's talk, in contrast to boring ones by some other economists, will be very interesting and stimulating since Löwe 'surely will have controversial discussions with Mises but probably also with Strigl and myself' (Oskar Morgenstern Collection, Special Manuscript Department, William R. Perkins Library, Duke University).

8. For a most thorough analysis and comparison of the 'vertical' and the 'horizontal' treatment of economic structure see the contributions in Baranzini and Scazzieri (1990).

9. Kuznets (1930b, p. 128).

10. See Hayek (1928a). For a detailed discussion of Hayek's notion of intertemporal equilibrium and the subtle subjectivist transformation of the equilibrium concept in his writings see Currie and Steedman (1989) and Böhm (1986).

11. In contrast to many new classical real business cycle models Hayek is looking less enthusiastic at exogenous shocks to technology as the decisive driving force. Another difference lies in the *endogeneity* of fluctuations in the volume of money and credit in Hayek's cycle theory and the *exogenous* nature of monetary disturbances in new classical monetary cycle theories in which the Hayek problem of how coordination can be achieved in a market economy is assumed away.

12. The Burchardt–Lowe critique was taken up by a variety of authors in the English language debate. See, e.g., Nurkse (1935).

13. See Hicks (1967, 1982, 1991).

14. This dates from his 1935 'Suggestion for Simplifying the Theory of Money', a landmark in the evolution of the theory of liquidity preference with which Hicks became a very influential monetary economist, via his 1967 *Critical Essays in Monetary Theory* to his last book *A Market Theory of Money* (1989).

15. It should be pointed out here that Hayek, while using the notions 'degree of roundaboutness etc.' in his contributions to business cycle theory, gave up that notion in his *The Pure*

Theory of Capital (1941) after Morgenstern (1935) had shown the period of production to be a dubious tool for the analysis of problems of capital theory.
16. For a detailed discussion of the role of fixed capital goods in Hicks's neo-Austrian model in comparison to a von Neumann–Sraffa approach see Hagemann and Kurz (1976).
17. For an analysis of the basic dilemma of Hayek's monetary theory see Trautwein (1992).

References

Baranzini, M. and R. Scazzieri (eds) (1990), *The Economic Theory of Structure and Change,* Cambridge: Cambridge University Press.

Burchardt, F. A. (1928), 'Entwicklungsgeschichte der monetären Konjunkturtheorie', *Weltwirtschaftliches Archiv,* **28**, 78–143.

Burchardt, F. A. (1931–32), 'Die Schemata des stationären Kreislaufs bei Böhm-Bawerk und Marx', *Weltwirtschaftliches Archiv,* **34**, 525–64, and 35, 116–76.

Böhm, S. (1986), 'Time and Equilibrium: Hayek's Notion of Intertemporal Equilibrium Reconsidered', in I. M. Kirzner (ed.), *Subjectivism, Intelligibility and Economic Understanding. Essays in Honor of Ludwig M. Lachmann,* New York: New York University Press.

Carell, E. (1929), *Sozialökonomische Theorie und Konjunkturproblem,* Munich and Leipzig: Duncker & Humblot.

Clark, D. (1984), 'Confronting the Linear Imperialism of the Austrians: Lowe's Contribution to Capital and Growth Theory', *Eastern Economic Journal,* **10**, 107–27.

Craver, E. (1986), 'Patronage and the Directions of Research in Economics: The Rockefeller Foundation in Europe 1924–1938', *Minerva,* **24**, 205–22.

Currie, M. and I. Steedman (1989), 'Agonising over Equilibrium: Hayek and Lindahl', *Quaderni di Storia dell'Economica Politica,* **7**, 75–99.

Garvy, G. (1975), 'Keynes and the Economic Activists of Pre-Hitler Germany', *Journal of Political Economy,* **83**, 391–405.

Hagemann, H. (1990a), 'The Structural Theory of Economic Growth', in M. Baranzini and R. Scazzieri (eds), *The Economic Theory of Structure and Change,* Cambridge: Cambridge University Press.

Hagemann, H. (1990b), 'Neisser's "The Wage Rate and Employment in Market Equilibrium": An Introduction', *Structural Change and Economic Dynamics,* **1**, 133–9.

Hagemann, H. and H.D. Kurz (1976), 'The Return of the Same Truncation Period and Reswitching of Techniques in Neo-Austrian and More General Models', *Kyklos,* **29**, 678–708.

Hayek, F. A. von (1925), 'The Monetary Policy of the United States after the Recovery From the 1920 Crisis', in F. A. von Hayek (1984).

Hayek, F. A. von (1928a), 'Das intertemporale Gleichgewichtssystem der Preise und die Bewegungen des "Geldwertes"', *Weltwirtschaftliches Archiv,* **28**, 33–76; English translation in Hayek (1984).

Hayek, F. A. von (1928b), 'Einige Bemerkungen über das Verhältnis der Geldtheorie zur Konjunkturtheorie', in K. Diehl (ed.), *Beiträge zur Wirtschaftstheorie. Zweiter Teil: Konjunkturforschung und Konjunkturtheorie,* Schriften des Vereins für Sozialpolitik, 173/II, Munich and Leipzig: Duncker & Humblot.

Hayek, F. A. von (1929a), *Geldtheorie und Konjunkturtheorie,* Vienna: Hölder–Pichler–Tempski. English edition *Monetary Theory and the Trade Cycle,* London 1933: J. Cape, Reprint New York 1966: Augustus M. Kelley.

Hayek, F. A. von (1929b), 'Diskussionsbemerkungen über "Kredit und Konjunktur"', in F. Boese (ed.), *Wandlungen des Kapitalismus. Auslandsanleihen. Kredit und Konjunktur* Schriften des Vereins für Sozialpolitik, 175, Munich and Leipzig: Duncker & Humblot.

Hayek, F. A. von (1931), *Prices and Production,* 2nd ed., London 1935: Routledge & Kegan Paul.

Hayek, F. A. von (1932), 'Money and Capital: A Reply', *Economic Journal,* **42**, 237–49.

Hayek, F. A. von (1939), *Profits, Interest and Investment,* London: Routledge.

Hayek, F. A. von (1941), *The Pure Theory of Capital,* London: Macmillan.

Hayek, F. A. von (1976), *Preise und Produktion,* reprint, New York and Vienna: Springer.

Hayek, F. A. von (1984), *Money, Capital and Fluctuations: Early Essays*, ed. R. McCloughry, London: Routledge and Kegan Paul.

Hicks, J. (1933), 'Gleichgewicht und Konjunktur', *Zeitschrift für Nationalökonomie*, 4, 441–55; English translation as 'Equilibrium and the Trade Cycle', *Economic Inquiry*, 18, 1980, 523–34.

Hicks, J. (1935), 'A Suggestion for Simplifying the Theory of Money', *Economica*, new series, 2, 1–19.

Hicks, J. (1950), A *Contribution to the Theory of the Trade Cycle*, Oxford: Clarendon Press.

Hicks, J. (1967), 'The Hayek Story', in: J. Hicks, *Critical Essays in Monetary Theory*, Oxford: Clarendon.

Hicks, J. (1973), *Capital and Time*, Oxford: Clarendon Press.

Hicks, J. (1982), 'Introductory: LSE and the Robbins Circle', in J. Hicks, *Money, Interest and Wages. Collected Essays on Economic Theory. Volume II*, Oxford: Basil Blackwell.

Hicks, J. (1989), A *Market Theory of Money*, Oxford: Clarendon Press.

Hicks, J. (1991), 'The Swedish Influence on *Value and Capital*', in L. Jonung (ed.), *The Stockholm School of Economics Revisited*, Cambridge: Cambridge University Press.

Hudson, M. (1988), 'Keynes, Hayek and the monetary economy', in J. Hillard (ed.), *J. M. Keynes in Retrospect. The Legacy of the Keynesian Revolution*, Aldershot: Edward Elgar.

Kuznets, S. (1930a), 'Equilibrium Economics and Business-Cycle Theory', *Quarterly Journal of Economics*, 44, 381–415.

Kuznets, S. (1930b), 'Monetary Business Cycle Theory in Germany', *Journal of Political Economy*, 38, 125–63.

Löwe, A. (1925), 'Der gegenwärtige Stand der Konjunkturforschung in Deutschland', in M. J. Bonn and M. Palyi (eds), *Die Wirtschaftswissenschaft nach dem Kriege. Festgabe für Lujo Brentano zum 80. Geburtstag,* vol. 2, Munich and Leipzig: Duncker & Humblot.

Löwe, A. (1926), 'Wie ist Konjunkturtheorie überhaupt möglich?' *Weltwirtschaftliches Archiv*, 24, 165–97.

Löwe, A. (1928), 'Über den Einfluß monetärer Faktoren auf den Konjunkturzyklus', in K. Diehl (ed.), *Beiträge zur Wirtschaftstheorie. Zweiter Teil: Konjunkturforschung und Konjunkturtheorie*, Schriften des Vereins für Sozialpolitik, 173/II, Munich and Leipzig: Duncker & Humblot.

Löwe, A. (1929), 'Diskussionsbemerkungen über "Kredit und Konjunktur"', in F. Boese (ed.), *Wandlungen des Kapitalismus. Auslandsanleihen. Kredit und Konjunktur.* Schriften des Vereins für Sozialpolitik, 175, Munich and Leipzig: Duncker & Humblot.

Lowe, A. (1959), 'F. A. Burchardt, Part I: Recollections of his Work in Germany', *Bulletin of the Oxford University Institute of Statistics*, 21, 59–65.

Lowe, A. (1976), *The Path of Economic Growth*, Cambridge: Cambridge University Press.

Lowe, A. (1988), *Has Freedom a Future?*, New York: Praeger.

Lowe, A. (1989), 'Konjunkturtheorie in Deutschland in den Zwanziger Jahren', in B. Schefold (ed.), *Studien zur Entwicklung der ökonomischen Theorie VIII*, Berlin: Duncker & Humblot.

Morgenstern, O. (1935), 'Zur Theorie der Produktionsperiode', *Zeitschrift für Nationalökonomie*, 6, 196–208.

Neisser, H. (1928), *Der Tauschwert des Geldes*, Jena: Gustav Fischer.

Neisser, H. (1932), 'Lohnhöhe und Beschäftigungsgrad im Marktgleichgewicht', *Weltwirtschaftliches Archiv*, 36, 415–55; English translation in *Structural Change and Economic Dynamics*, 1, 1990, 141–63.

Neisser, H. (1934), 'Monetary Expansion and the Structure of Production', *Social Research*, 1, 434–57.

Nurkse, R. (1935), 'The Schematic Representation of the Structure of Production', *Review of Economic Studies*, 2, 232–44.

Sraffa, P. (1960), *Production of Commodities by Means of Commodities*, Cambridge: Cambridge University Press.

Trautwein, H.-M. (1992), 'Kredit, Zins und Güterpreise: Über produktive Unklarheiten bei Wicksell und Hayek', Universität Hohenheim. Institut für Volkswirtschaftslehre, Discussion Paper no. 69, Stuttgart.

7 Trade cycle as a frustrated traverse: an analytical reconstruction of Hayek's model

Meghnad Desai and Paul Redfern

Hayek's model of the trade cycle as contained in *Prices and Production* excited much comment at the time he presented it at the LSE in 1931. [See for a bibliography Desai (1982).] In the recent revival of interest in Hayek's work there has been some further interest expressed, though unlike in the case of other parts of his work this interest has expressed itself mainly in going over the old ground rather than advancing the argument beyond where Hayek left it or filling in the gaps in his model. [See Desai (1991) for a defence of Hayek's model against Kaldor's criticism. See Colonna (1990) for a scholarly alternative account of Hayek's enterprise.]

Our purpose in this paper is to give an analytical reconstruction of Hayek's argument in *Prices and Production*. This involves constructing a simple numerical account of the *equilibrium traverse* of a growing economy which Hayek took as the background case in his triangular diagrams. Then we shall try to illustrate in the context of the same numerical scheme the Hayek model of the cycle as a *frustrated traverse*. This will, we hope, clarify the analytical anatomy of Hayek's theory.

Our reason for relying on numerical examples rather than a general algebraic formulation is two-fold. To begin with, apart from our own shortcomings as economic theorists, a numerical scheme may be comprehensible by many more economists. The Hayekians are by and large non-mathematical if not anti-mathematical. There is also the point that a general schema can be constructed if anyone wishes to (and has the talent for it) by using the tools set out in Hicks's *Capital and Time* (Hicks, 1973) and Zamagni's brilliant contribution 'Ricardo and Hayek Effects in a Fixwage Model of Traverse' (Zamagni, 1984).

An additional excuse (rather than reason) we could cite for using a numerical scheme is that Hayek used that device in his 1929 article 'The Paradox of Savings' to illustrate his point (Hayek, 1929–39). He took an economy with eight stages (sectors) of intermediate inputs using £1000 each and producing a consumption good output of £1000. Capital intensity is thus measured as total input cost of £8000 to output £1000 i.e. 8:1 (See Table 7.1, Column A). Then a voluntary decline in consumption from £1000 to £900 leads eventually (though Hayek does not trace out the traverse) to an economy with a capital intensity of 9:1. This economy contains an extra sector, but each of the nine intermediate sectors use £900 each and produces an output of £900 (Table 7.1, Column B). Hayek contrasts this with an artificial expansion whereby banks create credit worth an extra £100 to compensate for the decline in consumption. Hayek then presents this case (Table 7.1, Column C) as showing a capital intensity of 8.1:1 whereby there is merely an additional sector spending £100.

Table 7.1   Hayek's production structure

		A	B	C
		Initial £	With voluntary savings of £100	With credit of £100 to consumers compensating for £100 savings
Consumption goods demand	1	1000	900	1000
Intermediate stages demand	2	1000	900	1000
	3	1000	900	1000
	4	1000	900	1000
	5	1000	900	1000
	6	1000	900	1000
	7	1000	900	1000
	8	1000	900	1000
	9	1000	900	1000
	10	0	900	100
Intensity = Σ *intermediate consumption*		8:1	9:1	8.1:1

Source: Examples taken from Hayek (1929–39), pp. 229, 231, 257.

Hayek's example raises more questions than it answers. Compared to the presentation in *Prices and Production* where he speaks of the price gradient formed by the input–output structure of adjoining sectors and the rate of interest, there is little here that is clear. It is not clear whether the £1000 of each intermediate sector's output contains costs of input bought in from earlier sectors plus interest rate, and if so, how. Why do all sectors go down from £1000 to £900 plus an extra sector? Is this merely numerically convenient or is it necessary for the structure of production? Lastly, is the ratio of total input costs to output value a good way of measuring capital intensity?

Our analytical reconstruction began in an attempt to make sense of that table. A nine to ten stage economy is too big to be tractable. We therefore began with an original 'short' economy which consists of just two sectors. We then posit a 'long' economy with three sectors. Thus the second economy has two intermediate input sectors compared to only one in the first economy. Each economy produces a single consumption good. Having set up these two economies, we solve out for the wages and prices. We then construct an equilibrium traverse sequence by invoking a 'shock' of higher savings. This is designed to parallel the changeover in Hayek's table from Column A to Column B. We then construct equilibrium money demand in such an economy. The next step is to assume not higher savings but a credit expansion as a 'shock'. The traverse is then traced out and shown to be frustrated.

A model of equilibrium traverse

Let us call the original economy Economy A. It has two sectors labelled 1 and 2. The input–output structure is triangular (in line with the technology in *Prices and Production*). As we see from Table 7.2, Panel A, there are 1000 workers, 500 in each sector. Sector 1 produces inputs for itself (400) and for Sector 2 (600). It generates no net output. Sector 2 uses Sector 1's net output and also consumes its own output as input (500), to produce 2500 units of output. Net output of the economy is therefore 2000 units of consumption goods.

Economy B has three sectors labelled 0, 1 and 2. The input–output structure is triangular again. Sector 0 has been added as an extra 'deepening' element. The numerical magnitudes are displayed in Panel B of Table 7.2. Again there are 1000 workers. The lengthening of the economy allows labour productivity to rise in the consumption good sector as well as in Sector 1 compared to its level in Economy A.[1]

The net output of Economy B is 2500 units of consumption goods. Thus we have deliberately constructed the economy in such a way as to accommodate the Austrian claim that lengthening the process of production leads to higher output. In Hayek's example of Table 1 it is not at all clear whether Column B represents a lower money value but a higher physical amount of consumption goods, since the price is not explicitly worked out.

Before describing the process of traverse, let us work out the prices. The pricing formula is based on two alternative assumptions: wages paid at the onset of production and hence included in the costs which are marked up by the interest factor $(1 + \rho)$ or wages paid at the end of the process.

Table 7.2   Production, prices and money demand

Production

	Panel A					Panel B				
Sector	1	2	Labour	Output		0	1	2	Labour	Output
					0	500	0	0	400	1000
1	400		500	1000	1	500	500	0	300	1000
2	600	500	500	2500	2		500	500	300	3000

Prices

	p_1	p_2	w	ρ		p_0	p_1	p_2	w	ρ
Advance	1.25	0.833	1	0.25		1.33	3.24	0.95	1	0.25
Arrears	1.0	0.66	1	0.25		1.07	2.60	0.775	1	0.25
Advance	1.15	0.75	1	0.20		1.2	2.70	0.79	1	0.2
Arrears	0.96	0.63	1	0.20		1.0	2.25	0.66	1	0.2

Money demand

Sector	1	2	Total
	Advance ($\rho=0.25$)		
Incl. own output	1000	1666.67	2666.67
Excl. own output	500	1250	1750
	Arrears ($\rho=0.25$)		
Incl. own output	400	933.33	1333.33
Excl. own output	0	600	600

Sector	1	2	Total	0	1	2	Total
	Advance ($\rho=0.2$)				Advance ($\rho=0.2$)		
Incl. own output	961.54	1568.83	2530.36	1000.00	2250.00	2045.05	5295.05
Excl. own output	500.00	1192.31	1692.31	400.00	600.79	1650.00	2650.79
	Arrears ($\rho=0.2$)				Arrears ($\rho=0.2$)		
Incl. own output	384.62	917.00	1301.62	500.00	1625.00	1454.21	3579.21
Excl. own output	0.00	576.92	576.92	0.00	500.00	1125.00	1625.00

	Vertically integrated economy	
Advance	1000	0
Arrears	0	0

Thus, for wages paid in advance

$$p_1 = (1 + \rho) [a_{11}p_1 + wl_1]_{-1} \tag{1a}$$
$$p_2 = (1 + \rho) [a_{21}p_1 + a_{22}p_2 + wl_2]_{-1} \tag{1b}$$

where a_{ij} is the relevant input coefficient and l_i the labour input coefficient.

For wages paid in arrears

$$p_1 = (1 + \rho) [a_{11} \, p_1]_{-1} + wl_1 \tag{2a}$$
$$p_2 = (1 + \rho) [a_{21} \, p_1 + a_{22}p_2]_{-1} + wl_2 \tag{2b}$$

Similarly for Economy B, with, of course, an extra equation for p_0.

We take, somewhat arbitrarily, $\rho = 0.25$. In a stationary state, i.e., $p_{it} = p_{it-1}$; this value of ρ gives us in Equation (2a) $p_1 = w$ and $p_2 = 0.66$, that is, $p_2 = 0.66w$. For wages paid in advance (Equation 1a) we have $p_1 = 1.25w$, $p_2 = 0.833w$. The real wage is lower in the case where wages are paid in advance (alternatively, we could say that the rate of savings is higher/lower in the case where wages are paid in advance/arrears).

Given the structure of the two economies, we can further explore their nature by assuming that the wage rate is £1. Then the wage bill of £1000 will buy 1500 units of consumption goods in the 'arrears' case and 1200 units[2] in the 'advance' case, leaving 500 and 800 respectively for the capitalists, that is, profits of £333.3 in the arrears case, and £666.6 in the advance case.

But these economies have to be seen through time. If production takes one year then the output of Sector 1 of this year goes to provide the input for Sector 2 in the following year. Thus if we were to think of these two sectors as two separate firms (behaving as price takers rather than as monopolists), then the money costs and revenue in each sector can be easily traced out.

In the advance case, Sector 1 needs £1000 to start production.[3] At the end of the period, it sells its output of 1000 units for £1250 thus having enough to earn $\rho = 0.25$. Similarly Sector 2 requires £1666.7 to start production[4] and sells its output for £2082.3. Also the appropriate lags have to be specified in Equations (1a), (1b), (2a) and (2b).

If we exclude the purchase of own product from these calculations, profit on use of own input is retained inside the firm. Sector 1 then only needs to borrow money to pay the wage bill; and Sector 2 to borrow money to buy Sector 1 product, plus its wage bill. Sector 1 gets £1250 ({400 + 600}*1.25) at the end of the year, and so pays back its loan of £500 plus interest cost at 0.25, i.e. £625, and retains £625, its equivalent of 400 units of own product.[5] Sector 2 similarly borrows £500 for wage bill and £750 for buying Sector 1 input or £1250 in total and pays back £1562.5, retaining £520.83.[6]

We have set out these calculations in some detail, tedious though it may be, to clarify where the demand for money by business enterprises comes from. It is only in this way that we can model the phenomenon of excess credit creation and its impact on the structure of production.

In this matter if we were to view the economy as a *single integrated firm*, then the only demand for money by business is to pay the wage bill in the 'advance' case. Thus 'the coefficient of monetary circulation', money relative to value of output depends on the importance of intrafirm transactions, the degree of vertical integration and the conventions concerning wage payments. This is very much the way in which Hayek envisaged the coefficient of monetary circulation to be determined (*Prices and Production*, pp.120–122).

In solving for prices for Economy B, it is legitimate to assume that the rate of return will be lower. Short of adding a full savings-investment submodel, we have taken $\rho = 0.2$. At this value of ρ (Panel B), the real wage remains unaltered in the arrears economy but goes down in the advance economy. The gradient of prices – the ratio p_2/p_1 – is much lower with greater capital intensity in Economy B relative to Economy A, as one would expect.

The two economies A and B correspond to Figures 2 and 3 in *Prices and Production*. Hayek has a larger number of sectors/stages but the purpose of his example is similar. His measure of capital intensity is the ratio of the value of intermediate inputs to final output. In his example this goes up from 8:1 to 9:1. The fall in the value of final output however hides the result that the volume is larger but that the price of consumer goods has fallen. In our example, the value of *net* output (Economy A) is £1333.3 (arrears) or £1666.7 (advance),[7] while the value of inputs is £1333.3 (arrears) or £2666.7 (advance).[8] Thus the capital intensity for Economy A is 1 (arrears) or 1.6 (advance). For Economy B, the value of net output is £1650 (arrears) or £2250 (advance), while the value of inputs is £3583.3 (arrears) and £5350 (advance). Thus the ratio is 2.17 (arrears) or 2.38 (advance).

Now imagine that there is a voluntary increase in savings in Economy A and that these savings are made available to entrepreneurs to implement the blueprint for Economy B. The process of the traverse to the longer economy can be traced out with the help of our example. Of course the illustration is just one among the alternative paths that can be taken. The path illustrated here has been constructed under the assumptions that (a) full employment is maintained (i.e. total labour units of 1000) and (b) production period is of one year in each sector. No specific assumption is made about the savings ratio but a fairly rapid traverse is constructed and its consequence for required savings will be brought out. The details are given in Table 7.3.

In the first year after the shock, sector 0 of Economy B is set up, withdrawing 250 workers from Economy A. This leaves Economy A with 750 workers and the net output of consumer goods is reduced to 1500 units, exactly equal to the real value of the wage bill[9] in the original A situation.

In year 2, the output of Sector 0 is available to set up Sector 1 of Economy B. At the same time, Sector 0 can expand so as to have inputs available for Sector 1 in Year 3 etc. The labour force in Economy B expands from 250 to

Table 7.3 The Hayek equilibrium traverse

	Economy A				Economy B					
Sector	1	2	Labour	Output	Sector	0	1	2	Labour	Output
Year 1										
1	300	0	375	750	0	312.5	0	2	250	625
2	450	375	375	1875	1					
					2					
Consumption goods net output			**1500**						**0**	
Year 2										
					0	375	0	0	300	750
1	210	0	262.5	525	1	312.5	312.5	0	187.5	625
2	300	250	250	1250	2					
Consumption goods net output			**1000**						**0**	
Year 3										
					0	500	0	0	400	1000
1	80	0	100	200	1	375	375	0	225	750
2	105	87.5	87.5	437.5	2		312.5	312.5	187.5	1875
Consumption goods net output			**350**					**1562.5**		
Year 4										
					0	500	0	0	400	1000
1	32	0	40	80	1	500	500	0	300	1000
2	42	35	35	175	2		375	375	225	2250
Consumption goods net output			**140**					**1875**		
Year 5										
					0	500	0	0	400	1000
1					1	500	500	0	300	1000
2					2		500	500	300	3000
Consumption goods net output			**0**					**2500**		

487.5 leaving only 512.5 in Economy A. The net output of Economy A shrinks to 1000 units. There is a small unsold surplus of output of industry 1 in Economy A (525 – 510 = 15).

In Year 3, Economy B is ready to produce final consumption good with the excess output of 312.5 from Sector 1. This absorbs 187.5 workers in Sector 2 of Economy B producing 1875 units of output. There is a truncated Economy A left which again has a small surplus of the intermediate good. As can be seen from Table 7.3, by Year 5 the traverse is completed.

Any numerical example is bound to be artificial but we would argue that the essence of Hayek's argument in *Prices and Production* is captured in Table 7.3. The time sequence of production in Economy B is constrained by the amount of intermediate input available. Thus in Year 1, only Sector 0 can be set up. (We are assuming that it can produce input for own consumption *within* the production period. We could alternatively insist that the initial input for Sector 0 is imported.) In Year 2, the size of Sector 1 of Economy B is determined by the net output of Sector 0 in Year 1 and so on for Year 3, Sector 2 etc. Thus the setting up of a new longer economy means reduced consumption goods output for at least as long as it takes for the input inventory to become available for the final good.

The pattern of consumption goods output during the traverse is interesting. This is illustrated in Table 7.4 below. Output of consumption good sinks up to half of its original level by the end of the second period (Figure 7.1). Thus the real wage must fall also to two-thirds of its original level, even if capitalists' consumption were to fall to zero; or to one half (of the original level) if shares stay constant. But the rewards of abstinence are large. By Year 3, output is up to 1862.5 and exceeds its original level by Year 4.

The traverse is thus smooth as long as there is a willingness to save up to 50 per cent. (Obviously slower scenarios can be constructed.) Economy A shrinks steadily in employment and output while Economy B is built up. This is very much the picture of a regularly growing economy in an Austrian

Table 7.4   Consumption good output

Year	Economy A	Economy B
0	2000	0
1	1500	0
2	1000	0
3	350	1562.5
4	140	1875
5	0	2500

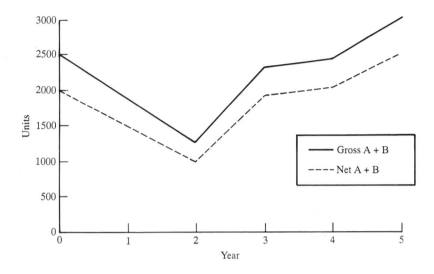

Figure 7.1 Total output (net and gross) during equilibrium traverse (from Tables 7.3 and 7.4)

sense. But we have not as yet introduced money or bank loans into our account. That is a consequence of the inessentialness of money during steady states. A smooth traverse financed by voluntary savings can be treated like a barter economy. But since money is crucial to the frustrated traverse, it is necessary to spell out the equilibrium story.

If the sectors were separate firms which bought and sold their outputs to each other, the monetary consequence of the traverse would be straightforward. The entrepreneur setting up Sector 0 would need only a one-year loan to buy the inputs. Thus in Year 1, Sector 0 entrepreneurs could borrow £250 for hiring workers paid in advance plus £375 for own inputs. At the end of Year 1, the entrepreneur (Economy B) would sell his/her output of 625 units for £750. This would give him/her the money to retire the old loan of £625 at $\rho = 0.2$ and renew borrowing. Of course, the demand for loans by Economy A entrepreneurs has shrunk in the meantime. The full path for the demand for money during the traverse can also be worked out. This is presented in Table 7.5 under the alternative wage payment arrangements in advance/arrears and with the three different assumptions about input purchase. These are (1) including payment for within-sector inputs (inclusive), (2) excluding payments for within-sector inputs (exclusive), (3) fully vertically integrated i.e., no payments for material inputs, only for labour (fully integrated).

Table 7.5 *Sectoral demand for money during equilibrium traverse*

Year	1	2	3	4	5
Advance/ incl.					
A	(721.15 + 1176.62)	(504.81 + 784.41)	(192.31 + 274.54)	(77.92 + 109.82)	
B	625	(750 + 1406.25)	(1000 + 1687.5 + 1278.16)	(1000 + 2250 + 1533.78)	(1000 + 2250 + 2045.05)
Advance/ excl.					
A	(375 + 894.23)	(262.5 + 596.2)	(100 + 208.65)	(41 + 83.46)	
B	250	(300 + 562.5)	(400 + 675 + 1031.25)	(400 + 900 + 1237.5)	(400 + 900 + 1650)
Advance/ fully integrated					
A	750	512.5	187.5	75	0
B	250	487.5	812.5	925	1000
Arrears/ incl.					
A	(288.46 + 668.05)	(201.92 + 445.34)	(76.92 + 155.87)	(30.77+ 62.35)	0
B	312.5	(375 + 1015.63)	(500 + 1218.75 + 908.88)	(500 + 1625 + 1090.66)	(500 + 1625 +1454.21)
Arrears/ excl.					
A	(0 + 432.69)	(0 + 288.46)	(0 + 100.96)	(0 + 40.38)	0
B	0	(0 + 312.5)	(0 + 375 + 703.13)	(0 + 500 + 843.75)	(0 + 500 + 1125)

130

Recall that in Economy A in the original equilibrium, the demand for money is constant since it is an economy that reproduces itself at the same scale. The traverse is obviously a scenario of changing demand for money. The first impact of the rate of interest falling from 0.25 to 0.2 is that prices in Economy A drop as shown in Table 7.2 Panel A. Thus there is a one-off fall in demand for money even at full employment in Economy A as can be seen from Table 7.5. In each of the four scenarios there is a slight drop in Year 1 in the total demand for money. This is a consequence of the new sector producing a cheaper product compared to the output produced by the labour previously employed in Economy A. Once, however, the new Sector 1 comes onstream, the demand for money goes up. Eventually the new longer economy requires double or more amount of money. This increase in the demand for money *is not inflationary* as a crude quantity theory of money would predict. Indeed Hayek's many remarks against the simplifications of the quantity theory expressed in *Prices and Production* are vindicated by these illustra-

Table 7.6   Total demand for money during equilibrium traverse

Year	Advance/incl.			Advance/excl.		
	Ec. A	Ec. B	Total	Ec. A	Ec. B	Total
0:ρ=0.25	2666.67		2666.67	1750.00		1750.00
0:ρ=0.20	2530.36		2530.36	1692.31		1692.31
1	1897.77	625.00	2522.77	1269.23	250.00	1519.23
2	1289.22	2156.25	3445.47	858.65	862.50	1721.15
3	466.85	3965.66	4432.51	308.65	2106.25	2414.90
4	187.74	4783.79	4971.53	124.46	2537.50	2661.46
5	0.00	5295.05	5295.05	2950.00	0.00	2950.00

Year	Arrears/incl.			Arrears/excl.		
	Ec. A	Ec. B	Total	Ec. A	Ec. B	Total
0:ρ=0.25	1333.33		1333.33	600.00		600.00
0:ρ=0.20	1275.30		1275.30	576.92		576.92
1	956.48	312.50	1268.98	432.69	0.00	432.69
2	647.27	1390.63	2037.89	288.46	312.50	600.96
3	232.79	2627.63	2860.42	100.96	1078.13	1179.09
4	93.12	3215.66	3308.77	40.38	1343.75	1384.13
5	0.00	3579.21	3579.21	0.00	1625.00	1625.00

tions. Note here especially that if one were to divide the total demand for money in any of the four scenarios in Table 7.6 by the total consumption output in Table 7.4, the ratio would be higher in the fifth year than in the first; 'the price level' would be predicted to rise by a quantity theorist (see Figure 7.2). As can be seen from our exercise this is a fallacious interpretation created by ignoring the increased volume of intermediate output and the higher ratio of capital goods to consumption goods. Thus it is the amount of money relative to the structure of production that matters in an Austrian model.

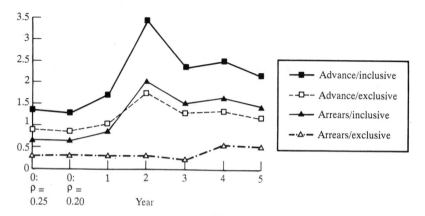

Figure 7.2   Money demand/consumption good output during equilibrium traverse (from Tables 7.4 and 7.6)

A model of frustrated traverse

We are now ready to outline Hayek's trade cycle as a frustrated traverse. While Hayek was persuasive in his rather condensed analytical argument in *Prices and Production*, many aspects will have to be clarified.

The story starts with creation of credit by the banking system. This credit offered at a lower interest rate goes to producers of capital goods. They try to undertake longer processes of production but are eventually defeated by the banks' unwillingness to go on creating credit. The boom collapses with the newer methods abandoned before they yield consumption goods. However, the abandoned unfinished products of the new industry are not usable as inputs in the old industry. Thus the output of the old industry cannot be expanded rapidly, nor can employment.

This is the Hayek cycle. In our example, we start with the proposition that there is no voluntary increase in savings. We shall also assume that we are in advance wage payment/own input inclusive scenario.

Year 1

The banks advance credit of £625 to the new entrepreneur who wishes to start Economy B, Sector 0. Now £250 of this loan is to hire workers away from the old economy. The entrepreneurs of the old economy (Economy A) have borrowed, as is their wont, money to finance production. With the lower rate of interest, they borrow £2525 (assuming zero interest elasticity for the time being). Of this £2525 they would like to spend £1000 on workers. It is clear that we have £1250[10] chasing 1000 workers and the money wage will rise to £1.25. This will mean that the new entrepreneur can only have 200 workers and the old economy 800 workers.[11]

This scenario is sketched in Table 7.7. The old economy produces 1000 units of consumption goods. This is because it has an adequate supply of input from Industry 1 from the past year. Now recall that in the original equilibrium with $\rho = 0.25$, the wage bill is £1000 and profits are £666. If the only shock was a fall of interest rate to $\rho = 0.20$, then, with wages remaining the same, profits would have fallen to 500. This is reflected in the fall in p_2 from £0.83 to £0.75 (cf. Table 7.2). Again, *ceteris paribus*, the 2000 units of consumption goods would have been divided in the ratio of 1200 to workers (1333 with $\rho = 0.2$) and 800 to capitalists (667). However in the first year of the traverse the wage bill has risen to £1250 with capitalists' consumption adding to the pressure of demand.

What is not clear is the role that capitalists' consumption plays in Hayek's model, or even its size. Thus a variety of assumptions is consistent with his model. We assume that capitalists' consumption depends on last period's realized profits. It is not implausible and it makes the calculation easy. The profit in Year 0 when $\rho = 0.25$ was £666. So let us say that with no revision in their consumption plans, capitalists spend all their profits on consumption. Thus £1250 + £666 = £1916 confronts the output of 2000. The market clearing price of the consumption good (p_2) is £0.958[12] compared to the cost of production price of £0.75. Workers get 1305[13] units of this consumption good and capitalists get 695.[14]

	Before $\rho = 0.25$	**Before** $\rho = 0.20$	**After** $\rho = 0.20$
Workers	1200	1333	1305
Capitalists	800	667	695

Table 7.7   The frustrated traverse

Sector	1	2	Labour	Output	Sector	0	1	2	Labour	Output
Year 1										
					0	250	0	0	200	500
1	240		300	600	1					
2	600	500	500	2500	2					
Prices(£)	1.44	0.94	1.25			1.25			1.25	
Year 2										
	Planned						**Planned**			
					0	312.5			250	625
1	400	0	500	1000	1	250	250	0	150	500
2	360	300	300	1500	2					
	Realized						**Realized**			
					0	156.25			208.33	520.83
1	333.33		416.67	833.33	1	208.33	208.33	0	125.00	416.67
2	300	250	250	1250	2					
Prices(£)	1.73	1.13	1.5			1.8	4.05	1.19	1.5	

(Sector 2A carries stocks of 360 – 300 = 60 of Year 1 forward to Year 3)

Sector	1	2	Labour	Output
Year 3				
	Planned			
1	308		385	770
2	560	466.7	466.7	2333.33

The crucial importance of inputs available from previous year's production is seen here. In the first year, the output of consumption good is maintained and the forced saving, i.e. reduction in consumption, is marginal for workers but the capitalists get a bit extra. This is a familiar event during inflation.

The higher wages at £1.25 get translated into higher prices. At the end of Year 1, we have

$$p_{1A} = 1.44 \ (1.15) \quad p_{2A} = 0.94 \ (0.75) \quad p_{0B} = 1.5 \ (1.2)^{15}$$

where p_{1A} is price of Sector 1 output in Economy A etc., and the figures in parentheses are the equilibrium traverse prices.

The crucial effect of the effort to divert resources to Economy B are felt by Sector 1 in Economy A. Given that the consumption good sector (2) can claim its full quota of labour (500 workers) because it has the complementary input available, Sector 1 has only 300 workers. Thus it will produce only 360 units[16] for the consumption good sector in Year 2.

Year 2

In Year 2 therefore Economy A will shrink. Sector 2 will have 360 units of inputs which will occupy only 300 workers and produce a net output of 1200. Let us assume that Sector 1 in Economy A would like to get back to its original plan of producing 1000 units with 500 workers. There is after all demand for their product down the line. In a parallel fashion, Sector 1 in Economy B is constrained by 250 units of inputs it has available from Industry 0. Sector 0 will, like Sector 1 in Economy A, plan to get back to its original scale of 250 workers from which it was frustrated.

Obviously not all plans can be fulfilled. The four sectors plan to hire 1200 workers at £1.25 each. Since there are only 1000 workers, the market clearing wage rate will rise to £1.5.[17] This immediately pushes up money demand.

In what follows, $M_{1A,1B}$ is planned demand for money by industry 1 in Economy A, B etc.[18]

$M1A$	576.92 + 0.00 + 625.00	=	1201.92
$M2A$	519.23 + 282.39 + 375.00	=	1176.62
	Sub-total	=	2378.54
$M0B$	468.75 + 0.00 + 0.00 + 312.50	=	781.25
$M1B$	375.00 + 843.75 + 0.00 + 187.50	=	1406.25
	Sub-total	=	2187.50
Total		=	4566.04

This demand for money, £4566.04, represents a 38 per cent rise in planned expenditures over actual expenditures in Year 1, £3307.19. However, these plans have been formulated independently of one another, on the assumption that last year's prices will hold. The impact of the increase in wages to £1.50 is immediately to increase money demand another 28 per cent (over the £3307.19 spent in Year 1) to £5479.25.

However, the realized levels of output[19] detailed in Table 7.7 tell us that the net consumption good output will only be 1000.[20] There are stocks of inputs left unused because of shortage of labour.[21] The actual demand for money[22] falls back to £4566.04, some 15 per cent less than if all plans had been realized at this year's prices, but still some 41 per cent higher than in Year 1.

The total demand for the consumption good is represented by a £1500 wage bill plus last year's profits. With net output of 1500 units in Year 1 and a (then) price of £0.94, capitalists' profits in Year 1 worked out at £160.[23]

Therefore, the market clearing price of the consumption good is now £1.56,[24] 38 per cent higher than last year's price of £1.13. Workers obtain 962[25] units of the consumption good and capitalists 38.[26]

Thus at end of Year 2, we have hit Hayek's fear of forced savings.

	Year 1	Year 2
Workers	1305	962
Capitalists	695	38

These numbers are relative to the original equilibrium of 1200/800 before credit began to expand. If workers wanted to restore their *ex ante* level of consumption of 1200 (rather than 1333 which they never actually experienced) they would want a wage rate of £1.87,[27] an increase of 15 per cent in one year.

Even before wages rise to such levels, the prices at the end of Year 2 are already showing signs of getting out of control. Thus $p_{1A} = £1.73$, $p_{2A} = £1.13$, $p_{0B} = £1.8$, $p_{1B} = £4.05$, some 20 per cent above the prices anticipated when plans were formed[28] and 50 per cent above the equilibrium traverse prices.[29]

Thus within two years, the price history of the economy is quite stark. Wages have risen by 50 per cent and threaten to rise by another 24 per cent. The price of the consumption good has gone up from £0.83 originally ($\rho = 0.25$) to £1.13[30] in terms of cost but sells at £1.56 in the market. This is an increase of 88 per cent. Hayek is not explicit as to what causes banks to stop credit. But as far as Economy B is concerned its prices have rocketed by 50 per cent and there is no sign of final output. An expansion of money demand of 75 per cent over two years (and which threatened to reach 105 per cent) is alarming.

Even worse, from the employers' (and banks') point of view, is the disastrous fall in capitalists' revenues. Whereas, in Year 0, capitalists' consumption accounted for 25 per cent of *all* consumption, rising to nearly 35 per cent in Year 1, their actual *personal* consumption falls continuously, by 13 per cent between Years 0 and 1, and by a precipitous 95 per cent between Years 1 and 2. In the meantime, the demand for money has been rising rapidly: from £2666.7 ($\rho = 0.25$, Year 0) to £3307.19 at end Year 1, money demand then threatens to explode; planned expenditures of £4566 suddenly become £5479 in response to labour shortages, an increase in two years of 105 per cent. The fact that the actual money demand, £4660, turns out only to be some 3 per cent, rather than 28 per cent above anticipated expenditures, will be cold comfort in the light of the fall in capitalists' incomes. It is likely that the volatility of the demand will be predominant in the bankers' (*qua* investors') minds. This, taken with the fall in capitalists' revenues and rises in wage rates, is not likely to dispose the banks towards continuing to pump money into the economy.

It would be reasonable to assume in our somewhat abstract case that banks would stop credit and put up interest rates. It would be reasonable so to assume because in Hayek's model the credit expansion stops before the new production process reaches the final stage.

Year 3

If now all credit to the Economy B stops, we are left with 240 units of Y_{0B} and 192 units of Y_{1B} at the beginning of Year 3. They are however useless for Economy A. In that economy, Sector 2 is limited by the amount of Y_{1A} available, i.e. 500 units[31] + 60 units of stocks carried over.[32] (It is not clear whether Hayek assumed storable inputs but that seems reasonable.) Sector 1 on the other hand may not decide to expand since its output was not sold last year. If it merely repeats its scale of Year 2, we could have unemployment of 148 workers.[33]

Thus at the outset of Year 3, Y_{2A} plans to use up all its supply of Y_{1A} and employs 466.7 workers. Its net output will be 1866.7 units, nearly back to equilibrium. Sector 1 hires 385 workers as before. The two sectors of Economy B have shut down and their loans[34] of £2187.5 will have to be written off by the banks. The interest rate will be raised above its old level of $\rho = 0.25$, say to $\rho = 0.4$. Such a steep rise in interest rate may by itself lead the entrepreneurs in Economy A to alter their plans downwards.

Hayek asserted that the recovery would take a long time. The original price gradient will take a long time in his view to be restored. In *Prices and Production* he did not spell this out but merely hinted that reflationary finance was not the solution. It would be possible to work out different scenarios of the path of recovery. Enough has been done here, we trust, to convey the phenomenon of the frustrated traverse. Credit expansion not backed by voluntary savings leads to hyperinflation. The traverse is not completed and losses and unpaid debts result. At the start of Year 3, the economy begins its long road to recovery.

Conclusion

The purpose of this paper is a simple one. It is to check whether Hayek's model of the trade cycle as a frustrated traverse can be worked out in detail under plausible assumptions. We have chosen the method of constructing numerical schemes (following the long established precedents of Hayek and Marx) but there is a clear analytical structure behind these schemes. We have worked out an equilibrium traverse and contrasted that with the cycle. Hyperinflation emerges clearly and quickly as a possibility and the crisis is plausible with doubling of consumer prices and wages and an 80 per cent rise in money demand.

This is merely a beginning. Having filled out the details Hayek only hinted at, there is now scope for others to test the robustness of our model. We look forward to such further work.

Notes

1. Since the input commodities – 'capital goods' – are heterogeneous as between economies A and B, labour productivity comparisons across the two economies are not strictly legitimate for Sector 1. We may just assume that the consumption good is less heterogeneous across the two economies although even this need not be true. The quality of the consumption good could be different.
2. £1000/£0.66, arrears; £1000/£0.833, advance.
3. From Table 7.2, Panel A: 400 * £1.25 + 500 * £1.
4. From Table 7.2, Panel B: 600 * £1.25 + 500 * £0.833 + 500 * £1.
5. From Table 7.2, Panel A: 400 * £1.25 = £500, $(1 + \rho) = 1.25$, and £500 * 1.25 = £625.
6. Which equals cost of own product plus 25%, i.e., 500 * £0.833 * 1.25.
7. 2000 * £0.66 (arrears); 2000 * £0.833 (advance).
8. 1000 units @ p_1 + 500 units @ p_2 (arrears); 1000 units @ p_1 + 500 units @ p_2 + 1000 labour @ w (advance).
9. Whether wages paid in advance or arrears:
   1500 * (£0.833/1.25) = £1000 (advance); 1500 * £0.66 = £1000 (arrears).
10. I.e., £1000 from Economy A plus £250 from Economy B.
11. We have assumed flexible money wages and a simple market clearing rule.
12. £1916/2000 = £0.958 [i.e., $p_2 = (wL + \prod_{t-1})/x_2$].
13. £1250/£0.958.
14. 2000 – 1305.
15. 1.2 * 1.25 = 1.5.
16. Net output from Sector 1, Economy A, Year 1.
17. 1.2 * £1.25.
18. Planned output in Year 2 multiplied by prices in effect at end Year 1.
19. Each sector is only able to employ 1/1.2 (83%) of the workforce it had planned for.
20. 1250 – 250.
21. Hayek does assume a fixed coefficient technology.
22. Actual output multiplied by this year's prices. Realized money demand comes to equal actual money demand because output plans have been scaled back in the same proportions as market prices have risen.
23. (0.94 * 1500) – £1250 = £160 [£1250 – Sector 1 outgoings in Year 0 – (advance/exclusive scenario)].
24. Price of £1.56 obtained from £(1500+160)/1000.
25. £1500/1.56 = 961.54.
26. 1000–961.54 = 38.46.
27. (1200 * £1.56) + 1000.
28. I.e., at end Year 1.
29. £2.7.
30. Cf. Table 7.7.
31. Net output of Sector 1, Economy A, Year 2, i.e., 833.33–333.33.
32. 360 (planned to be used in Sector 2, Year 2) – 300 (actually used) = 60.
33. 1000 – (466.7 + 385) (Table 7.7).
34. $M_{0B} + M_{1B}$.

References

Baranzini, M. (ed.) (1982) *Advances in Economic Theory*, Oxford: Basil Blackwell.
Colonna, M. (1990) 'Hayek on Money and Equilibrium', *Contributions to Political Economy*, **9**, 43–68.

Desai, M. (1982) 'The Task of Monetary Theory: the Hayek–Sraffa Debate in a Modern Perspective' in Baranzini (1982).
Desai, M. (1991) 'Kaldor between Keynes and Hayek, or: Did Nicky Kill Capital Theory?' in Nell and Semmler (1991).
Hayek, F. A. von (1929/31/39) 'The Paradox of Saving', published in German in *Zeitschrift für Nationalökonomie*, **I**, III, 1929 under the title 'Gibt es einen Widersinn des Sparens?' translated by N. Kaldor and G. Tugendhat and published in *Economica*, May 1931; also in Hayek (1939).
Hayek, F. A. von (1931), *Prices and Production*, London: Routledge.
Hayek, F. A. von (1939), *Profits, Interest and Investment*, London: Routledge.
Hicks, J. R. (1973), *Capital and Time*, Oxford: Oxford University Press.
Nell, E. J. and W. Semmler (eds) (1991), *Nicholas Kaldor and Mainstream Economics: Confrontation or Convergence*, London: Macmillan.
Zamagni, S. (1984) 'Ricardo and Hayek Effects in a Fixwage Model of Traverse' in *Oxford Economic Papers*, new series, **36**, November, 135–51.

Appendix: Money demand under current and lagged prices

When analysing equilibrium, there is no problem with assuming that $p_t = p_{t-1}$ therefore the question of whether the prices faced by producers and consumers are this year's or last (market or producer prices) does not pose a problem. When analysing a frustrated traverse, however, this question needs to be addressed. In the main text, it is assumed that producers always face market prices; constraints created by the events of previous periods (lags) occur only in the physical quantities available for production. For completeness, and for interest's sake, presented below is a comparison of money demand under the assumptions, first that current prices only apply (as in the main text), and second that the input prices faced by producers are lagged one year. As both Tables 7A.1–7A.3 and Figure 7A.1 show, the effect is to dampen the money demand trajectory marginally. Money demand is slightly higher in the early stages of the traverse, and slightly lower during Year 2. Realized money demand turns out to be slightly higher than planned, but its threatened rise is slightly less than in the unlagged case. In both cases, it has continued to be assumed that consumers (workers) always face current (market) prices for the consumption good.

The production technology is assumed in this paper to be Leontieff, as given below:

Economy A

$$x_{1t} = a_{11}x_{1t} + a_1 l_{1t}$$
$$x_{2t} = a_{12}x_{1t-1} + a_{22}x_{2t} + a_2 l_{2t}$$

Economy B

$$x_{0t} = b_{00}x_{0t} + b_0 l_{0t}$$
$$x_{1t} = b_{01}x_{0t-1} + b_{11}x_{1t} + b_1 l_{1t}$$
$$x_{2t} = b_{12}x_{1t-1} + b_{22}x_{2t} + b_2 l_{2t}$$

The binding constraints are (a) the quantity of bought input, i.e., x_{ij} ($i{\neq}j$) and (b) total labour availability $\sum l_{it} = L_t = 1000$.

The prices for p_1 and p_2, as derived from Equations (1) and (2) above are as follows:

Arrears case
$$p_1 = [1 - (1+\rho)a_{11}]^{-1}*a_1 w$$
$$p_2 = [1 - (1+\rho)a_{22}]^{-1}*\{a_{12}(1+\rho)p_{1t-1} + a_2 w\}$$

Advance case
$$p_1 = [1 - (1+\rho)a_{11}]^{-1}* a_1(1+\rho)w$$
$$p_2 = [1 - (1+\rho)a_{22}]^{-1}*\{a_{12}(1+\rho)p_{1t-1} + a_2(1+\rho)w\}$$

and similarly for Economy B.

Table 7A.1　Money demand during frustrated traverse (current prices – as in main text)

Economy A					Economy B						
YEAR 0											
	Advance (ρ=0.25)										
Sector	Sector 1	Sector 2	Labour	Total							
1.00				1000.00							
2.00				1666.67		Advance (ρ=0.2)					Grand total
Total				2666.67							2666.67
						Sector 0	Sector 1	Sector 2	Labour	Total	
	Advance (ρ=0.2)										
					0					*1000.00*	
1				961.54	*1*					*2250.00*	
2				1568.83	*2*					*2045.05*	Grand total
Total				2530.36	*Total*					*5295.05*	2530.36
YEAR 1											
1	346.15	0.00	375.00	721.15	0	375.00	0.00	0.00	250.00	625.00	
2	865.38	470.65	625.00	1961.03	1					0.00	
Total				2682.19	2					0.00	Grand total
					Total					625.00	3307.19
YEAR 2 (planned)											
					0	468.75	0.00	0.00	312.50	781.25	
1	576.92	0.00	625.00	1201.92	1	375.00	843.75	0.00	187.50	1406.25	Grand total
2	519.23	282.39	375.00	1176.62	2					0.00	(planned)
Total				2378.54	Total					2187.50	4566.04
YEAR 2 (Threatened)											
					0	562.50	0.00	0.00	375.00	937.50	
					1	450.00	1012.50	0.00	225.00	1687.50	Grand total
1	692.31	0.00	750.00	1442.31	2					0.00	(threatened)
2	623.08	338.87	450.00	1411.94	Total					2625.00	5479.25
Total				2854.25							
YEAR 2 (realized)											
					0	468.75	0.00	0.00	312.50	781.25	
					1	375.00	843.75	0.00	187.50	1406.25	Grand total
1	576.92	0.00	625.01	1201.92	2					0.00	(realized)
2	519.23	282.39	375.00	1176.62	Total					2187.50	4566.04
Total				2378.54							

Table 7A.2   Money demand during frustrated traverse (input prices lagged one year)

Economy A

	Sector 1	Sector 2	Labour	Total
YEAR 0				
Advance (ρ=0.25)				
1				1000.00
2				1666.67
Total				2666.67
Advance (r=0.25)				
1	461.54	0.00	500.00	961.54
2	750.00	376.52	500.00	1626.52
Total				2588.06
YEAR 1				
1	346.15	0.00	375.00	721.15
2	692.31	470.65	625.00	1787.96
Total				2509.11
YEAR 2 (planned)				
1	576.92	0.00	625.00	1201.92
2	415.38	282.39	375.00	1072.77
Total				2274.70
YEAR 2 (threatened)				
1	692.31	0.00	750.00	1442.31
2	519.23	338.87	450.00	1308.10
Total				2750.40
YEAR 2 (realized)				
1	576.92	0.00	625.00	1201.92
2	432.69	282.39	375.00	1090.08
Total				2292.00

Economy B

	Sector 0	Sector 1	Sector 2	Labour	Total	Grand total
YEAR 0 (see above)						2666.67
Advance (ρ=0.2)						
0	600.00	0.00	0.00	400.00	1000.00	
1	666.67	1350.00	0.00	300.00	2316.67	
2	0.00	1611.11	395.05	300.00	2306.16	Grand total
Total					5622.83	2588.06
					(5295.05)	
YEAR 1						
0	375.00	0.00	0.00	250.00	625.00	
1					0.00	
2					0.00	Grand total
Total					625.00	3134.11
YEAR 2 (planned)						
0	468.75	0.00	0.00	312.50	781.25	
1	375.00	843.75	0.00	187.50	1406.25	Grand total
2					0.00	(planned)
Total					2187.50	4387.20
YEAR 2 (threatened)						
0	562.50	0.00	0.00	375.00	937.50	
1	450.00	1012.50	0.00	225.00	1687.50	Grand total
2					0.00	(threatened)
Total					2625.00	5300.40
YEAR 2 (realized)						
0	281.25	0.00	0.00	312.50	593.75	
1	375.00	843.75	0.00	187.50	1406.25	Grand total
2					0.00	(realized)
Total					2000.00	4417.00

Table 7A.3   Comparison of money demand trajectories with input prices current and lagged

YEAR 0	
(ρ=0.25)	
Grand total	Grand total
2666.67	2666.67
YEAR 0	
(ρ=0.2)	
Grand total	Grand total
2530.36	2588.06
YEAR 1	
Grand total	Grand total
3307.19	3134.11
YEAR 2	
Grand total	Grand total
(planned)	(planned)
4566.04	4387.20
Grand total	Grand total
(threatened)	(threatened)
5479.25	5300.40
Grand total	Grand total
(realized)	(realized)
4566.04	4417.00

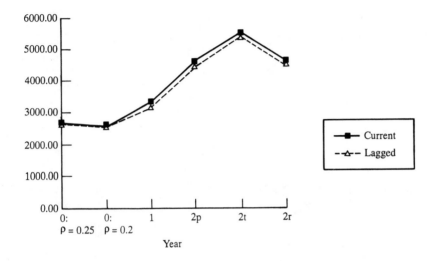

*Figure 7A.1   Money demand trajectories under assumptions of current and
lagged input prices*

PART III

HAYEK AND EQUILIBRIUM BUSINESS CYCLE THEORIES

8 The formation and evolution of Hayek's trade cycle theory*

Gilles Dostaler

> It is equally obvious that the very selection of our problems for scientific exami-
> nation implies valuations and that therefore the clear separation of scientific
> knowledge and valuations cannot be achieved by avoiding all valuations, but only
> by an unmistakable statement of the guiding values. It seems equally incontest-
> able that the academic teacher should not pretend to be neutral or indifferent but
> should make it easier for his audience to recognize the dependence of his practical
> conclusions on value judgment by openly stating his personal ideals as such.
> (Hayek, [1963] 1967, p. 254)

In June 1962, the above declaration by Hayek, delivered on the occasion of
his inaugural lecture as professor of political economy at the University of
Freiburg im Breisgau, could well have been taken from the work of Myrdal,
his corecipient of the Nobel Memorial Prize in Economics in 1974. Although
these authors were poles apart in political terms, they nonetheless shared
some aspects of methodology, including the claim that there are narrow links
between an author's theoretical analysis, his political philosophy and his
ethical convictions, a methodological stance which renders problematic the
traditional division between the normative and the positive. This does not
mean that the convictions dictate the nature of the answers an economist
might give to the questions he raised, but rather that they establish, among
other things, the nature of the questions themselves: '... it seems to me a
clear duty of the social scientist to ask certain questions the mere raising of
which will seem to imply the taking of a political position' (Hayek, [1963]
1967, p. 255; see also 1933b).

Such was the case with the theory of cycles which Hayek elaborated from
the mid-1920s to the end of the 1930s. Ethical and political convictions, most
of which he had developed earlier, coloured several of the theory's aspects.
Above all, they explained the continuity of the theoretical core, beyond the
technical modifications Hayek was led to make both as a reaction to the
events and as an answer to the increasingly virulent criticisms that his ideas
had provoked. Thus in the preface to the French translation of *Prices and*

*The translation of this paper from the French by Valérie Cauchemez was made possible by a
grant from the University of Québec at Montréal. I would like to thank Richard Arena and
Hans-Michael Trautwein for their comments on a first draft of this essay, Robert Leonard for
revising the English translation and Ianik Marcil for research assistantship.

Production, published in 1975 more than 40 years after the first English edition, Hayek could affirm that the analysis delivered in his small book deserved recognition as being more credible than Keynes's. And even in his last book, *The Fatal Conceit* (1988), Hayek maintains the ethico-political basis of both his interpretation of business cycles and his opposition to Keynesianism.

But it was with *The Pure Theory of Capital*, published in 1941, that Hayek completed what he called '… the first half of my career as an economist … wholly devoted to pure theory' ([1963] 1967, p. 253). In the following pages, we intend to examine the genesis and the evolution of Hayek's theory of business cycles. It is not a matter of presenting a formalized model of one version of this theory and examining its inner workings. This has been done on several occasions;[1] moreover, it is not even certain that such an exercise would conform with Hayek's project, a system which is, as pointed out by Tinbergen (1935), essentially 'open' and 'non-mathematical'.[2] Neither is it our intention to examine in detail the criticisms provoked by this theory, nor its links with current theories, several of which ostensibly draw on Hayek. This has already been done in other articles, some of which are found in this book.

Instead, we would like to present an internal reading of the evolution of Hayek's ideas, based on his texts. It is very often the case that an author, particularly one as famous as Hayek, has his thesis simplified or even altered. One reads other people's comments on the author's work, rather than reading the original text itself. And thus one becomes Keynesian without once open-ing *The General Theory*, or Marxist without reading *Capital*. Therefore, we offer more of a reading guide, with the hope that the reader will seek in the texts the evolution of a line of thinking whose richness and complexity have to be acknowledged, even if he does not agree with Hayek's vision. We distinguish three steps within this evolution: the conception, which was nur-tured by, amongst other things, his reflection on the recovery from the 1920s crisis in the United States; the consolidation, which coincided with the begin-ning of the Great Depression; and the revision, which was a reaction both to critics and to the events that marked the slow and painful recovery from the 1930s crisis.

Conception

Hayek obtained a doctorate in law in 1921, followed in 1923 by a doctorate in political sciences. He became interested in both economics and psychol-ogy, and hesitated between the two disciplines. Later, he would explain that fortuitous events were responsible for the beginning of his interest in the study of industrial fluctuations. He first devoted a year and a half to writing, under Friedrich von Wieser's supervision, a thesis on the problem of imputation. Employed in a governmental agency around the same time, he worked under Ludwig von Mises 'who for the next ten years, became the chief guide in the development of my ideas' (Hayek, 1984, p. 1).

In 1912, Mises published *The Theory of Money and Credit*, which constitutes the first elaboration of the Austrian theory of cyclical fluctuations, based on the Wicksellian distinction between the natural and monetary rates of interest, and on the conception of capital as roundabout production, formulated by Böhm-Bawerk. The English translation of the 1924 second edition was not published until 1934, so that, for the English-speaking public, the Austrian theory of cycles is associated with the name of Hayek. But it is clear that Mises was one of Hayek's primary inspirers and the former, moreover, quoted a passage from *The Theory of Money and Credit* in the epigraph to the third part of *Prices and Production*.

Besides the theoretical inspiration, Mises also provided Hayek with a political influence. His 1922 book on socialism, following the article published in 1920, launched a polemic that would continue for several years, and in which Hayek's intervention would become increasingly important (1935a). For Mises, an uncompromising liberal, socialism was not only reprehensible on moral and political grounds, but was logically unworkable. The aim of an important part of Hayek's work was to give rigorous foundations to liberalism, and to reveal what he called in his last book 'the errors of socialism' (1988).

But the political convictions Hayek defended with so much consistency until the end of his life had an origin prior to Mises's influence. They certainly had connections with the environment in which Hayek was formed. This milieu was profoundly marked by fast transformations and the crisis experienced by Vienna, a city which was, at the turn of the century, one of the great cultural centres of the world and the capital of the Austro-Hungarian empire.[3]

Part of a wealthy Viennese family, Hayek bore witness to this empire's collapse and the succeeding birth of the Austrian republic, following the rise of the Austrian socialist movement, which came to power in 1919.[4] He observed the rise of an inflation which duped the savings of the well-off classes. He lived through the insecurity, the political crisis and the fear of an uprising from the extreme left. Vienna's social–democratic municipal administration, by means of heavy taxation, financed, among other projects, a programme of public housing which, at the end of the 1920s, would inspire Hayek to write a polemical pamphlet (1929c). This conjunction of events could explain some characteristics of the economic analysis Hayek would subsequently develop. Undoubtedly, it was around this time he forged his conviction concerning the motor role of saving, to which he would remain faithful. He would later blame Keynes for considering saving as a vice and for elaborating an economic theory on immoral grounds, themselves linked to the self-proclaimed immoralism of their author (1988, pp. 57–8). On numerous occasions, Hayek established links in his work between saving reprobation and civilization crisis. Here, Vienna's decline had to be remembered. Here also lay the origin of Hayek's mistrust regarding inflation, and more generally of the harmful role that the monetary system can play in the mechanism of the economy. So, such are some of the preliminary value judgements which would contribute to the development of his business cycle analysis.

During 1923 and 1924, Hayek stayed fifteen months in the United States and there developed a more active interest in the study of business cycles and, in particular, in the attempts made to control these cycles using monetary policy. Spending time at the New School for Social Research, Columbia University and New York University, he was in close contact with the institutionalist economists, circumstances which would contribute to his distrust for empirical and statistical analysis. The American economy had vigorously resumed its activities after the 1920–21 depression. Hayek's studies and observations of the attempts made to control the cyclical fluctuations – by means of, *inter alia*, the monetary policy of the Federal Reserve System, with the logistic support of the Harvard Economic Service – engendered in him a scepticism regarding monetary stabilization policies, something which would constitute a *leitmotiv* of his subsequent works.

The research conducted during this stay in the United States, and notably that for a doctoral thesis on the problems of monetary stabilization – begun under the supervision of J. D. Magee but never completed – gave birth to a long study 'Die Währungspolitik der Vereinigten Staaten seit der Überwindung der Krise von 1920', published in two parts in 1925 in the Austrian journal *Zeitschrift für Volkswirtschaft und Sozialpolitik*. The sixth section, 'The Theoretical Foundations of Attempts to Influence the Level of Economic Activity by Banking Policy', published in English under the title 'The Monetary Policy of the United States after the Recovery from the 1920 Crisis' (Hayek, 1984, pp. 5–32), already contained the fundamental elements of his theory of cycles, and an assertion of a political nature which coloured his analysis. Hayek believed that crises could be eliminated, but at a politically unacceptable price, because it would imply making a sacrifice in terms of economic progress. As in the opinion of his compatriot Schumpeter, cyclical fluctuations and crisis were therefore linked to economic progress: 'Hence economic fluctuations must probably be regarded as a necessary accompaniment of the accelerated development experienced by countries of the Western world in the last 150 years' ([1925] 1984, p. 21).

The article also presents considerations of a methodological nature to which Hayek would often return later, and which should cause us to at least question the commonly held conception that Hayek moved gradually from pure economic theory to multidisciplinary research. Indeed, it was said in the essay that economic science could not itself contain all the answers to the problems raised by the alternation of phases of progress and depression: 'But on the other hand, it will thereby become evident that the practical questions arising in this context cannot be answered in any clear-cut way by science alone. For they are also partly questions of one's outlook on life, and hence are in the widest sense matters of judgments upon which sharply divergent views may be held' (p. 22).

Besides his criticism of 'the dominantly statistical basis and the lack of interest in theory characteristic of American researchers that prevents them from taking up the most difficult problems' (p. 20), Hayek already expresses his mistrust regarding analysis in terms of aggregates and what he called 'very simple quantity theory conceptions' (p. 13). As to the propositions about the stabilization of the general level of prices, which he associates with the name of Fisher and Keynes, he wrote that '... the economic situation is not revealed by the movement of any one of the factors that they take as their indicator, such as the level of output, employment, or commodity stocks, or their relationship to one another or to the movement of prices. Rather it is in the first instance the relationship between the behaviour of these factors in the individual sectors of the economy that reveals the situation' (p. 20).

The relation between the movement of relative prices and the temporal structure of production, the responsibility of the elasticity of the modern credit system, the concept of overinvestment, the necessity of crisis in order to restore equilibrium, all these ingredients of Hayek's theory of cyclical fluctuations were already clearly spelled out, as shown, in particular, in a long paragraph of which it is worth quoting a rather large excerpt:

> The excessive development of the industries producing raw materials and capital goods, whose regular recurrence is thus to be regarded as the main cause of the periodic economic crises, necessarily arises from and is chiefly due to the much praised elasticity of our modern credit system. ... This can take place only because the extension of credit by the banking system is not strictly linked to the growth of savings. ... The most significant phenomena of the upswing, over-investment and a general rise in prices, and at the same time the causes of the crises which always follow upon the upswing, are therefore largely a result of an extension of credit. ... This extension of credit gives rise to a short-lived inflation and leads to the emergence of the disproportions between the individual sectors of the economy to which the accompanying stimulation of business always gives rise. The crisis then becomes the only way of eliminating these disproportions. (Hayek, [1925] 1984, p. 10)

Hayek compares this recurrent inflation to a drug that would provide an ephemeral sensation of well-being while at the same time preparing later nightmares. In a long note added to this passage, he explains the link between the decline of bank interest rate and the lengthening of the production process: 'A rate of interest which is inappropriately low offers to the individual sectors of the economy an advantage which is greater the more remote is their product from the consumption stage. This is so because the time over which interest is saved with respect to the ultimate final product is correspondingly longer, and the price which the purchaser at the next stage can offer is higher by the entire amount of the interest saved on the path to the consumer' (p. 27). The only economic policy likely to attenuate the cyclical fluctuations would then be evident: 'If it is changes in the volume of credit in use which are to be considered as the chief cause of the unequal development of supply and demand, and hence of cyclical movements, a policy which maintained the volume of bank credit approximately stable would have most to contribute to the prevention of cyclical fluctuations' (p. 23).

'Intertemporal Price Equilibrium and Movements in the Value of Money', published in 1928 and presented as 'part of a hitherto uncompleted larger work on the goals of monetary policy' ([1928] 1984, p. 113) has been justly considered one of Hayek's major theoretical contributions with respect to the project of integrating money in the theory of general equilibrium, of rendering dynamic the latter, and more generally of taking the time factor into account in economic analysis. As he seldom did in his work, Hayek claimed originality: 'To my knowledge, no one has hitherto analysed the function fulfilled by the relative levels of prices at different points in time' (p. 100).

For Hayek, prices have to be considered as regulators and guides in temporal processes, thus allowing the adaptation to changes in exogenous data determined through time. A given price structure should then be compatible with an intertemporal equilibrium based on the behaviour of the agents and the conditions of production. In the analysis of this process, money had to be taken seriously: 'We will have to come to terms with the idea that money always exerts a determining influence on the development of the economy, that the principles derived for an economy without money can be applied to an economy with money only with substantial qualifications...' (p. 103). This implied taking some distance from what he called the 'naive conception of the Quantity Theory' (p. 89).

The intertemporal equilibrium of natural prices, corresponding to the equality of supply and demand, is broken by variations in the quantity of money, whose effect on so evanescent an entity as the 'general price level' is of no interest. This rupture of price equilibrium provokes transformations in the structure of production; these transformations corresponding, when the money stock is raised, to lengthening the structure mentioned, to 'the exaggerated stimulus to the expansion of output for more distant points in time at the expense of that for nearer points' (p. 93). The conditions for severe crisis are set up when these excessive stimulations of investment translate into transformations which are irreversible or hardly reversible in the production system. The only way to prevent these difficulties is to avoid any change in the quantity of money in order to allow 'the establishment of that natural structure of prices through time corresponding to the intertemporal exchange relations originating from barter, and alone able to ensure undisturbed self-reproduction in a monetary economy as well' (p. 95). Hayek admits that such a policy in the modern monetary and financial context is absolutely unachievable. Besides, it is neither credit in itself nor the existence of a gap between natural and monetary rate of interest that is questioned. Rather, it is the existence of a means of exchange, which permits the separation in time of the acts of selling and buying.

Consolidation

Two short books contributed the most to publicizing the Hayekian vision of trade cycles: *Prices and Production* (1931a) and *Monetary Theory and the Trade Cycle* (1933a). While the first was initially published in English in 1931, the second was first published in German in 1929, before it was translated into English by N. Kaldor and H. M. Croome. It stemmed from a text presented at a meeting held in Zurich in September 1928. In the preface to the English edition of *Monetary Theory and the Trade Cycle*, Hayek thus described the connection between his two books:

> In particular, my *Prices and Production*, originally published in England, should be considered as an essential complement to the present publication. While I have here emphasized the *monetary causes* which *start* the cyclical fluctuations, I have, in that later publication, concentrated on the *successive changes in the real structure of production* which *constitute* those fluctuations. (Hayek, 1933a, p. 17, emphasis in original)

But there is much more in *Monetary Theory and the Trade Cycle* than the mere analysis of the monetary causes of the cyclical fluctuations. In the first place, there are important methodological considerations. It was in this book that Hayek most clearly presented his mistrust regarding the utilization of mathematics and statistics in economic theory, even if at the same time he declared that theoretical analysis should take the notion of equilibrium as its starting point and that: 'By "equilibrium theory" we here primarily understand the modern theory of the general interdependence of all economic quantities, which has been most perfectly expressed by the Lausanne School of theoretical economics' (p. 42).[5] As to statistics, he asserted that they 'can never prove or disprove a theoretical explanation, they can only present problems or offer fields for theoretical research' (p. 232).[6]

Monetary Theory and the Trade Cycle is mainly a treatise on the history of economic thought. Besides, if there is one characteristic of Hayek's work as a whole, it is a continual concern with making reference to the past, and in particular with revealing the origins of the ideas he is putting forward. (Thus, only rarely does Hayek claim originality, a feature which puts him in a minority among social thinkers.) Hayek here puts forward a taxonomy in terms of monetary/non-monetary, but relativizes its importance right away, not only in an oft-quoted note added to the English translation,[7] but in the body of the text: 'Once this point is agreed upon, it naturally becomes quite irrelevant whether we label this explanation of the Trade Cycle as a monetary theory or not' (p. 183).

This point refers to the fact that, following a modification in the data of an economic system, characterized by what Hayek calls a structure of production, the system, rather than reacting in order to reach a new equilibrium, 'begins a particular movement of "boom" which contains, within itself, the seeds of an inevitable reaction' (p. 183). This phenomenon is due to monetary factors, to the elasticity of the credit system, which, for that matter, leads him to call his theory the 'Additional Credit Theory of the Trade Cycle' (p. 177). But the factor triggering the process can as much be real as monetary. The initial impulse can come from the demand side or from the supply side, it can be a question of 'New inventions or discoveries, the opening up of new markets, or even bad harvests, the appearance of entrepreneurs of genius who originate "new combinations" (Schumpeter), a fall in wage rates due to heavy immigration; and the destruction of great blocks or capital by natural catastrophe, or many others' (p. 168). The common effect of these factors is to modify the natural rate of interest, which Hayek prefers to call the equilibrium rate, the one that equalizes the proportion of productive resources committed to lengthening the production process and the fraction of their actual income that consumers want to save. Therefore, the bank system is not responsible for cyclical fluctuations (pp. 143, 147, 189). Nonetheless, it does make possible the gap between the two rates which produces fluctuations: '*The determining cause of the cyclical fluctuation is, therefore, the fact that on account of the elasticity of the volume of currency media the rate of interest demanded by the banks is not necessarily always equal to the equilibrium rate, but is, in the short run, determined by considerations of banking liquidity*' (pp. 179–80, emphasis in original). Hayek's conclusion is that only by maintaining the stability of total bank deposits can we get rid of cyclical fluctuations, but he adds also that this appears to him 'purely Utopian'. It is necessary to live with a monetary system which 'loosens that finality and "closedness" of the system which is the fundamental assumption of static theory' (p. 93).

Despite the reference to Walrasian general equilibrium, we need to stress the fact that Hayek is already far from the traditional notion of prices. They are viewed as means of conveying information scattered among numerous individuals: 'in the exchange economy, production is governed by prices, independently of any knowledge of the whole process on the part of individual producers' (p. 84). 'Wrong' prices can therefore prompt 'wrong' allocations of resources (p. 85). It is not actual but expected prices 'which renders it profitable, under the new conditions, to extend production' (p. 71).

For the first time, in May 1931, the English readership had access to a presentation of Hayek's vision of cyclical fluctuations, in an article entitled 'The "Paradox" of Saving'. This is the translation by N. Kaldor and G. Tugendhat, of a text published in German in 1929 (1929b), whose point of departure is a long criticism of Foster and Catchings's theses, then very much in vogue in the United States. This great energy Hayek shows in demolishing Foster and Catchings's underconsumptionist arguments also illustrates well the political intention which constantly accompanied his theoretical work. Evidently, Hayek regards the popularity of Foster and Catchings's books as a danger. At stake is the fight against a trend of thought which originated with the mercantilists and developed from the writings of Lauderdale and Malthus through to those of Tougan-Baranowsky, Veblen and Hobson. In Hayek's view, Keynes would subsequently soon stand out as this tradition's most distinguished heir and spokesperson, and it was therefore in his direction that he would direct his attack.

As far as Hayek's theory of cycles is concerned, this text constitutes a transition between *Monetary Theory and the Trade Cycle* and *Prices and Production*. Hayek introduces in it the idea relating to the harmful effect of the growth of the consumption demand during a crisis. The crisis is aggravated, not because the demand for consumption goods is insufficient, but because, on the contrary, 'it is too large and too urgent to render the execution of lengthy roundabout processes profitable ([1929b] 1931, p. 160). In this manner, the idea is expressed for the first time that it is necessary to let the crisis develop in order to restore the equilibria shattered by the excessive stimulation of investment. Far from being at the origin of crisis, the growth of voluntary saving is the only way to stimulate investment, bringing about a new equilibrium in which the production processes, lengthened, become more productive. This process of contraction and expansion of the production structure is continuous, in modern economies: 'This frantic game of now enlarging, now contracting the productive apparatus through increases in the volume of money injected, now on the production, now on the consumption side, is always going on under the present organisation of currency' (p. 167). By means of arithmetical examples, Hayek illustrates this process. While Kaldor (1942) would subsequently call it the concertina effect, Hayek, in *Prices and Production*, where the arithmetical sketches are transformed into triangles, would designate it the fan.

Published in September 1931, *Prices and Production* is the compilation of four conferences held at the London School of Economics in February of that year, during which Hayek described to his audience the development of the crisis with the aid of triangles used to illustrate the Austrian conception of capital and production. Once again, an excursion through the history of economics thought opens *Prices and Production*. Here, Hayek goes back even further than in *Monetary Theory and the Trade Cycle*, being careful, as usual, to reveal the ideational thread in minute detail, no element being presented as totally original: 'Locke and Montanari, at the end of the seventeenth century, had stated quite clearly the theory I have been discussing. Richard Cantillon ... provides the first attempt known to me to trace the actual chain of cause and effect between the amount of money and prices' ([1931a] 1935, p. 79). With regard to the concept of forced saving – an idea of such prominence in his theory that he was at times considered to be its founder – Hayek shows that it goes back to at least Bentham, who himself might have borrowed it from earlier authors. In 1932, Hayek published a long historical note meant to complete the first chapter of *Prices and Production* on the genealogy of the forced saving concept (1932e). In a reply to Sraffa, he wrote that his theory stood or fell depending on the truth of the following point: 'the tendency for capital accumulated by "forced saving" to be, at least partly, dissipated as soon as the cause of the "forced saving" disappears' (1932c, p. 239). Moreover, he adds that, to his knowledge, he is original in making this exposition.

It is to Wicksell that he attributes the concept of neutral money, that is money which does not disrupt the equilibrium of relative prices determined by supply and demand: 'Not a money which is *stable* in value, but a *neutral* money must therefore form the starting point for the theoretical analysis of monetary influences on production...' ([1931a] 1935, p. 31). In an article published in German in 1933, Hayek insists again on the fact that he had not invented this concept and moreover, he added, in an answer to Marget (1932), that it was not a norm of monetary policy, but an instrument of theoretical analysis (1933d, p. 160). And as for his triangles, intended to illustrate what he called the structure of production, he claims that he has traced their origin back to Jevons, and that Marschak was thus justified in suggesting that they be called 'Jevonian Investment Figures' ([1931a] 1935, p. 38).

His description of a mechanism by which economic activity is stimulated through the extension of bank credit – rather than through an increase of voluntary saving which lengthens the production structure – is well known. But it is interesting to give here, *in extenso*, the summary the author himself offered 40 years later:

> The fundamental argument developed in this book is that the expansion of credit leads to an erroneous allocation of the factors of production, and in particular labour, by directing them into employments which cease being profitable as soon

as inflation stops accelerating. Once this has taken place, there is no means of avoiding a reaction and all the attempts to postpone the day of reckoning risk worsening it even more. As I have maintained for over forty years, the moment for preventing these depressions is to be found during the expansionary phase and it is therefore essential not to use credit growth to create jobs, which, of their nature, can only be temporary. (Hayek, 1975, p. 56; translated from French)

Controversy

The arrival in England of Hayek's theses was a source of enthusiasm for some and annoyance for others. Hicks (1967) witnessed the perplexity faced by those young economists who had to choose between Keynes's explanations, presented in *A Treatise on Money*, and Hayek's. Keynes, incidentally, was one of the first to criticize *Prices and Production*, 'one of the most frightful muddles I have ever read, with scarcely a sound proposition in it beginning with page 45... It is an extraordinary example of how, starting with a mistake, a remorseless logician can end up in Bedlam' (Keynes [1931] 1973, p. 252). Hayek had commenced hostilities by publishing the first part of a long critical analysis of Keynes's book in the August 1931 issue of *Economica* (1931b). Keynes responded with a counter-attack in November, before Hayek, the following February, published the second part of his critique (1932a; see also 1931c), which he concluded by stating that Keynes, in the end, presented only a rather simple explanation of cyclical fluctuations which fell into the same category as the underconsumptionist theses of Foster and Catchings. To the latter he opposed his 'true explanation of the crisis', which could only be resolved by 'the slow and painful process of readjustment of the structure of production' (1932a, p. 42).[8]

Following that of Keynes, much diverse criticism was forthcoming, and we do not have the space here to offer an exhaustive account.[9] Both Hayek's reaction to these critiques and the manner in which his work subsequently developed are rather complex. He proceeded on several fronts. His main project was to reconstruct the theory of cycles based on a correct theory of capital and investment. He perfected his theory of cycles, giving it a final formulation in *Profits, Interest and Investment* (1939), while his considerable efforts to modernize the Austrian theory of capital yielded *The Pure Theory of Capital* (1941). At the same time, he deepened further his critique of socialism, developing more systematically his critique of its intellectual foundations, which he would name in turn scientism and constructivist rationalism. Finally, reflections of a philosophical and methodological nature led him to develop a much more critical attitude regarding the Walrasian theory of general equilibrium.

In 1932, Hayek stated in 'The Fate of the Gold Standard' (1932b) that the prolongation of the crisis showed the soundness of the analysis he had developed. The policies carried on had contributed to worsen rather than solve it.

The remote cause was the induced inflation up to 1929, while the immediate cause came from the resulting disequilibria in the structure of production. In 'Capital Consumption' (1932d), presented as a complement to *Prices and Production*, 'providing a somewhat more detailed representation of the mechanism of depressions' ([1932d] 1984, p. 157), Hayek criticizes the underconsumptionist theories, insisting that the surplus of current receipts over costs which, according to Keynes and his followers, leads to the boom, is, on the contrary, a cause of crisis. In particular, the growth of the share of workers' income beyond their contribution to production must result in a decline in the capital stock. One of the main causes of capital consumption 'is the result of excessively high costs of production, especially of wages which are too high' (p. 153).

In his contribution to the *Festschrift* in honor of Spiethoff (1933c), Hayek again criticizes the theories of underconsumption whose falsity, he finds, is obvious when one understands the role of the interest rate: the latter stays positive even in a stationary state, contrary to the claims of some fashionable theories, 'based on purely "dynamic" considerations or merely on considerations of banking liquidity' ([1933c] 1939, p. 173). He points out that it was the unsatisfactory state of the theory of interest, which is situated at the nexus of capital, monetary and price theories, which encouraged him to edit a book on monetary theory, which includes texts by Myrdal and Wicksell, among others (1933e).

Responding to the criticisms of Hansen and Tout (1933), which he considered positive, he developed his analysis of the role of forced saving in relation to the lengthening and then shortening of the production process, emphasizing that one of his book's weaknesses was the lack of explanation of the fact that the forced saving rhythm could sustain itself for a while. In particular, forced saving has the paradoxical effect of leading to an increase in the demand for consumer goods. The causality runs as follows: an increase in factor income, growth in consumer goods demanded, a rise in their prices, a shift of resources towards the consumer goods sector, a decrease in demand and employment in the investment goods sector, eventually also in the consumer goods sector and then generalized unemployment. The forced saving which begins the process can be maintained only by a constantly increasing credit injection: otherwise, contrary forces would set in motion to cancel the effect as soon as a certain inflation rate is reached (1934a, p.161).

Hayek continued his revision of *Prices and Production* in an article 'On the Relationship Between Investment and Output' (1934b), nearly all of which would be included, almost verbatim, in *The Pure Theory of Capital*. Here, he proceeds to replace the concept of the structure of production with that of the investment period, developing his theory of the interest rate. Asked to write a text on saving for the *Encyclopedia of the Social Sciences*, he launched a new attack on the underconsumption theories by underlining that the modern systems of social insurance, retirement support, and protection against accidents, illness and unemployment, 'are, no doubt, a very important factor decreasing the aggregate supply of savings' ([1934c] 1939, p. 169), which fact contributes to the instability of modern economies.

It was during a conference held in Copenhagen in December 1933, with proceedings published in German in 1935 (1935b), that Hayek most clearly drew the attention to the role of expectations, accusing the traditional approach of rendering the time factor completely abstract. Praising the Scandinavian approaches to uncertainty and risk, he wondered at the critique offered by Myrdal in his *Monetary Equilibrium* (1931), which blamed him, as well as Keynes, for not taking expectations into account. In 'The Maintenance of Capital' (1935c), Hayek continued the reflections that would lead to *The Pure Theory of Capital*, in the context of an analysis of the link between investment and saving. Their size cannot be determined by reference to changes in an undefinable quantity of capital. We have 'to compare directly the intentions of the consumers and the intentions of the producers with regard to the income stream they want to consume and produce respectively' (1935c, p. 270). It is at this point that Hayek, while discussing once more the concepts of time and prediction, truly began the critical revision of the equilibrium concept that would be completed in 'Economics and Knowledge' (1937a).[10]

In 1936, when Keynes's *General Theory of Employment, Interest and Money* was published, Hayek, for his part, published three other preliminary articles on the new theory of capital (1936a, 1936b and 1936c). There, one may read that 'in today's economy the scarcity of the other means of production required is often not a natural scarcity but frequently artificially caused, namely by an arbitrary fixing of minimum prices, above all for labour services' ([1936a] 1984, p. 177). In 'Investment that Raises the Demand for Capital', Hayek attempts to give a new formulation to what he henceforth calls 'the modern "monetary over-investment theories" of the trade cycle' (1937b, p. 174). It goes through the critique of the erroneous extension in dynamic analysis of the static proposition according to which a rise in the quantity of capital leads to a reduction in marginal productivity. The article's aim is to demonstrate that, on the contrary, the effect might be to increase the future demand for loanable funds and, therefore, the interest rate. Only at the margin does the demand for capital react to a change in the interest rate. Otherwise, it is very inelastic with respect to interest rate changes, which means that 'much of the argument based on the supposed tendency of the "marginal efficiency of capital" to fall more rapidly than the money rate of interest' will have to be abandoned (1937b, p. 177). The rise in the interest rate witnessed at the end of the boom is produced not by monetary factors, but by real factors which affect demand.

The last version of Hayek's theory of cycles appeared in 1939, under the title *Profits, Interest and Investment*. In fact, it is a collection of articles, most of which had been published between 1932 and 1939. The book includes a 1929 text in its appendix. Hayek presents these texts as attempts to improve and develop the theses of *Prices and Production* and *Monetary Theory and the Trade Cycle*. The volume is opened by a previously unpublished long essay bearing the same title as the book, 'Profits, Interest and Investment', and this contains the new version of Hayek's thesis.

In this new version, Hayek avoids the Austrian terminology that had brought him so much criticism. The equilibrium interest rate becomes the profit rate, a concept that had unfortunately been abandoned because of its use by Marx. The goal of the analysis is, as before, to show how a rise in the demand for consumer goods can prompt a reduction of that for investment goods, in the conditions usually prevailing at the beginning of a recovery. However, the sequences are different from those of the 1931 model. Hayek now relies on what he calls the Ricardo effect: 'a rise in the price of the product (or a fall in real wages) will lead to the use of relatively less machinery and other capital and of relatively more direct labour in the production of any given quantity of output' (1939, p. 10). Now, 'probably one of the best established empirical generalisations about industrial fluctuations' (p. 11) is that, about half-way into the recovery, prices of consumer goods start to rise and, therefore, real wages start to fall. The result of this fall of real wages is to create a tendency to substitute labour for capital. Profits rise in labour-intensive industries and fall in the others. Now, these groups correspond in part to consumer and capital goods industries, respectively, although one must be careful of making too simplistic a partition of total production between these two sectors. The reduction of profits in the investment goods industries eventually provokes a decline in employment, first in the sectors hit by the initial reduction of profits, then in all the others. Hayek states he has thus demonstrated his first thesis, 'namely that an increase in the demand for consumers' goods may lead to a decrease in the demand for capital goods' (p. 31). This decline can be postponed by maintaining the interest rate at a low level, but the fall will be even greater the higher the profit rate in labour-intensive sectors. Conversely, if interest rates are allowed to rise, then the harmful consequences of the process are lessened. A weak propensity to consume would have the same effect. So, in all cases, growth is finally brought to an end by 'capital scarcity', regardless of the interest rate. During the period of depression, in the same manner, it is not interest rates, but 'the rate of profits and real wages, which govern the decline and eventual revival of investment' (p. 37).

Therefore, it is not a reduction in investment opportunities that provokes the crisis. Neither is it the growth of investment which lies at the origin of the profit rate reduction. The causal link is the opposite. The increase in investment beyond voluntary saving produces a growth in profits, and 'the process can only come to an end when the rise of profits begins to operate as a curb to investment in the way explained before' (p. 56). The rise of profits in the consumer goods sector creates an unstable situation, the development of which can be prevented only if, from the beginning of the recovery, interest rates are allowed to rise to meet profit rates: 'A policy designed to mitigate fluctuations will therefore have to watch the recovery from its very beginning' (p. 61). And one of the most effective ways is 'preventing the rate of profit from falling too low, and real wages from rising too high' (p. 62). If the process cannot be avoided, i.e. the profit rates in the consumer goods sector are too low and real wages too high, 'the proper remedy appears to be a reduction of wages' (p. 63). Any attempt made to improve the situation by lowering the interest rates would only accentuate the difficulties. Hayek granted Keynes the idea that employment could be artificially stimulated in the short term by a monetary policy. But this type of full employment is unstable and results in future problems: 'But the economist should not conceal the fact that to aim at the maximum of employment which can be achieved in the short run by means of monetary policy is essentially the policy of the desperado who has nothing to lose and everything to gain from a short breathing space' (p. 64).

In 1941, Friedrich Hayek published *The Pure Theory of Capital*, his last large scale contribution to pure economic theory. This long treatise was intended to present the basic theoretical instruments for the analysis of cyclical fluctuations, but was also meant to answer certain objections raised by his previous works. It covers only the first part of the terrain, and its hasty publication was prompted by the war. In fact, the remainder would never be published. This might explain the abruptness of tone beginning in chapter 25, where one finds Hayek's sharpest criticism of Keynes's theory, and in particular of the latter's political basis. Again, Hayek strongly asserts the virtue of saving and austerity in the face of what he calls the economy of the desperado based on the short run and on the principle of '*après nous le déluge*', regarded 'not only as a serious and dangerous intellectual error, but as a betrayal of the main duty of the economist and a grave menace to our civilisation' (1941, p. 409).

This was for Hayek, at least at this moment, a cry in the desert. His two books did not have the same impact as the two publications in the early 1930s. Far from it. Not only were they published at the beginning of the war, but they also appeared at the moment when Keynes's theses were very much in the foreground. So they remained almost unknown, even if they prompted diverse critiques, including a virulent one by his former disciple Kaldor (1942),[11] whose tone compared to Sraffa's. In 1942, Hayek responded to

Townshend's (1940) and Wilson's (1940) critiques in the context of clarifying what he called the Ricardo effect (Hayek 1942a). Standing by his methodological precepts, Hayek admits that any attempt to verify the Ricardo effect by statistical methods is doomed to the greatest difficulties.[12]

To Kaldor, who saw a significant contradiction between the Hayek I of *Prices and Production* and the Hayek II of *Profits, Interest and Investment*, the author replied: 'Though I hope that in the dozen years since I wrote *Prices and Production* my understanding of the problems involved has somewhat increased, I find it impossible, hard as I try, to find any irreconcilable conflict between the earlier and the later version' (Hayek, 1942b, p. 383). He specified regarding the change in terminology from interest rate to profit rate that he supposed in 1930, and still supposed in parts, that the variations of 'price margins' – which in *Prices and Production* play the same role as the profit rates – end by causing movements in interest rates in the same direction, except in cases of major inflation or deflation. In *Profits, Interest and Investment* he tries to ascertain if the harmful effects of margin increases remain, even given the hypothesis of constant interest rates. Moreover, there is no contradiction between these two visions of the connections between lengthening and shortening of the period of production. The succession of phases remains the same, with only the analytical approach towards the process analysis differing. Finally, in his critique, Kaldor mixes up total profits and profit margins. The effect of the former and latter are different:

> But the whole point is that expanding final output and expanding the volume of investment are not necessarily the same thing, and that the endeavour to provide a large output quickly, such as may be caused by a large 'profit *margin*', may be the cause of a decrease in the volume of investment – in other words, that an increase of the 'profit margins' may create a situation where each entrepreneur aiming to maximise his aggregate profits may result in a smaller volume of total investment. (Hayek, 1942b, p. 385, emphasis in the original)

It is the increase in the price of consumer goods that induces the abandonment of investments undertaken when their prices were low. The question is to know if this problem would be solved by distributing money in order to maintain the interest rate at a low level. Such is the popular solution, to which Kaldor subscribes according to Hayek. Evidently, this is not the latter's opinion.

Conclusion
We find ourselves back at our point of departure. For Hayek, the measures advocated by Kaldor, Keynes and their friends for getting out of economic depression are the same as those put forward by Foster, Catchings and the underconsumptionists in the 1920s. It was the critique of the theoretical

foundation of the latter theses that motivated Hayek's intense theoretical effort, between 1925 and 1940, to posit a firmly based alternative explanation. This, after some initial success, was largely forgotten before regaining popularity in recent years, as a source of inspiration for several economists sharing Hayek's political vision. Beyond modifications, improvements and revisions, there is, a *leitmotiv*.

This *leitmotiv* is already found in writings by Turgot, Smith and Say. It concerns the key role of preliminary, that is voluntary saving, as the motor for accumulation. Investment is determined by saving, and saving is linked to thrift, to frugality, as expressed by the agents' intertemporal preferences. The natural or equilibrium rate of interest is a real price that brings to equality saving and investment. Money allows the introduction of an artificial motor for investment, which creates temporary additional energy, in the same way that a drug can stimulate the energy of the artist, writer or athlete. But for these it can also be lethal. This conception of money is the kernel of Hayek's thesis. Hayek states clearly, in his early work, that money plays an essential part in the economy, that a monetary economy is quite different from a real-exchange economy, and he even criticizes on this ground the naïve quantity theory of money. But he then turns back to a conception of money considered, not as an integral part of the economy, but as a veil, or as the oil of the engine, according to Hume's vision. Money, considered as an exogenous element, is thus the villain, responsible in the last resort for crises and cycles.

To this can be opposed an endogenous vision of money, and a conception of investment as the active part of the story. This is almost always linked to the absence of faith in the automatic stabilization of market economies, and thus to the affirmation of the necessity of State intervention. These views cannot be compared and criticized on purely rational or empirical grounds. This explains why these debates are ever lasting. Different conceptions of man, of life, and of the relation of man to society are in question.

Of course, no one should encourage the use of dangerous drugs to stimulate the economy as well as the artist – even if Baudelaire did not die from the use of the artificial paradises that maybe inspired some of the marvellous poems of *Les fleurs du mal*, or if Rimbaud survived the absinthe which doubtless coloured some miraculous pages of his *Illuminations* and *Une saison en enfer*. Illness is part of human experience, and the necessary means of combating it inevitably bring on secondary effects. In the same way, it appears highly doubtful, after a few centuries of experience, that the smooth functioning of the free market is of such a nature as to insulate the open society against those evils which perhaps risk destroying it with greater certainty than the non-neutrality of money.

Notes

1. In particular, see Benassi (1987), Klausinger (1986), Thalenhorst and Wenig (1984), Tsiang (1949) and Zamagni (1984).
2. It is interesting to note that Tinbergen characterized Keynes's system in this manner as well as Hayek's. In contrast with the analysis developed by Frisch, Kalecki or himself: 'Both are examples of "open" systems. The number of variables referred to in the discussion is larger than the relations that are precisely and explicitly stated. An attempt at a mathematical "translation" leads the reader to many unsolved questions' (Tinbergen, 1935, p. 264).
3. On this subject, see Mendell and Polanyi-Levitt (1988).
4. Schumpeter then became the finance minister of the governmental coalition of the Social-Democrat Party and the Christian Socialist Party, a coalition which pushed a programme of gradual and limited socialization.
5. Alluding to the 'mathematical school, following Walras' (1926, p. 53), in an article on imputation and drawn from his doctoral dissertation, Hayek, however, already expresses his scepticism regarding the practical possibility of taking into account all the complex interrelations found in a given economic system, a scepticism which would grow stronger in the course of his career.
6. In his article on intertemporal equilibrium, he gave 'a beautiful example of how dangerous it is to derive theoretical propositions from the results of statistical investigations' (1928, p. 116).
7. 'Since the publication of the German edition of this book, I have become less convinced that the difference between monetary and non-monetary explanations is *the most important* point of disagreement between the various Trade Cycle theories' (Hayek 1933a, p. 41, emphasis in original).
8. This controversy has been described in detail in Dostaler (1991).
9. Among the most important papers, we should mention, in chronological order, those of Marget (1932), Hawtrey (1932), Sraffa (1932), Hansen and Tout (1933), Hawtrey (1933), Shackle (1933), Tinbergen (1935), Knight (1935). A detailed presentation of the critiques of Hayek's thesis in the 1930s may be found in Saulnier (1938). On the debate between Hayek and Sraffa, see Desai (1982) and Mongiovi (1990).
10. See also Hayek (1933b).
11. On the controversy between Kaldor and Hayek, consult M. Desai (1991).
12. The question of the Ricardo effect constitutes perhaps the only element of *Profits, Interest and Investment* which, in the decades following its publication, prompted a sustained debate, in which Hayek himself took part. On the subject, consult Moss and Vaughn (1986).

References

Benassi, C. (1987), 'An Input–Output Formulation of the "Coefficient of Money Transactions": A Note on Hayek's Trade Cycle Theory', *Economia Internazionale*, **1**, 1–19.

Desai, M. (1982), 'The Task of Monetary Theory: The Hayek-Sraffa Debate in a Modern Perspective', in M. Baranzani (ed.), *Advances in Economic Theory*, Oxford: Basil Blackwell.

Desai, M. (1991), 'Kaldor Between Hayek and Keynes, or: Did Nicky Kill Capital Theory?', in E. Nell and W. Semmler (eds), *Nicholas Kaldor and Mainstream Economics: Confrontation or Convergence?*, London: Macmillan; New York: St Martin's Press.

Dostaler, G. (1991), 'The Debate Between Hayek and Keynes', in W. J. Barber (ed.), *Perspectives on the History of Economic Thought*, vol. 6, *Themes in Keynesian Criticism and Supplementary Modern Topics*, Aldershot, Hants: Edward Elgar.

Dostaler, G. and D. Éthier (eds) (1988), *Friedrich Hayek: Philosophie, économie et politique*, Montreal: ACFAS; Paris: Économica, 1989.

Hansen, A. H. and H. Tout (1933), 'Annual Survey of Business Cycle Theory: Investment and Saving in Business Cycle Theory', *Econometrica*, **1**, 119–47.

Hawtrey, R. G. (1932), '*Prices and Production*. By F. A. Hayek', *Economica*, **12**, 119–25.

Hawtrey, R. G. (1933), '*Monetary Theory and the Trade Cycle.* By F. A. Hayek', *Economic Journal*, **43**, 669–72.

Hayek, F. A. von (1925), 'Die Währungspolitik der Vereinigten Staaten seit der Überwindung der Krise von 1920', *Zeitschrift für Volkswirtschaft und Sozialpolitik*, new series, **5**, (1–3), 25–63 and (4–6), 254–317; partial English trans., 'The Monetary Policy of the United States after the Recovery from the 1920 Crisis', in Hayek (1984).

Hayek, F. A. von (1926), 'Bemerkungen zum Zurechnungsproblem', *Jahrbücher für Nationalökonomie und Statistik*, **69**, 1–18; English trans., 'Some Remarks on the Problem of Imputation', in Hayek (1984).

Hayek, F. A. von (1928), 'Das intertemporale Gleichgewichtssystem der Preise und die Bewegungen des "Geldwertes"', *Weltwirtschaftliches Archiv*, **28**, 33–76; English trans., 'Intertemporal Price Equilibrium and Movements in the Value of Money', in Hayek (1984).

Hayek, F. A. von (1929a), *Geldtheorie und Konjunkturtheorie*, Vienna and Leipzig: Hölder–Pichler–Tempsky; English trans., 1933a.

Hayek, F. A. von (1929b), 'Gibt es einen "Widersinn des Sparens"? Eine Kritik der Krisentheorie von W. T. Foster und W. Catchings mit einigen Bemerkungen zur Lehre von den Beziehungen zwischen Geld und Kapital', *Zeitschrift für Nationalökonomie*, **1** (3), 387–412; augm. version, Vienna: Springer, 1931; English trans., 'The "Paradox" of Saving', *Economica*, **11**, 1931, 125–69.

Hayek, F. A. von (1929c), *Das Mieterschutzproblem: Nationalökonomische Betrachtungen*, Vienna: Steyrermühl.

Hayek, F. A. von (1931a), *Prices and Production*, London: Routledge & Son; 2nd ed., 1935.

Hayek, F. A. von (1931b), 'Reflections on the Pure Theory of Money of Mr. J. M. Keynes', *Economica*, **11**, 270–95.

Hayek, F. A. von (1931c), 'A Rejoinder to Mr Keynes', *Economica*, **11**, 398–403.

Hayek, F. A. von (1932a), 'Reflections on the Pure Theory of Money of Mr. J. M. Keynes (*continued*)', *Economica*, **12**, 22–44.

Hayek, F. A. von (1932b), 'Das Schicksal der Goldwährung', *Der Deutsche Volkswirt*, no. 20, 642–5 and no. 21, 677–81; English trans., 'The Fate of the Gold Standard', in Hayek (1984).

Hayek, F. A. von (1932c), 'Money and Capital: A Reply', *Economic Journal*, **42**, 237–49.

Hayek, F. A. von (1932d), 'Kapitalaufzehrung', *Weltwirtschatfliches Archiv*, **36**, 86–108; English trans., 'Capital Consumption', in Hayek (1984).

Hayek, F. A. von (1932e), 'A Note on the Development of the Doctrine of "Forced Saving"', *Quarterly Journal of Economics*, **47**, 123–33; in Hayek (1939).

Hayek, F. A. von (1933a), *Monetary Theory and the Trade Cycle*, London: Jonathan Cape; New York: Augustus M. Kelley, 1966.

Hayek, F. A. von (1933b), 'The Trend of Economic Thinking', *Economica*, **13**, 121–37.

Hayek, F. A. von (1933c), 'The Present State and Immediate Prospects of the Study of Industrial Fluctuations', in G. Clausing (ed.), *Der Stand und die nächste Zukunft der Konjunkturforschung: Festschrift für Arthur Spiethoff*, Munich: Duncker & Humblot; in Hayek (1939).

Hayek, F. A. von (1933d), 'Über "neutrales Geld"', *Zeitschrift für Nationalökonomie*, **4**, 659–61; English trans., 'On "Neutral Money"', in Hayek (1984).

Hayek, F. A. von (ed.) (1933e), *Beiträge zur Geldtheorie*, Vienna: Julius Springer.

Hayek, F. A. von (1934a), 'Capital and Industrial Fluctuations', *Econometrica*, **2**, 152–67.

Hayek, F. A. von (1934b), 'On the Relationship Between Investment and Output', *Economic Journal*, **44**, 207–31.

Hayek, F. A. von (1934c), 'Saving', *Encyclopedia of the Social Sciences*, New York: Macmillan, vol. 13; in Hayek (1939).

Hayek, F. A. von (ed.) (1935a), *Collectivist Economic Planning: Critical Studies on the Possibilities of Socialism*, London: Routledge & Sons.

Hayek, F. A. von (1935b), 'Preiserwartungen, Monetäre Störungen und Fehlinvestionen', *Nationalökonomisk Tidskrift*, **73** (3); English trans., 'Price Expectations, Monetary Disturbances and Maladjustments', in Hayek (1939).

Hayek, F. A. von (1935c), 'The Maintenance of Capital', *Economica*, new series, **2**, 241–76.

Hayek, F. A. von (1936a), 'Technischer Fortschritt und Überkapazität', *Österreichische Zeitschrift für Bankwesen*, **1**, 9–23; English trans., 'Technical Progress and Excess Capacity', in Hayek (1984).

Hayek, F. A. von (1936b), 'The Mythology of Capital', *Quarterly Journal of Economics*, **50**, 199–228.

Hayek, F. A. von (1936c), 'Utility Analysis and Interest', *Economic Journal*, **46**, 44–60.

Hayek, F. A. von (1937a), 'Economics and Knowledge', *Economica*, new series, **4**, 33–54.

Hayek, F. A. von (1937b), 'Investment that Raises the Demand for Capital', *Review of Economic Statistics*, **19**, 174–7.

Hayek, F. A. von (1939), *Profits, Interest and Investment: and Other Essays on The Theory of Industrial Fluctuations*, London: Routledge and Kegan Paul.

Hayek, F. A. von (1941), *The Pure Theory of Capital*, London: Routledge & Kegan Paul; Chicago: University of Chicago Press.

Hayek, F. A. von (1942a), 'The Ricardo Effect', *Economica*, **9**, 127–52.

Hayek, F. A. von (1942b), 'A Comment', *Economica*, **9**, 383–5.

Hayek, F. A. von (1963), *Wirtschaft, Wissenschaft und Politik*, Freiburg im Breisgau: H. F. Schulz; English trans., 'The Economy, Science and Politics' in Hayek (1967).

Hayek, F. A. von (1967), *Studies in Philosophy, Politics and Economics*, London: Routledge & Kegan Paul; Chicago: University of Chicago Press.

Hayek, F. A. von (1975), *Prix et production*, Paris: Calmann-Lévy.

Hayek, F. A. von (1984), *Money, Capital, and Fluctuations: Early Essays*, ed. R. McCloughry, London: Routledge & Kegan Paul; Chicago: University of Chicago Press.

Hayek, F. A. von (1988), *The Fatal Conceit*, vol. 1 of *The Collected Works of F. A. Hayek*, ed. W. W. Bartley III, London: Routledge; Chicago: University of Chicago Press, 1989.

Hicks, J. R. (1967), 'The Hayek Story', in *Critical Essays in Monetary Theory*, Oxford: Clarendon Press.

Kaldor, N. (1942), 'Professor Hayek and the Concertina-Effect', *Economica*, **9**, 359–82.

Keynes, J.M. (1931), 'A Reply to Dr Hayek', *Economica*, **12**, 387–97; in *The Collected Writings of John Maynard Keynes*, London: Macmillan, vol. 13, 1973.

Klausinger, H. (1986), '"Hayek Re-analyzed": A Note', *Jahrbücher für Nationalökonomie und Statistik*, **201**, 422–8.

Knight, F. H. (1935), 'Professor Hayek and the Theory of Investment', *Economic Journal*, **45**, 77–94.

Marget, A. W. (1932), '*Prices and Production*. By Friedrich A. Hayek; *Preise und Produktion*. By Friedrich A. Hayek', *Journal of Political Economy*, **40**, 261–66.

Mendell, M. and Polanyi-Levitt, K. (1988), 'Hayek à Vienne', in Dostaler and Éthier (eds) (1988).

Mises, L. von (1912), *Theorie des Geldes und der Umlaufsmittel*, Munich and Leipzig: Duncker & Humblot; 2nd ed., 1924; English trans., *The Theory of Money and Credit*, London: Jonathan Cape, 1934.

Mises, L. von (1920), 'The Wirtschaftsrechnung in sozialistischen Gemeinwesen', *Archiv für Sozialwissenschaften und Sozialpolitik*, **47** (1), 86–121.

Mises, L. von (1922), *Die Gemeinwirtschaft: Untersuchungen über den Sozialismus*, Jena: Gustav Fischer.

Mongiovi, G. (1990), 'Keynes, Hayek and Sraffa: On the Origins of Chapter 17 of *The General Theory*', *Économie appliquée*, **43**, 131–56.

Moss, L. S. and K.I. Vaughn, (1986), 'Hayek's Ricardo Effect: A Second Look', *History of Political Economy*, **18**, 545–65.

Myrdal, G. (1931), 'Om penningteoretisk jämvikt. En studie över den "normala räntan" i Wicksells penninglära', *Ekonomisk Tidskrift*, **33**, 191–302; German version in F. A. Hayek (1933e), English version, *Monetary Equilibrium*, Glasgow: William Hodge, 1939.

Saulnier, R. J. (1938), *Contemporary Monetary Theory: Studies of Some Recent Theories of Money, Prices and Production*, New York: Columbia University Press.

Shackle, G. L. S. (1933), 'Some Notes on Monetary Theories of the Trade Cycle', *Review of Economic Studies*, **1**, 27–38.

Sraffa, P. (1932), 'Dr Hayek on Money and Capital', *Economic Journal*, **42**, 42–53.

Thalenhorst, J. and A. Wenig (1984), 'F. A. Hayek's *Prices and Production* Reanalyzed', *Jahrbücher für Nationalökonomie und Statistik*, **199**, 213–36.

Tinbergen, J. (1935), 'Annual Survey: Suggestions on Quantitative Business Cycle Theory', *Econometrica*, **3**, 241–308.

Townshend, H. (1940), '*Profits, Interest and Investment*. By F. A. von Hayek', *Economic Journal*, **50**, 99–103.

Tsiang, S. C. (1949), 'Rehabilitation of Time Dimension of Investment in Macrodynamic Analysis', *Economica*, **16**, 204–17.

Wilson, T. (1940), 'Capital Theory and the Trade Cycle', *Review of Economic Studies*, **7**, 169–79.

Zamagni, S. (1984), 'Ricardo and Hayek Effects in a Fixwage Model of Traverse', *Oxford Economic Papers*, **36**, 135–51.

9 The transformation of business cycle theory: Hayek, Lucas and a change in the notion of equilibrium*

Christof Rühl

> ... *the good old days: when*
> *everything was simple and more confused.*
> (J. Morrison, *An American Prayer*)

I. Introduction

This paper addresses three issues. First, it examines Hayek's contribution to interwar business cycle theory by concentrating on the primary methodological problem of this period: how to reconcile contemporary equilibrium theory and the empirical phenomenon of a regular business cycle. Second, it scrutinizes the claim that Hayek was an important forerunner of modern equilibrium business cycle theory – falling short simply for a lack of technical devices. Third, it briefly addresses the change in the concept of equilibrium which underlies the different attempts to explain persistent economic fluctuations now and in the interwar period.

The following section provides an outline of the argument. The next introduces the contemporary debate on equilibrium and business cycle theory. Part IV presents a detailed discussion of Hayek's position and its relation to modern equilibrium theory, while the final section contains a brief conclusion.

II. Outline of the argument

We start this investigation by reviving a German language debate which took place between the mid-1920s and the early 1930s. Hayek's contribution was an offspring of this debate and is best appreciated in this context. A more compelling reason to return to this particular 'crossroad' in the history of economics, however, is that the participants in this early debate were concerned with an issue relevant to modern macroeconomics, and that they addressed this issue in a manner more frank, more clear-cut, and in some respects more useful than current discussions.

*I would like to acknowledge the support I had in preparing this paper, and I am particularly grateful to Barbara Link for her help and encouragement. All translations in this Chapter are my own.

At issue is the compatibility of an explanation of 'the' business cycle with general equilibrium theory. As long as regular fluctuations of important economic indicators are recognized as an accurate empirical observation, a well known conflict between that observation and explanations based on the axioms of equilibrium theory exists. It is a conflict between axiomatic theory on the one hand and subject of inquiry on the other, with a theory *prima facie* not designed to explain dynamic processes, and an economy exhibiting, of all things, a recurrent pattern of changing activity levels which is accompanied by regular fluctuations in key variables. The debate referred to covers all four possible escape routes out of this dilemma: to deny the regular character of the observation; to reconcile the notion of a gravitational centre, determined by general equilibrium theory, with recurrent oscillations by developing an endogenous propagation mechanism; to find reasons for the equilibrium attractor itself to move systematically, in a recurrent fashion; or to abandon the axiomatic approach underlying these attempts.

The problem can also be approached, in slightly more modern language, by simply asking whether the behaviour of competitive economies over time can be appropriately understood by modelling an attractor (or a 'centre of gravitation', as it was referred to in earlier debates) around which the economy fluctuates but which itself is determined independently from these short-run deviations; or whether economic behaviour has to be modelled as path-dependent in the sense that the trend-rate of output growth is contingent on the observed cyclical fluctuations. With the second hypothesis the notion of a trend may denote nothing but a statistical *ex-post* average, devoid of all economic content. Only with the first can 'the last dogma' (Tichy, 1989) of textbook business cycle theory, the independence of trend and cycle, be maintained – and the process of economic growth be analysed by separating it into two theoretical compartments, entitled growth and business cycle theory.[1]

No conclusion on these issues was reached in the interwar period. That the fundamental problem – how to reconcile an economy which so clearly seemed to exhibit a pattern of regular oscillation with an axiomatic approach not designed to explain recurrent fluctuations at all – had been left unsettled became obvious during the early 1970s when business cycle theory once again rose to the centre of attention in macroeconomics. This time, however, there was not much room for hesitant methodological inquiries. The new approach was based on a developed aggregate growth model which successfully had translated the static properties of equilibrium theory into the steady state. Perhaps more importantly, it came with the often acclaimed 'rigour and consistency' supposedly entailed in employing the hypothesis of rational expectations. The confidence from having wreaked havoc to (comparative static) mainstream Keynesian models translated neatly into the claim of representing the successful completion of an earlier research programme (on dynamics) of which Hayek was thought to be the leading protagonist.

This claim, however, has to be distinguished from the criticism of Keynesian macro models, which by and large relied on the Hicksian device of temporary equilibrium. It is explicitly directed at the development of a dynamic intertemporal analysis, as opposed to the critique of models relying on comparative statics. Evaluating the new classical attack by the damage done to mainstream Keynesian models therefore reflects, though it may look more familiar, in our context only the more or less destructive end of a detour. The alleged integration of business cycle and general equilibrium theory, on the other hand, constitutes the constructive part of the argument. In this paper we are concerned only with the constructive part – i.e. with developments within the neoclassical camp, methodological and theoretical.

It is true that Hayek's writings on the 'trade cycle' and the emerging new classical literature on the business cycle were both directed at reconciling their respective equilibrium frameworks with the presumably regular and recurrent fluctuations in economic activity we still label business cycles, and that the latter was defined in almost identical terms. But that history was convenient enough to pose the same problem all over again almost exhausts what both approaches have in common. The attempted solution, the tools, and the perception of success all differ.[2]

The problem itself certainly is not new. Walras had likened recurrent oscillations in economic activity to the regular waves of an ocean, and conceived his theory as prepared only to deal with the 'flat surface' which, he thought, could nowhere be observed. Perhaps still the best description of the dilemma faced by those willing to save the inherited axiomatic approach was Hayek's own. He identified the tension between (contemporary) 'static' equilibrium theory and 'that regular wave-like appearance which we observe in cyclical fluctuations', stating that the latter should

> ... be explained only by widening the assumptions on which our deductions are based, so that cyclical fluctuations follow from these as a *necessary* consequence, just as the general propositions of the theory of price followed from the narrower assumptions of equilibrium theory. (1933, p. 30, italics added)

Cyclical fluctuations 'with all their peculiarities' had to be explained by a 'purely deductive method', and this explanation was to be firmly grounded in the territory of equilibrium theory. The point is made over and over again – but apparently to little avail. For the quest for an explanation of economic fluctuations about trend, which at the same time is coherent with the theory explaining that trend, has celebrated a remarkable revival only recently. 'Why is it', asks Lucas (1977, p. 7) 'that, in capitalist economies, aggregate variables undergo repeated fluctuations about trend, all of essentially the same character?' And he continues to quote, with approval, Hayek's statement that the incorporation of said cyclical fluctuations into equilibrium theory, 'with which they are in apparent contradiction', would constitute and would remain the crucial problem of trade cycle theory. Both authors suggest that the optimal growth path around which these fluctuations occur does not represent the theoretical problem.

Rather than carrying the attempts of the interwar period to a logical conclusion, however, the new approach changed the question by changing the method of analysis. It did not attempt to identify reasons for systematic coordination failures in order for them to be reconciled with the underlying structure of equilibrium theory. Instead, the issue of *systematic* coordination failures was evaded. New classical models (in the present context *alias* equilibrium business cycle theory) rely on white noise to generate fluctuations. Neither a systematic explanation of technological or structural change, nor a systematic account of oscillations deduced from maladjustments in the price system, is part of that picture. In the background we observe a change in the concept of equilibrium dominating macroeconomic analysis – from the concept of temporary (or 'short-run') equilibrium, developed by Hicks (1939) and employed in most Keynesian models, to that of continuous equilibrium with instantaneous adjustment in principle, but contingent on information sets of agents with mutually consistent beliefs, constructed in the wake of the rational expectation 'revolution'.[3]

As far as new classical macroeconomics is concerned, it will be this shift in method which marks its lasting legacy – not the content of its business cycle theories, nominal or real, and not the provocative neutrality postulates derived early on. In the process, macroeconomics has switched from (comparative) statics to dynamics and in that sense from Keynesian economics back to topics more openly addressed in the interwar period. But in the course of redefining the dominant equilibrium concept from a position with no inherent tendency to change ('position at rest') to stochastic rational expectation equilibria with 'no gains from trade left unexploited', the old-fashioned distinction between equilibrium and disequilibrium analysis was squandered in favour of processes with the presumption of demand and supply moving in line continuously. As a result, the old division of agents (and their behaviour) by the economic function they perform disappeared; the signals to which they react came to be characterized in categories of arbitrary shocks, no longer themselves subject to feedback mechanisms and therefore in principle open to an economic explanation. Agents with mutually consistent beliefs optimize plans which are subject to perceived constraints, as rationally as they can; if they err, it is due to limits imposed on the system from the outside, or to exogenous 'shocks' (in themselves left unexplained), or, to adhere to the language of the *genre*, because their information sets have been restricted. That excess demands or supplies should not matter in attempting to model 'real' adjustment processes when analysing the intertemporal coordination of a growing economy is different from both (comparative-static) Keynesian and (dynamic) pre-Keynesian theory.

Theorists of the interwar period, on the other hand, could not rely on the Hicksian notion of temporary equilibrium. But Hayek's idea of an intertemporal equilibrium also differs from stochastic rational expectation equilibria. So do the questions he (and his colleagues) tried to answer: they tried to explore precisely what later became precluded by the Hicksian device – the adjustment processes in between the non-trading periods. This meant focusing on intertemporal coordination to determine how equilibrating processes in the aggregate are brought about or why, as in the context of the business cycle puzzle, they are not brought about perfectly well. It also implied utilizing the functional separation of economic agents to explain why agents should react to different signals, or react differently to the same signal. The obvious way of reconciling the business cycle phenomenon with the equilibrium framework included attempts at modelling the interaction between signals and agents' behaviour in such a way as to include the feedback effects of induced economic behaviour on the relevant economic variables constituting such signals, typically nominal prices and the interest rate. In summa, the cycle was not perceived as an equilibrium phenomenon, for the task was to explain the recurrent pattern of movements *away* from the equilibrium configuration of relative prices and quantities as endogenous systemic behaviour. These were situations in which the presumed equilibrating tendencies not only seemed to fail but to reverse themselves; dynamic processes over time, therefore, in which the notion of equilibrium serves as an abstract benchmark, without the instantaneous adjustment and therefore the continuity presumed in modern business cycle theory. In this respect, the difference between both approaches cannot be more striking.

However, the notion of continuous equilibrium does not *per se* preclude the discussion of coordination failures – as long as the latter are perceived to be equilibrium phenomena which can be Pareto-ranked. Today, the bread and butter problems of macroeconomics are increasingly tackled by using the resulting multiple-equilibrium framework. The ultimate question then becomes whether the new approach provides better explanatory tools than the old idea of distinguishing equilibrium positions from adjustment processes which have to be characterized as disequilibria – or whether our enhanced modelling capacities fail, as critics claim, to explain unwarranted aggregate outcomes as the result of systemic interaction. In what follows, this question will be addressed with reference to interwar theories of economic growth and development, as opposed to the more common scenario of Keynesian/new classical comparisons. The claim advanced here is that, in this particular respect, new classical macroeconomics falls short of what had been accomplished decades ago and, 'technically' speaking, with an undoubtedly more limited toolbox.[4]

Thus, retrospection is not only helpful in the passive sense of denoting how the means of analysis have changed. It provides a handle to assess the progress economics has made with regard to particular problems. Business cycle theory is particularly well suited to such an investigation. There are significant lessons to be learned even from the more narrow approach of comparing early and modern attempts at explaining the business cycle within the Walrasian tradition. Though not attracting the attention it deserves, a full understanding of the change in the method of equilibrium analysis which separates these alternative approaches seems to us an important first step if the goal is to weigh the merits and demerits of competing explanations of 'unsteady growth in an unsteady world' (Nell, 1993). Since the new concept of equilibrium is now firmly established, we will focus the investigation on the implications arising for modern equilibrium analysis from a German language debate which addressed precisely this issue of compatibility between the dynamics of industrial fluctuations and equilibrium analysis as it was understood before the change took place.

'The' business cycle can now be defined in a manner sufficiently general to cover the arguments alluded to. We define it as regular and recurrent co-movements of aggregate economic variables, prominent among them real output and nominal prices. Periodicity, as in 'recurrent', implies turning points and allows for the possibility of oscillations around an independently determined attractor, without prejudicing that issue. 'Regular' implies common characteristics in the behaviour of serially correlated key variables, without pre-judging the question of unique causation. The common extension 'with a relatively regular period and a roughly constant amplitude' (e.g. Tichy, 1989, p. 5) may be added, but it is not essential.[5]

The compatibility of the cycle in the sense just defined with the axiomatic theory descending from Walras constitutes the object of inquiry. But a similar, unique definition of the notion of equilibrium cannot be given for 'old' and 'new' business cycle theories alike – because this instrument of inquiry has changed. The concept of equilibrium, therefore, will have to be considered on a case-by-case basis when comparing old and new theories. What we then have, at the outset, is on the most basic level a conflict between empirical observation and axiomatic theory with economists agreeing that the former defies the rules of deduction laid down by the latter. Interestingly, both components of the problem emerged at about the same time.

III.   Equilibrium and the business cycle: a case study

It took time for 'the' business cycle to become an independent and accepted object of study. For most *classical* authors the interesting problem was the decline in industrial output associated with the feasibility of a 'general glut'. Even Marx, the most prominent exception did not, though he denied the validity of Say's Law, consider the business cycle as an object worthy of independent study. Others, for example Lord Overstone, tied their analyses so closely to the issues of monetary policy they were concerned with that their derived interest on business cycles seems almost accidental. From both angles there was little need to reconcile cyclical fluctuations with the standards of contemporary theorizing. Moreover, nineteenth century authors were largely concerned with price movements, reflecting a genuine feature of that period (Nell, 1993) as well as the limited availability of data (at the time almost exclusively confined to time series observations of nominal prices). Recurrent fluctuations involving price *cum* quantity movements became a generally accepted feature of economic development only after the 1870s, and only slowly.[6] As a theoretical problem the business cycle was thus recognized at a time when classical political economy had by and large already been replaced by the results of the marginal revolution.

In considering the interwar period, a time when economics still developed quite independently at different locations, this order implies that common traits can be identified whatever the particular version of equilibrium theory adopted. Most importantly, all authors discussed in this section share the general properties of an equilibrium position as representing a *unique* and *stable* social *optimum*. The concept was, though sometimes indirectly derived, reminiscent of Walras. The equilibrium position therefore was determined by the same set of data employed today: endowments, technology and preferences.

The point of reference for discussing economic dynamics was the stationary and, much less frequently, the steady state. Translating the static equilibrium configuration of prices and quantities (and its properties) into the stationary state 'in the tradition of Cassel, Walras and Wicksell' (Löwe) seems just as simple and legitimate as to allow for growth by transforming the latter into a steady state system. Yet, while references to steady state growth are scattered throughout all of the writings discussed here, the concept is nowhere developed in a formal way. One of the reasons certainly is that it was not considered a particularly revealing extension. We will nevertheless use an optimal *steady state* growth path as our scheme of reference. It provides the most useful organizational principle for a comparative study of the different approaches, without violating the concepts and intentions actually found.[7]

Furthermore, contemporary writers perceived equilibrium theory as very well capable to explain irregularities in economic growth – as long as the latter could be attributed to exogenous disturbances of the data set. Changes in relative prices and quantities, or their growth rates, could then be accounted for by employing the 'variation method', that is, by modelling the adjustment process to a new equilibrium configuration induced by the change in the initial configuration of the system's fundamentals. The equilibrating process could be time consuming, but in the end the new equilibrium would exhibit the old optimality properties, as well as those of stability and uniqueness. However, it was understood that the economy *during* the adjustment process was in a state of *dis*equilibrium. This capability of mainstream economic theory to explain the mitigation of exogenous shocks by tracing the adjustment process is 'general' in that it was conceived as a characteristic feature of contemporary theory by all the authors discussed in this section.

The empirical observation of a regular business cycle poses a severe problem against this set-up. It requires the explanation of two phenomena for which contemporary theory was inadequately prepared: the *recurrent* pattern of the observed fluctuations in economic activity in general, and the existence of periods of falling output, increasing unemployment, and falling prices as movements *away* from the equilibrium position in particular. The main trouble with the empirical pattern created by oscillatory movements was that the existing toolbox – the variation method – could not account for it.[8] We have already mentioned the four choices then available. However, it seems appropriate to localize the starting point of that remarkable discussion before taking a closer look at the proposed solutions.

The problem
Even a casual glance into Hayek's little book (1933) reveals the somewhat puzzling appearance of Adolph Löwe. Only von Mises and Wicksell are quoted more often, for good reasons of course. Löwe, however, is not part of the constructive argument. He populates the footnotes and even a thorough reading never entirely clarifies what provoked the many references. In the aftermath, we have learned that Löwe played a role analogous to that of the child identifying the naked emperor: a contribution of his had triggered the subsequent debate.[9]

The nature of the provocation is revealed in a paper with the indicative title 'How is Business Cycle Theory Possible at All?' (Löwe, 1926). After the loss of analytical rigour during the period dominated by the inductive mania of the Historical School, and after a short but fruitless exchange along the confused lines of real *versus* nominal business cycle theories (Burchardt, 1928), someone finally asked the simple yet fundamental question: given that a regular cycle was an accurate empirical observation – was static equilibrium theory capable *in principle* to explain it?

Löwe flatly denied it. The analytical assumptions in his paper – the definition of the business cycle, the concept of equilibrium, the use of stationary and steady state, the variation method – are as we have just sketched them. But his task was not to develop yet another explanation of the cycle. Rather, it was to check whether this analytical apparatus could be employed to reconcile what was considered an empirical truth with the premises of deductive reasoning, as shared within the profession. 'Economics, contrary to mathematics, is an empirical science. It therefore has to take into account contradictions between its results and reality' is Löwe's starting point.[10] The connection between axiomatic theory and empirical observation is established very cautiously:

> There is no need for the additional effort of a special theory of the business cycle arising out of *systematic* reasons, since the variation method is capable of explaining all the problems of a circular flow following from the system's interaction. And business cycle theory has indeed not emerged out of systemic considerations. It owes its existence to the fact that since more than a century real market movements exhibit peculiarities which can not be explained by the variation method. The results of this method can not be *verified* against reality.' (Löwe, 1926, p. 173)

Such an approach, however, involves a serious problem and requires integrity, for it addresses the subject from the outset with the attitude that, if whatever is perceived a basic fact of economic life cannot be answered within a theoretical framework, little patience should be wasted in defending that framework. It risks the conclusion that an entire, well established theoretical edifice has to be abandoned.

Given the empirical observation of the business cycle, Löwe's argument is straightforward. The contemporary notion of equilibrium could be translated into an optimal and, with some abstraction, a steady growth path. Such a system may exhibit temporary difficulties following exogenous shocks in the real world, but it is permissible, for all analytical purposes, to abstract from these arbitrary disturbances. No explanation for a regular cycle is left – and none is required. Alternatively, an explanation has to be given why a general equilibrium system should endogenously create cyclical fluctuations.[11] This, then, was the logical dilemma:

> The solution of the problem must be capable of being integrated into the static system. A theory of the business cycle which has a logical structure linking it to a different type of system may well be in accordance with the facts. But as a supplement to the method of variation and as the completion of the theoretical system underlying this method it is worthless. The 'general glut' will drive not only the economy but also economic theory into a crisis, should constructing a business cycle theory in accordance with this generic system fail. (Löwe, 1926, p. 175)

Hayek's strong reaction can be explained as an attempt to show that equilibrium theory could deliver against this challenge.

A case study

In principle, there are the four ways of handling the problem identified above. We shall use them to structure the following discussion.[12]

(a) First, the methodological difficulty of a correct explanation of the business cycle may indeed force the theorist to abandon economic theory in the Walrasian tradition. This, of course, was the consequence drawn by economists in the Marxist tradition, but also a prominent feature of those willing to give up 'abstract' theorizing altogether (such as several members of the Historical School). Löwe (1926, 1926a) represents a theoretical variant of this solution.

(b) Second, the question of path dependence may be raised. Given the agreement that observed cycles are of a systematic nature and hence subject to deductive explanation, one can extend the equilibrium approach by explaining why changes in the fundamentals themselves (the system's data) should exhibit a regular pattern. In our context, this is a very different enterprise from Jevons's original formulation of 'sunspots', or agricultural cycles, since the recurrent shifts in data commonly taken as parametric in equilibrium theory, now have to be explained as the endogenous results of regular economic interaction. Modelling the feedbacks from the stationary state which cause the parameters of the 'static' system to change was the road taken by Schumpeter (1926).

(c) Third, the 'old dogma' may be defended. If an attempt at deriving endogenous fluctuations can be reconciled with the theory determining the stationary (or steady) state, the independent determination of the equilibrium attractor (the optimal growth path) can be maintained without sacrificing the study of systematic fluctuations. Note, that this desire for an endogenous explanation in the older theories did *not* evolve around the idea of defining a propagation mechanism capable of turning arbitrary shocks into regular fluctuations. There should, of course, be no contradiction, but in principle the analysis of the attractor was to be dichotomized from that of short-run fluctuations, such that the attractor can be taken as given when analysing the latter. This is the line taken by most of the mainstream literature, including Hayek (1933).

(d) Finally, if the development of the economic system over time is conceived as an idealized optimal growth path subject to exogenous and random disturbances, a theory of the business cycle may not even be necessary. Although affected by these changes, the growth path can in principle be determined independently; the equilibrium toolbox will suffice since only exogenous shocks to the system's fundamentals and their propagation need investigation. Obviously, this solution requires denial of the 'metaphysics' of regular and systematic oscillations in the sense defined above – or it has to include the possibility of a propagation mechanism capable of translating arbitrary impulses into regular fluctuations, thus resembling the approach chosen by modern real business cycle theory. In our example, the argument is advanced by Friedrich Lutz (1932).

Claims that Hayek's theory is related to new classical analysis often rest on the implicit assumption that both have successfully applied the third hypothesis (e.g. Laidler, 1986). But the fourth hypothesis, in so far as it allows for the seemingly absurd case of inventing propagation mechanisms (and reasons for persistence) capable of turning all arbitrary initial disturbances into regular fluctuations is not at all irrelevant from a modern perspective either, as an overview of today's literature will easily confirm. It very much resembles the approach chosen by modern real business cycle authors. It ought to be noted that Lutz did not extend the argument to define such a 'modern' propagation mechanism, nor did he claim that such an extension would have made much economic sense.

We will emphasize the contrast between path dependent behaviour (b) and the alleged independence of a long run trend from short-run fluctuations (c) in what follows. These topics demonstrate how far an endogenous explanation of the business cycle can be derived. They therefore mark the extent to which the framework of perceived economic wisdom was sustainable.

Abandoning the equilibrium approach: Adolph Löwe   Löwe's constructive argument is a joint product of Luxemburg's theory of imperialism and the Marxian characterization of technological change as inevitably leading to an increase in the capital/ labour ratio (the 'organic composition' of capital), and causing periodic recessions due to the impossibility of maintaining the expected rate of profits. The problem of finding markets to realize the surplus product, Löwe thought, could be solved by the spatial extension of the capitalist system.

It is less the theoretical content of this approach that is of interest here than two of its implications. 'Static' Walrasian equilibrium theory was perceived as contingent on two propositions, both violated as soon as capital accumulation was made an issue to account properly for the dynamic process. It was supposed to represent an interdependent and a closed system. Identifying technological change as the *raison d'être* for the periodic emergence of crises in the process of circulation transferred the cause of cyclical fluctuations into the sphere of what, for general equilibrium theory, is taken as parametric. Any systematic interruption of the stationary circular flow violates the requirement of interdependence. And the alleged solution to the problem of systematic overproduction was the conquest of new markets – the spatial extension of capitalism, necessitated by economic forces. Thus, as Löwe argued, this solution also violates the second tenet of Walrasian equilibrium: the static system could not be regarded as 'closed'.

For Löwe, reviewing the literature seemed to suggest that the 'problem of the business cycle' had been tackled successfully only where someone had questioned what standard theory took as its data. The parameters were in fact variables certain to change for systematic reasons. 'It basically is a misunderstanding to ask the static system for a complete discussion of the process of circulation' writes Löwe and continues to denounce the 'typical sense of a "disturbance" of the basic equilibrium configuration' as a valid explanation of structural change initiated by economic growth. From this perspective, neoclassical equilibrium theory was wrong because it treated as parametric factors which could not legitimately be taken as given when investigating the laws of motion of a decentralized free market system. Capital accumulation renders economic development path dependent. Consequently, economic theory can not be subdivided into growth and business cycle theories.

The constructive part of Löwe's argument, as opposed to the criticism of general equilibrium theory, can easily be dismissed as blurred by misty logic, dubious terminology and Marxist mistakes. Today we know that the vision of a theory of accumulation and structural change along classical lines has never been realized. In Löwe's own judgement, however, the development of such a dynamic system was already under way. His contribution was designed to 'knock off the inorganic rests of the old system' which still clung to theories such as Schumpeter's.[13] Löwe's proposed solution resembles the first point mentioned above: accepting the systematic nature of the observed phenomenon and the challenge of finding an endogenous explanation, but finding it impossible to provide for such an explanation within the narrow boundaries of the Walrasian framework. The consequence was obvious.

Endogenous data changes: Alois Schumpeter   Schumpeter published the first version of his *Theory of Economic Development* long before Löwe's article appeared (1911). Especially after the profoundly revised second edition he tried to promote the essentials towards an international audience and we owe it to these attempts that summaries of his theory became available in English, just at the time when the German debate took off.[14]

Like Löwe, Schumpeter localized technological change as the driving force behind capitalist development; unlike Löwe, however, he saw no reason to abandon general equilibrium theory. On the contrary, 'static' theory only had to be supplemented with the necessary ingredients to delineate correctly the cyclical character of the growing economy. The stated goal was to bring home the idea of the 'cycle as the form development takes under capitalism', but without giving up the inherited doctrine at least as a useful point of reference. Thus, we find a dichotomy in Schumpeter's writings, with 'static' theory on the one hand and 'dynamic' theory on the other. Dynamic theory addresses shifts of the attractor; static theory addresses the adjustment processes towards the new equilibrium configuration once this shift has taken place. Furthermore, while the cycle ultimately is caused by discontinuous changes in the data determining the gravitational centre, these shifts themselves appear to be endogenous in that they represent the inevitable results of regular economic interaction; they are 'springing from the economy itself'. Consequently, dynamic theory was also supposed to depict the necessary feedback and possible spillover effects creating the periodic vacillations inducing the 'center of gravitation' to shift. The resulting theory of development was perceived as complementary to Walrasian wisdom. Both addressed different issues.[15]

The regular economic interaction depicted in the circular flow is interrupted by the introduction of 'new combinations'. Taking his famous entrepreneurs as vehicles,[16] Schumpeter describes a process with three characteristics: first, the stationary state or circular flow, characterized by the famous hypothesis of absent time preference (zero interest) or, more justifiable, the absence of windfall profits, is interrupted by technological change as soon as it has reestablished itself. Second, diffusion will tend to cluster since innovations in one sector spread throughout the economy, ultimately affecting even remote corners, so that technological change is diffused in a wave-like fashion to which the system as a whole needs to adapt. Third, the possibility of credit creation is the *conditio sine qua non* for this process: starting from the full employment equilibrium of the stationary state (and 'static' theory), the role of credit enables entrepreneurs *via* the modern banking system to free resources by bidding them away from the existing allocation.

The cyclical upswing is created by the introduction of new techniques, organizational improvements or, not quite the regular case, by the invention of new products. The necessary resources are made available through an increase in the volume of outstanding loans, and the process of wrestling them away from their former use explains the procyclical behaviour of important nominal as well as relative prices (most notably, real wages and the interest rate). Innovative 'leaders' are rewarded by productivity increases (and higher product prices) in the first place. Others have to follow suit if they want to avoid punishment by the competitive mechanism. A 'secondary wave' of adaptation to the new standards sweeps through the economy, ushering in a slow-down with latecomers going out of business, a decline in profit margins for the group of pioneers brought about by the elimination of windfall profits, with the total volume of credit shrinking and interest rates, prices and wages if not falling, then adjusting to (zero) growth rates, and resettling to uniform levels (in the zero interest case, as well as in the steady state translation, productivity gains presumably are retained in the new real wage structure).

The average length of this cycle was predicted at four to six years which seemed to fit the facts quite well. However, it was only part of the grand scheme of evolution: Schumpeter never pretended to have developed a general analysis in the lunatic sense of having *one* theory fitting all the different stages of economic development. The short-run cycle was conceived to be a phenomenon typically associated with the early stages of capitalism, namely the stage of competitive (as opposed to 'trustified') capitalism. Expanding trustification, with research more and more delegated to research departments within large corporations, would not only dampen the amplitude of the typical cycle but also lengthen its period. The activities of entrepreneurs would lose importance since the race among 'leaders' would now find expression mainly as personal rivalries within the structure of corporate governance, thus mitigating the violent character of cyclical fluctuations under highly competitive conditions.

The analysis had two consequences which are important in that they relate to Hayek's reasoning – one fully worked out, the other of a more hidden nature. The first concerns the role of 'prior savings'. At the time generally held as the prerequisite to gain the financial strength necessary for an economic upswing, the concept helps to explain why, in the midst of the great depression for example, many contemporary economists would still argue that a 'recession' always has to bottom out first, before recovery is conceivable. Not the least among them was Hayek, famous for his untimely advice on the need to increase savings at the expense of aggregate consumption as the prerequisite for any future increase in activity levels. Not so the young Schumpeter: he had pointed out as early as 1911 that credit creation could be 'productive', i.e. that it could foster accumulation by creating additional productive capacity. Schumpeter and the neglected Nicholas Johannsen were perhaps the first economists to argue that case by denoting precisely the preconditions under which credit creation becomes 'the parent, not the twin' (Keynes) of a sustainable increase in aggregate investment: underutilized capacity (and labour) on the one hand, technological change with productivity improvements on the other. Hayek never wasted much thought on this possibility.

The second feature is the exact nature and timing of technological change and its connection to increasing returns to scale. For Schumpeter, new technologies, inducing cyclical fluctuations, are implemented relatively quickly so that the productivity gains become available within the period confined by the boom. However, he never managed to bring into the open the implicit link which exists between economies of scale and his theory of economic development.[17] What Adam Smith had accomplished so elegantly for growth theory, Schumpeter failed to achieve for his explanation of the business cycle: to depict also external increasing returns, resulting from organizational and technical improvements, as the prime reason why the new equilibrium configuration should be associated with higher productivity levels. Hayek, on the other hand, tried to avoid the issue; confronted with the potential output increase resulting from a successful 'saving-traverse' after implementing a more 'roundabout' production structure *before* the boom was cut short, he limited his upswing to a period shorter than the gestation period for new capital goods. Doing so maintained the feature of decreasing marginal productivity of aggregate net investment. But doing otherwise would also have led him to admit a causal role of credit creation in the process of economic growth, similar to Schumpeter's reasoning; and it would, in the present context far more important, have led to the consideration of systematic changes in the gravitational centre itself – which now would be an equilibrium configuration associated with relatively higher activity and productivity levels than before.

In terms of our questionnaire, Schumpeter represents the prototype of the second case. Accepting the premise of regular and recurrent fluctuations required a deductive explanation; and the acceptance of Walrasian wisdom meant finding reasons for systematic change in the system's fundamentals. Although his endogenous mechanism is directed at changing what generally is taken as parametric, Schumpeter was not interested in exogenous shocks. The apparent contradiction (is there really one?) is the result of trying to combine what is so difficult to reconcile: general equilibrium theory and an explanation of economic growth tied to the institutional characteristics of contemporary capitalism. Such an endeavour will formulate a path-dependent system. Consequently, the independence of short run fluctuations from long run development was indeed considered a useless myth, and Schumpeter's economy is best depicted as developing in discrete 'jumps', without the comfort of an *a priori* trend line, which can unify these movements over time by serving as the path of reference (see Figure 9.1(b)):

> We could, of course, even fit trend lines through the facts succeeding one another historically; but they would merely be expressions of whatever has happened, not of distinct forces or mechanics; they would be statistical, not theoretical; they would have to be interpreted in terms of particular historic events ... and not in terms of the working of an economic mechanism *sui generis*. (Schumpeter, 1928, p. 374)

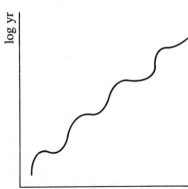

(a) Löwe (1926): Growth cycles
without the possibility of separating
long-run trend and short-run cycle.

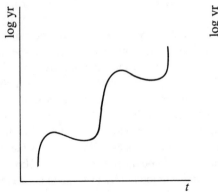

(b) Schumpeter (1926): Economic
development with cyclical
movements of the attractor.

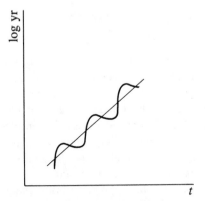

(c) Hayek (1933): Equilibrium
growth path with regular
cyclical fluctuations about
trend.

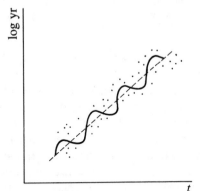

(d) Equilibrium business cycle
theory: regular fluctuations
created by imposing an
appropriate propagation
mechanism (defying the law
of large numbers for any
isolated period).

Figure 9.1   Long-run growth and short-run fluctuations

Endogenizing a propagation mechanism: Friedrich von Hayek   This brings us to the second attempt to integrate equilibrium and business cycle theory under the same roof. The theory advanced by Hayek was explicitly designed to identify a propagation mechanism responsible for movements first *away* and then back to an existing equilibrium configuration. The optimal growth path denotes the reference position by serving as the attractor around which the system oscillates – with an initial divergence triggering a process of systematic, perpetual overshooting. Similarly to Schumpeter, Hayek's problem was *not* an uneven growth path caused by random, exogenous disturbances; differently from Schumpeter, he was concerned with adjustment processes during which a stable attractor could be taken for granted.[18] Hayek thus addressed exactly the dilemma earlier pointed out by Löwe. But he made clear that any attempt to withdraw from the established mode of reasoning had to be considered premature.

The 'obvious and only' way out of Löwe's impasse seemed to integrate money into intertemporal equilibrium analysis.[19] Introducing the 'monetary factor' allows for an analytical

> ... starting point which fulfils the essential conditions for any satisfactory theory of the Trade Cycle. It shows, in a purely deductive way, the possibility and the necessity of movements which *do not* at any given moment tend towards a situation which, in the absence of changes in the economic 'data', could continue indefinitely. It shows that ... these movements lead to such a 'disproportionality' between certain parts of the system that the given situation cannot continue. (Hayek, 1933, p. 45)

What was called for amounts to localizing generic reasons for coordination failures without violating the system's global stability requirements. An elastic supply of 'credit money' provides the vehicle for doing so, and the assumed characteristics of the structure of production guarantee that the process constitutes itself (1933, p. 17). 'Money' is best understood as inside money in a system of fixed exchange rates. The 'disproportionalities' referred to are mismatches between the aggregate structure of production, i.e. the ratio of capital to consumption goods, and the rate of consumer's time preference. The interest rate acts as the mechanism supposed to bring about this synchronization. The underlying theory of capital, of course, is derived from Böhm-Bawerk, and the integration of the monetary factor closely resembles the route taken by Wicksell.

The easiest way to approach Hayek's trade cycle theory is to start out from his reference path, the notion of an optimal growth path which we will conceive as a steady state.[20] Into this *reference scheme*, money is introduced as a means of payment similar to Abba Lerner's 'peanuts': as a numeraire which fulfils the additional requirement that it has to be used to carry out all transactions, including real savings. Per capita output is a positive function of the existing capital stock, with the vertically integrated stock of productive capacity mimicking societies' preferences in a very convenient way: more 'roundabout' processes of production (a higher capital/labour ratio) imply lower unit costs of final (or consumption) goods. Hence, increases in capital intensity today will be translated into increased per capita consumption tomorrow and *vice versa*. That is to say that total labour productivity in the future can be increased with the increased quantity of capital goods employed 'tomorrow', i.e. *after* investment today has been sped up at the expense of consumption. However, productivity increases will not come into effect immediately – only after the new capital goods have been successfully implemented. This simple device guarantees avoiding some of the complications arising from increasing returns, since the investment ultimately leading to the more roundabout processes by extending productive capacity remains associated with decreasing marginal productivity the moment it is undertaken.[21]

The question then becomes where to penetrate the model to introduce the desired 'disturbing factor' without violating its 'axiomatic structure'. Hayek's claim was to have accomplished this task by taking proper account of money. But it really is the price for money, the 'market' rate of interest, which ought to be singled out. It drives the propagation mechanism by providing a signal which is subject to feedback effects. The market rate can therefore be singled out as performing a function different from that of other prices.

In equilibrium, the unique *natural* rate of interest, in Wicksell's tradition a real rate reflecting the intersection of aggregate saving and investment schedules, is equal to the marginal product of producing additions to the capital stock. Intertemporal saving and consumption decisions, in turn, are contingent on the interest rate, just as investment is; the natural rate therefore is determined solely by 'productivity and thrift'. Now a well-working system can be envisaged, translating the optimality properties of the static equilibrium into a dynamic setting with balanced growth. Suppose, for example, a sudden change in preferences, manifesting itself as an increase in voluntary savings, starting from a position of equilibrium. An increase in the supply of saving will cause the rate of interest to fall, leading to additional investment which, in turn, will generate the additional capital goods required to increase the future production of final (or consumption) goods. Intertemporal equilibrium will always be restored, following a change in data, with saving/consumption decisions synchronized over time.

By equipping his reference model with an Austrian theory of production in the first place, Hayek implicitly makes allowance for some characteristics of commodity production by means of commodities which distinguish his base model from, say, the Solow growth model utilized in modern business cycle theory: output may consist of capital or consumption goods, but capital goods can not be consumed immediately. Further, capital goods are specific to their use and cannot be transferred to other uses, or at least not without cost. The gestation period needed to transform investment into additional capital goods has already been mentioned. Into this system Hayek now introduces a banking system with fractual reserve requirements, i.e. the potential to create 'paper credit'.

These are the ingredients needed to generate systematic fluctuations. The new ability of the banks to create purchasing power combined with the possible distortion of the production structure arising from a 'wrong' price of the coordinating device – the rate of interest – will result in cyclical fluctuations *if* it is combined with upper and lower boundaries. Obviously, the process has initially to be set in motion by an appropriate impulse.[22] If the *market* rate of interest, i.e. the actual real rate charged by the banking system, deviates from the natural rate, processes of expansion or contraction will be triggered which are distinct from the smooth adjustment in the reference model. If, to compare it with the saving traverse, an increase in time preferences is not translated immediately into a fall of the market rate, a real contraction and the possibility of a 'credit crunch' will follow, without any violation of Walras's Law.

Should the market rate for some reason fall below the natural rate, an investment boom will be triggered since entrepreneurs now face the possibility of acquiring loanable funds (or 'purchasing power') at a rate below the relevant rate of return. Resources are bid away from the consumption goods sector; wages and, subsequently, the price of final goods increase. Given unchanged time preferences, these resources will be transferred to the capital good sector where quantity effects will result. The process of 'forced savings' due to the availability of fewer consumption goods than needed to cover the voluntary consumption/saving decisions of the public will continue as long as additional credit funds are made available at a rate below the marginal productivity of investment. In the first example, the process would be reversed by banks forced by competition to lower the market rate in order to stop the shortening of their balance sheets; in the second, they would be forced to raise it as soon as they run up against the reserve requirements limiting the credit multiplier.

However, no built-in mechanism provides any guarantee for the banks to hit the natural rate after such an adjustment, other than by pure accident. Since the process continues with any deviation between market and natural rate and since the natural rate is assumed to be unobservable for the functionally divided groups populating the economy,[23] overshooting seems likely; but Hayek perceived even a gradual process of interest rate adjustment as unlikely to occur.

Three features of this mechanism deserve to be pointed out before entering a discussion. Connected to the sustainability of the boom is the afore mentioned problem which Hayek glosses aside but which has the potential of changing some of his policy conclusions: if the period of expansion lasts long enough for the investment goods to be actually implemented and to increase productive capacity, the upswing may enhance labour productivity at the margin. The problem, as we have seen, originated in attempts to avoid Schumpeterian shifts in the equilibrium attractor (and the conclusions with respect to the connection between credit creation and economic growth they would have led to). But Hayek also did not intend to discuss changes in the attractor and attempted to keep the gravitational centre stable, and his optimal growth path intact. Nevertheless, according to the implied structure, the roundaboutness of production will have been increased as soon as the gestation period is over and, by definition, more final goods will be forthcoming at the same rates of labour input as before. However, Hayek did not discuss the matter any further.[24]

Second, his insistence that the difference between 'peanuts' and pieces of paper denoting an obligation to pay later – the capability of 'manufacturing' credit – drives the system (rather than incomplete information on the part of the functionally separated groups he identifies) goes hand in hand with a focus on endogenous variations in the quantity of money which is substantially different from the price level effects due to variations in outside money encountered in Lucas et al.[25]

However, the major role in making this mechanism possible is played by incomplete information on part of the agents populating the model. Their behaviour is restricted since they do not know, and cannot discover, the equilibrium interest rate. The third point therefore concerns the peculiar role of a signalling problem in this analysis. What we have are functionally differentiated groups who react to a signal (the observable or market rate of interest) in predictable ways; by so doing, however, they change the signal. On a very basic level, it is a coordination game where the signal is constantly altered by means of the very behaviour it helps to determine. Given the persistence of a restricted information set, one price thus 'loosens up' the static version of equilibrium theory. The interest rate is a parameter, determining economic interaction, and an endogenous variable, subjected to constant feedbacks, at the same time. That 'signal chasing' is certainly different from the signal *extraction* problem of rational expectation models where agents may find out all dimensions (the 'truth') of the signal, contingent on how fast asymmetric information is removed, but always step in step with each other.

Granted the impulse, can the model generate *and sustain* recurrent fluctuations around the attractor? How successfully was it, measured with the yardstick of providing an answer to Löwe's quest? The answer comes in three steps: by contemporaries, by Hayek himself, and through the glasses of modern theory.

Denying the regular business cycle: Friedrich Lutz   The last word in this debate was left to Lutz (1932), one of the most splendid books on the history of business cycle theory ever written. To some extent it contains the final verdict on the positions we have attempted to sketch. Lutz traces the development of business cycle theory from the advent of the subject in classical analysis to the interwar period. In terms of demarcating the relevant economic theory, equilibrium theory in the tradition of Walras is once more the only game in town. Lutz's main conclusion is that a systematic theory of the business cycle within the equilibrium framework is not possible, and that it is not necessary either.

To substantiate this point, different approaches are evaluated with respect to how far they managed to accomplish what Löwe had asked for – to reconcile what was considered an empirical truth by the authors in question with the only axiomatic theory available. We shall limit the discussion to point out very briefly the implications for the solutions previously discussed.

First, Löwe's constructive argument was easily tackled. Technological change in the form needed to generate the law of the falling rate of profit could not be sustained on logical grounds. It had to be perceived as an exogenous change in data. Such a change in fundamentals, however, cannot destroy the 'interdependence' of equilibrium analysis. Moreover, it is a basic misunderstanding that the spatial extension of markets can violate the postulate that the theoretical system be 'closed'; analysis can always proceed under that postulate without being inhibited by any spatial extensions in reality. Löwe, therefore, had asked an important question, but not given a particular valuable answer.

Second, Schumpeter is criticized on two grounds: either he had to assume that technological change occurs exogenously – in which case, again, anything of interest is a change in data which can be analysed with the existing toolbox. Or his theory violates the rationality postulates of equilibrium analysis, as indicated by the disruptive nature of technical change (and its diffusion) which hints at irrationality on the part of the entrepreneurs: they would leave gains from trade unexploited if, for some presumably psychological reason, they are hesitant to implement 'new combinations' even though they already know about them.[26]

Third, a similar point can be made with respect to Hayek: the initial disturbance is not explained; and even if an exogenous impulse is taken for granted, it should be obvious that rational behaviour would lead to a dampened cycle, not to continuous oscillations around an otherwise stable attractor, since agents (banks!) would inevitably learn how to decipher the relevant signal. They have an interest to do so.

All of the theories Lutz investigated entertained one of the following hypotheses in order to generate regular and recurrent oscillations: either facts not explained in a sound manner (such as the peculiar nature of technological change, causing the rate of profits to fall, in Löwe); or exogenous changes in the system's fundamentals, in itself not explained (such as the impulse needed in Hayek's system); or frictions and changes in the standard behavioural assumptions (e.g. rationality in Schumpeter's reasoning). For Lutz, the debate had come full circle:

> They may all happen in practice but they don't need to happen from the standpoint of economic theory; and with that, an explanation of the business cycle ... does not contradict the premises of equilibrium theory any longer. (Lutz, 1932, p. 79)

Consequently, the observed economic fluctuations had to be investigated within the existing theoretical framework, by means of the equilibrium toolbox. Industrial fluctuations could result from multiple causes and had therefore to be investigated on the more modest basis of a day to day approach to economic history. To use the inherited toolbox was just fine, since a business cycle theory as a separate branch was not only impossible – there was no need for it either.[27] Methodologically speaking, the position of Lutz comes closest to the modern equilibrium approach – were it not for the latter's grandiose claim of having, once again, established a 'general' theory of cyclical fluctuations.

IV. Hayek's failure and its consequences
Much ink has been spilled in trying to explain what later caused Hayek to abandon 'hard' economic theory and to concentrate on questions relating to knowledge, learning and the dissemination of information. Sometimes the apparent failure of establishing a general theory of the business cycle has been mentioned in this respect. There is not much point in entering such discussions if the aim is to juxtapose Hayek's theory with its modern counterparts. It might be of interest, however, that Hayek himself had admitted his failure quite openly.

Admitting failure
In a very little known passage, published in the Journal of the (British) *Royal Statistical Society* the old argument is taken up once again; even though Hayek is just supposed to give a short comment on someone else's paper on measurement problems, he echoes a theme of the past.[28] It reads, as a matter

of fact, almost like an answer to Löwe or Lutz. It contains the concession that the attempted integration of general equilibrium and business cycle theory had failed – that Lutz *and* Löwe were right, both in the sense that there is no unique phenomenon which can be labelled 'the' trade cycle and because there is no way of constructing a general theory of the business cycle within the premises of the Walrasian tradition.

As a sideline, 'statisticians, or at any rate the statistically minded economists' are blamed for having 'sinned', that is for having been 'particularly dogmatic' in concentrating their efforts on tracking down the 'common characteristics' of economic fluctuations. This, of course, might have given the theorist the wrong idea of what to explain. But there is more to the argument than just putting the blame on the econometricians for having supplied the wrong observation:

> Perhaps these efforts would be better spent if, instead of a vain search after the common characteristics of all cycles, we tried to provide really careful historical accounts of the course of events preceding and following particular crises, and then investigated how far our theoretical knowledge enabled us to explain these events. The theoreticians would then have an opportunity to test their views about particulars of the theory of money or capital by applying them to these particular situations. ... [W]hether beyond this there is scope for a separate theory of *the* trade cycle must for the time being remain at least doubtful. (Hayek, 1938, p. 579)

For Hayek, it now appears 'doubtful' whether the 'various causes which influence industrial fluctuations always combine in such a regular manner as to produce a distinct and uniform phenomenon which can be accounted for by some single theory' (Hayek, 1938, p. 579). If trade cycles are not all alike, then they cannot – and, as Lutz had put it, they need not – be explained by a unified theoretical approach.[29] That, of course, was exactly what Hayek himself had tried to accomplish only a few years earlier. Yet, the dominant axiomatic theory might be maintained, despite the fact that it had proved incapable to offer a solution – because the problem has been talked away. It doesn't read like a particularly glorious victory:

> It seems to me by no means certain that even in this more general sense we are entitled to speak about *the* trade cycle. This suggests that all or most of the ups and downs of trade which we observe are manifestations of a single phenomenon, caused by a distinct set of circumstances, and therefore to be explained by some single theory. It must be admitted that probably the majority of economists, or at any rate a great many, believe in the existence of a trade cycle in this sense. Although I am not guiltless in this respect, I feel now more and more that there is reason for a good deal of skepticism. (Hayek, 1938, p. 578)

Has the problem been talked away to rescue a theoretical approach which could not handle it? Or was the observation of a regular business cycle wrong from the beginning and equilibrium theory had been playing Sisyphus all along, confronted with a senseless task? The return of the question four decades later seems to suggest the former; but the way it was approached, the ultimate reliance on exogenous shocks, lends support to the view that the application of the old set of axioms even with the help of a more sophisticated (technical) toolbox cannot lead out of the dead end in which theory had found itself once before. However that may be, even if there is no regular cycle, economic fluctuations and coordination failures are still observed; and the really interesting question becomes whether economics has made advances at least in the modest sense of dealing with these unpleasant occurrences. It is at this point that we can learn from attempts at developing a theory of 'the' business cycle now and then.

Recent criticism

Of the many points of criticism advanced against Hayek's trade cycle theory, two seem more relevant than others in order to enter a discussion of today's equilibrium business cycle theory. These are, first, the question whether Hayek succeeded in correctly delineating turning points; and second, the complaint that the concept of intertemporal equilibrium underlying Hayek's theory could and should not be used for investigations aimed at elucidating the role of money.[30] As indictments I believe both to be wrong, but the underlying misunderstandings are useful in that they already hint at some of the major differences between Hayek's theory and its modern counterpart.

That Hayek (or Wicksell) failed to explain turning points is hard to argue. The idea that a constant increase in the rate of credit creation cannot be maintained in the face of reserve requirements seems well founded; Hayek repeatedly refers to the gold standard and, at least as often, mentions cash reserves from which he distinguishes payments made by cheques. (A system with fixed exchange rates and inside money, quite in accordance with the historical Austrian situation, would have served the same purpose.)[31] Essentially, the idea that banks will counter a demand for credit threatening their reserve ratios by raising the market rate and that they will try to stay in the loan business by lowering it in the case of a credit crunch, seems to be sensible. As pointed out above, one might legitimately wonder whether and why the upper turning point should always be brought about before the system's performance has been increased (due to the increase in labour productivity associated with the implementation of the additional capacity) – but that is quite a different issue.

And the argument, indeed, seems not so much whether turning points can be defined once allowance for reserve requirements is made; rather, it questions the legitimacy of assuming the presence of reserve requirements. Is this assumption one of the 'ad hoceries' superimposed on an otherwise unconstrained equilibrium model which we have learned so well to reject as violating the 'first principles' of economic analysis? That question leads straight to the second query, whether it is permissible to integrate credit as a means of payment into an intertemporal equilibrium framework or, to take the issue a little further, whether it is legitimate at all that intertemporal equilibrium serves as a reference path for the disequilibria connected with economic fluctuations.

Modern variants of neoclassical descent, at least as far as equilibrium business cycle theory is concerned, do not incorporate monetary phenomena, or they limit its role to the transmission mechanism of arbitrary shocks, not explained in itself. In models of continuous equilibrium one may limit the information available, or allow for mistakes, or for sudden changes in beliefs ('sunspots'), etc. But the structure of the behavioural assumptions, under rational expectations, is such as to make it hard to introduce *systematic* reasons for coordination failures: agents' beliefs have to remain mutually compatible. The new concept of equilibrium is precise in that it excludes arbitrarily different behaviour of agents who share access to the same information set. But this accomplishment has a price – namely, that groups of agents now are separated solely by the information they have access to. The 'representative agent' did not become so fashionable out of the blue: to sustain the informational separation requires to exclude that agents are capable of eliminating the difference – a restrictive hypothesis and, in macroeconomic models, perhaps not a very practical starting point. The modern approach (and the reduced form of methodological 'individualism' it propagates) is different from Hayek's in that vein. On the one hand, it is more precise in that it allows for a 'sub-optimal' outcome only in the truly limited sense that it is not to be perceived as sub-optimal the moment it occurs – on the other hand, it presents the result of unavoidable mistakes, and not of systematic interaction of functionally divided agents. It does not clarify how socially unwarranted outcomes can emerge as the consequences of rational individual behaviour.

Hayek (1933), on the other hand, had taken great pains to state explicitly which modifications had to be introduced to generate 'false trading' in an equilibrium system, and how the introduction of new state variables (such as credit money) could perpetuate the malfunctioning of a system where everyone is rational but badly informed. For the modern reader the problem arises that Hayek's agents should be clever enough to find out about the consequences of their actions in order not to perpetuate second best outcomes. Although it is true that learning in that sense would eliminate the cycle, Hayek insisted on formulating a model with the *ad hoc* assumption of fixed but obviously less than complete information set.[32] He thus chose to model fluctuations as the result of almost mechanical interaction among groups. Why should he have done that?

The argument referred to states that, on methodological grounds, a theory of intertemporal equilibrium cannot provide the logical underpinning for a theory of the business cycle as long as it refers to a situation where all expectations are correct (and future prices fully anticipated), whereas the cycle is based on false trading. The alternative formulation for both, the full information and its ancient counterpart, the fixed expectation assumption is a stochastic equilibrium where price expectations cannot be systematically disappointed because they relate to random processes (Desai, 1982). The claim then becomes that the jump from Hayek's 'perfect foresight' economy to the persistently ill-adjusted credit economy is illegitimate. However, modern rationality requirements need not be taken as the sole purpose of Hayek's exercise. The trade cycle booklet does not presuppose perfect foresight. Rather, a thought experiment is performed of the sort we are not particularly used to any more: extending theory to integrate perceived characteristics of the real economy. That procedure moves from the real world to modify the model – not the other way round.

Hayek's theoretical starting point is a 'pure' equilibrium setting which differs from standard assumptions only in that it delineates outside money as a means of payment, also denoting savings, and allows for banks as intermediaries, thus reducing them to 'the role of brokers, trading in savings' (1933, p. 190). Money is qualitatively neutral; it is an unexplained medium, introduced *ad hoc* just as banks are, and playing the role of the '*n*th good' in Walras law. The purist may argue that this model as a point of reference for a subsequent discussion on the effects of 'paper credit' does not provide any justification for the existence of money (or peanuts) at all: the case can always be made that money has no place in general equilibrium analysis. This supposition leads either to the new classical attitude or to a somewhat nihilistic criticism. But perhaps it also would mean to jump to conclusions, since Hayek's conceptual experiment can be understood as being of a much more limited nature.

Let us suppose that all the construct should demonstrate was what Hayek and his contemporaries took for granted anyway, namely that under these conditions (plus competitive markets populated with rational and optimizing agents) the equilibrium price vector can *always* be established. The reference model thus becomes a conceptual device, hypothetical for it constructs the world without account for the proper function of banks. It establishes merely the conditions under which agents can produce the warranted outcome *with the sheer power of market forces as their sole coordinating device*. The 'power of the market' guarantees the translation of preferences into the appropriate allocation of resources, and shocks to fundamentals will only induce adjustment processes. Heavy irregularities following these exogenous influences are conceivable, no doubt, but not the regular fluctuations Hayek was after.

This scenario, allowing for the 'normal' market mechanism, keeps the interest rate in line with the requirements imposed by productivity and thrift. The second scenario, with an elastic supply of purchasing power due to the existence of credit, does not. The first scenario represents the stable attractor with changes contingent on changes in fundamentals; the second maladjustments caused by false trading, regular overshooting and, possibly but not here addressed, spillovers, in turn always capable of causing changes in the data. The rationale provided for the second scenario is the familiar one: 'The process of interest fixation, which is at the basis of pure theory, never in fact follows the same course in a modern credit economy; for in such an economy the supply of, and the demand for, credit never directly confront each other' (Hayek, 1933, p. 200). It is here where the limited availability of information has its origin: the hypothesis of 'fixed but limited' information availability actually is in place because it seems to be a central feature of the world the model is supposed to depict. So central that the model would be considered based on obviously wrong premises, were its simplistic structure abused as an excuse to remove this feature.

The prerequisite for the second scenario is that agents are less than fully informed; but it is not this prerequisite which distinguishes both scenarios. The difference is that in case two the correction mechanism of the reference scenario is put out of order. The importance of establishing turning points by assuming reserve requirements and competitive behaviour for the banking system lies in defining a corridor around the optimal growth path; this way the system could, as Hayek put it, be 'extended' and the inquiry could proceed by analysing a *sequence* of events (without bothering about the stability of the attractor). Today, this may be considered a crude device, but the set-up certainly differs from equilibrium business cycle models and their (more sophisticated?) assumptions of vibrating production functions or sudden changes in the money supply, in itself left unexplained.

Lessons for today?
From this simple observation follow some basic distinctions between equilibrium business cycle theories and Hayek's mechanical picture of coordination failures. Many we have already pointed out: employing the behavioural assumptions beyond the modern notion of continuous equilibrium means to lose the capability of depicting systematic feedback effects. That greatly limits the pool for endogenous explanations other than belief changes or structural impositions, almost excluding those based on the distinction between individual rationality and aggregate outcomes. If reasons for endog-

enous growth are grounded in the system's structure itself (cf. Romer, 1986) one presupposes the results of the inquiry; thus diminishing the potential for gaining insights into the unsteady process of growth we observe. Modelling stochastic processes by employing the rational expectation hypothesis, on the other hand, restricts the capacity of depicting systematic economic interaction by restricting the capability to subdivide economic agents by the economic functions they perform. It limits attempts to model the importance of economic signals.

Hayek's model, on the other hand, is too mechanical to take us very far. Any reasonable assumption about expectation formation (or learning) would lead to the disappearance of his cycle. Unsteady growth can be modelled in this vein only by superimposing assumptions about lags in structural adjustment which would be no less dubious than the structural additions just referred to. There seems to be a curious coincidence: equilibrium business cycle models are capable of delivering propagation mechanisms, but they lack economic reasons for them. Hayek emphasizes the economics behind the process, but lacks a consistent model of how the propagation mechansim prevails. By placing so much emphasis on the adjustment processes following random disturbances equilibrium business cycle theories have succeeded in modelling an important aspect of the actual process of economic growth with simplified but consistent behavioural assumptions. But at a great expense, too: since rational expectations is considered the consistency axiom of macroeconomics it has become increasingly more complicated to discuss reasons for failure without introducing silly restrictions. The set of acceptable hypotheses to explain ongoing events has *de*creased compared to the interwar period, and so, perhaps, has the 'relevance' of economics (Harberger, 1993).

When all is said and done, these general observations translate into specific characteristics of the two branches of modern equilibrium business cycle theory which distinguish it from what Hayek had proposed. He violently opposed exactly the kind of explanation modern *nominal* business cycle theory advanced. His theory was labelled 'monetary' not to characterize the impulse. Money is important only as inside money; to rely on exogenous variations of the quantity of money and the subsequent price level effects was out of the question. 'We are in no way concerned to explain the effect of the monetary factor on trade fluctuations through changes in the value of money and variations in the prices level' (1933, p. 103). Variations in the quantity of money are a consequence rather than a cause, and so are price level changes:

> Theories which explain the Trade Cycle in terms of fluctuations in the general price level must be rejected ... because their fundamental hypothesis is, from a theoretical standpoint, every bit as naive as that of those theories which entirely neglect the influence of money. (Hayek, 1933, p. 106)

The reason is threefold: the insistence on localizing signals which correctly can be emphasized as representing the system's most important coordination devices (the interest rate); the belief that movements in the general price should, in principle, be considered as neutral[33]; and the related aversion against 'unsystematic' explanations, i.e. unexplained exogenous events which therefore were considered incapable of accounting for the periodicity of the observed fluctuations. These differences are not confined to a discussion of new classical *vs* interwar business cycle theory. Owing ultimately to the fact that equilibrium business cycle theory needs to rely on exogenous shocks to generate movements of the equilibrium position, a similar problem has been observed with respect to another, old-fashioned, approach:

> Output and employment fluctuations such as we observe in the real world are, according to New Classical Economics, voluntary responses to misperceived price signals. They occur because prices change. Keynesian economics (including its monetarist variant) explains quantity changes as occurring because prices do not change fast enough to keep markets cleared. In this vital matter the contrast between the two approaches could not be more stark. (Laidler, 1986, p. 31)

The reason, obviously, is the change in the equilibrium concept pointed out above. Whereas new classical theory relies hardly on anything else, 'mistakes' in general are not among the devices considered capable of creating the type of endogenous explanation Hayek wanted to mimic. The argument translates into the importance attached to depicting forecast errors as the source for cyclical fluctuations. As long as no explanation is given why they should be mistaken in a systematic fashion, forecast errors cannot fill the gap, as Hayek made clear unmistakenly.[34]

Finally, the argument applies to *real* business cycle theory (in the tradition of Kydland and Prescott, 1982, 1991) just as it does to nominal business cycle theory. It might, of course, be possible that the cycle is triggered by a real impulse, such as technological change. But that would only superimpose it upon Hayek's *causa causans*. A 'systematic' explanation of the cycle, it seems fair to conclude, which basically relies on the unit root properties of a dominant technology would have been just as inconceivable as sudden shifts in the quantity of outside money. 'In other words, *any* non-monetary Trade Cycle theory must superimpose its system of explanation on that of the monetarily determined fluctuations; it cannot start simply from the static system as presented by pure equilibrium theory.' (Hayek, 1933, p. 186, italics added).

The list could be continued but it should be obvious by now that the new and the old theories of the business cycle discussed here hardly have more in common than Löwe's (and Lucas's) starting point. But this is not all we can say.

V. Conclusion

For the underlying problem really is whether this change in the notion of equilibrium can help us in discerning the extent to which general equilibrium theory is useful in describing an economic system which seems to work reasonably well most of the time but fails to perform some of the time. Periodic poor performance has, within the equilibrium approach, been explained quite differently. Hayek stands as an example of using this approach to define coordination failures and their origin by comparing the 'pure' state of affairs with his more worldly picture of an economy where money, production over time, and information are important. True, the system has initially to be disturbed from the outside for any endogenous process to be set in motion. Granted also, if agents in his model are capable of learning at all, it will not generate a persistent cycle: endogenous fluctuations will be limited due to rational individuals acquiring more of the knowledge which, in principle, is available to them; and they have incentives to do so. However, as we have tried to show, the assumption about restricting the available information can be understood as being rooted in conceiving reality as limited in precisely this respect. That is to say, *it can be re-phrased as an attempt to take note of the fact that all human rationality is bounded.*

Rational expectations models are, in many respects, different. They too rely on outside shocks and again, reasons for persistence have to be invented. The price for being complacent about these limitations is something vaguely familiar from the post-Keynesian debates. It is the foregone opportunity to design simple mechanical systems to find sources of ill-coordinated behaviour at least remotely related to the world we live in. Agents in new classical models would, by definition, never fall for the traps set up in the interwar tradition. In addition, the prerequisite that expectations have to be mutually consistent seems to exclude the possibility of modelling feedback effects in an economy which has not been twisted by introducing indivisibilities, non-convexities, or the like. Rational expectation models, as long as this prerequisite is fulfilled, have even trouble in defining heterogeneous agents by the economic function they perform: bounded rationality can be introduced in the guise of asymmetric information – but any process resulting from here describes the discovery of truth in however many dimensions, not the trial and error processes we actually observe. The modern alternative of using multiple equilibria which can be Pareto ranked to model coordination failures seems, for the moment, also to require imposing restrictions on the underlying generality of the Arrow–Debreu world – as opposed to Hayek's attempts to 'widen' it.

In this chapter, we have confined ourselves to the discussion of economic fluctuations in the context of general equilibrium theory. We have not mentioned alternative approaches, new or old. We also refrained from discussing models subsequent to equilibrium business cycle theory, such as attempts to model coordination failures by depicting them as multiple equilibria. In that sense, any conclusion is limited.

What, then, can be said about equilibrium business cycle theory – does macroeconomics behave like the famous hunted hare, coming back to the same issues all over again if only the public waits long enough? How does the picture of the spiral staircase hold up, according to which it comes back, but on a higher technical level? Higher technical level certainly is true, and the same issue is partially correct – but with regard to the questions asked and the roads travelled in search of an answer, the picture does not hold up too well. The reason, however, seems less connected to economic history repeating itself. Rather, it appears that our basic framework is amazingly ill-suited to explain some fairly straightforward observations arising out of the fact that the process of economic growth is almost always unbalanced. In that respect, economic theory seems not to have made much progress at all.

Notes

1. Strictly speaking the trend *need* not become an economically meaningless notion in the second case. With a unique amplitude (due, for example, to a unique cause) it would be predetermined since floor and ceiling would be known. Not even in the textbook case can it be independently determined, however, if feedback effects result in data changes (changes in parameters or 'fundamentals') which are unknown *ex-ante*: an attractor can only be defined for a given set of data.

2. Critics may add that both approaches also share ultimate failure as far as the provision of a *systematic* explanation of recurrent fluctuations based on respective variants of equilibrium theory is concerned.

3. Cf. Rühl (1994a) for a detailed analysis of this change in method.

4. Restricting the comparison to one particular episode in the development of business cycle theory raises the question of opportunity costs. In what follows, the US development (from Clark to Mitchell to the Cowles commission), the pre- and post-Keynesian debates originating in the UK (from Harrod to Hicks to the multiplier/accelerator models of the 1950s and 1960s) and, perhaps most significantly, the Stockholm school and its successors are left out of consideration. Out of the second grew the mainstream approach targeted by new classical theory. It really is the third which resembles most closely the issues discussed above. Yet, all of these debates are better known; reference to any of them would not change the argument advanced here.

5. The above definition differs – for obvious reasons – from its often quoted modern counterpart (Lucas, 1987) in that it does not include the extension 'about trend', and also in that we do not *a priori* exclude that cycles may be explained by changes in the availability of factors of production.

6. Juglar (1889), often celebrated as the 'father' of business cycle theory as an independent branch of economics, is a good example – concentrating on the general price indices at his disposal (mainly bank's balance sheets) and focusing his analysis on the aspect of economic crises. In general, we follow Cassel (1921) who dates the 'slowly emerging ... uniform typos of cyclical fluctuations' (understood as price *and* quantity movements) as a generally accepted phenomenon to the 1870s.

7. For example, it guarantees to some degree comparability between Schumpeter's rather peculiar definition of the stationary state and Hayek's construct of an intertemporal equilibrium, without imposing on the 'regression line' of either author's thought (see also Samuelson, 1982).

8.   'By the early thirties, business cycle theories had come to realize that use of the equilibrium toolbox could be strictly justified only for stationary and perfect foresight processes. This pretty much excluded business cycles – and there was no other toolbox. Keynes' new method successfully evaded this dilemma. Lucas' new method attempts to solve it' (Leijonhufvud, 1983). See also Kohn (1986).

9.   When the German version of Hayek's book appeared (1929), Löwe was a well-established figure, presiding over the Kiel Institute for World Affairs. He had presented his paper in Vienna. Cf. Hagemann's contribution to this volume (Chapter 6).

10.   This statement would, it is fair to assume, have been signed by all participants in the subsequent debate.

11.   In fact, he formulated a bit more sharply: 'Either the subject of a business cycle problem is beyond the scope of economic theory and belongs to the large number of events which, like an earthquake or war, may have the most profound economic consequences but for theory can present only a *datum* and never a *task* ... [or] the solution of the problem is possible *in principle* but only *in contradiction* to the logical requirements of the present [theoretical] system; in our case that would mean that business cycle theory is possible at all only if we adopt a logic different from the logic of the theoretical system currently employed.' (Löwe, 1926, p. 170)

12.   It is necessary to curtail the extent to which this debate proliferated to focus on Hayek's contribution. Cf. Rühl (1994b) for a more detailed account.

13.   Quoted are also Lederer and, of course, Franz Oppenheimer (1924) who strongly influenced Löwe's reasoning. In an earlier article Löwe (1925) had accused Schumpeter's theory of failing to account for the 'periodicity' of the business cycle. Schumpeter (1926) could legitimately brush aside this claim by employing an argument in accordance with the definition of the cycle used in this paper: if 'periodicity' is taken to mean the determination of turning points, then he had delivered; if it was supposed to refer to a unique length or amplitude (of boom and recession) then neither Schumpeter nor most of the other writers in the interwar period meant to account for that. What Löwe denoted was a growth cycle as depicted in Figure 9.1(a): with fluctuations integral to economic growth, the idea of an independent growth path (idealized as a steady state) cannot be superimposed.

14.   The first edition (1911), together with some early articles (e.g. his celebrated paper on the quantity theory 1917/18), provide a far more concise version of Schumpeter's business cycle theory than the second edition (1926). As for his English language publications, the articles of the interwar period (e.g. 1927, 1928) seem, again, more to the point than the later two-volume tract.

15.   'A theory of changes in the course of the circular flow, of the transition of the economy from a given center of gravitation to a new one (i.e. dynamics) as opposed to the theory of the circular flow itself, of continuous adaptation to different centers of gravitation and, *ipso facto*, of the consequences of these changes (i.e. statics)' (Schumpeter, 1926, p. 99).

16.   And not much more: Large parts of the second edition of the *Theory of Economic Development* are devoted to (and suffer from) Schumpeter's desire to come clean against the accusation of being too apologetic towards the "slave-trading and brandy producing puritans at the historic threshold of the subject" (Schumpeter 1928, p. 379).

17.   Schumpeter (1928) is an example of trying to connect himself to the debate on 'empty economic boxes' which had filled the pages of the *Economic Journal* shortly before.

18.   'The real problem presented to economic theory is: Why does not this adjustment come about smoothly and continuously, just as a new equilibrium is formed after every change in the data? Why is there this temporary possibility of developments leading away from equilibrium and finally, without any changes in the data, necessitating [a turning point]? ... Why do the forces tending to restore equilibrium become temporarily ineffective and why do they only come into action again when it is too late?' (Hayek, 1933, p. 55 and 65)

19.   One should not be distracted by Hayek's use of words, however. He called his business cycle theory 'monetary' because he thought the existence of inside money in a general equilibrium setting to be ultimately responsible for cyclical fluctuations to persist at all. Despite the arbitrary wording, the distinction between 'real' and monetary business cycle

theories is not drawn along the simplistic lines of distinguishing the nature of the impulse: in Hayek's account, real impulses are more likely than nominal ones; money matters not so much as an impulse but it is important to establish the propagation mechanism.

20. Though the concept of a steady state was not alien to Hayek (1933) it is, similar to other authors discussed in this section, not spelled out in formal detail. However, the concept of an intertemporal equilibrium (such as the trend line depicted in Figure 9.1(c)) is most conveniently depicted as an optimal growth path, reflecting an undisturbed set of preferences, endowments, and technology – and growth at a steady rate.

21. This is different from Schumpeter, where the introduction of 'new combinations' may increase overall productivity instantaneously. That Hayek should use a unique interest rate, inversely related to the quantity of what essentially is conceived to be a stock of heterogenous capital goods is strange; the device of the 'natural' rate, together with the conceptual use of 'peanut money' along the lines discussed above in *Prices and Production* had been subject to early criticism – with Sraffa asking for the missing own rate of interest on money.

22. Three impulses inducing the initial divergence between real and market rate are conceivable, two of them 'real' (changing the natural rate), and one 'nominal' (changing the market rate): (i) a shift in preferences, changing the supply of savings; (ii) a shift in technology, inducing changes in investment demand; (iii) maladjustments of the market rate caused by the banking system. Hayek discusses all three.

23. These functionally divided groups could, at best (that is by treating them as homogeneous and not as groups made up of heterogeneous agents) only observe 'their side' of the natural rate: time preference on the part of the consumers, marginal productivity on the part of the entrepreneurs and no *directly* verifiable observation on the part of the banks. Why, at least, the banks should not gradually learn to deduce the correct values from what essentially amounts to the demand and supply of loanable funds they are supposed to equilibrate is, of course, subject to considerable doubt (see below).

24. This also must have suited his determination to maintain the optimality properties of the system if 'left alone'. Hayek maintained that credit creation has to 'keep ahead' of the (rising) purchasing power of the consumer during the boom, should new plants come to be operated. Nowhere does he disentangle that issue from new plants still under construction, which allows for the (too) easy conclusion: 'If a new process of roundabout production can be completed ... it can contribute temporarily to a lowering of the natural rate of interest; but this provides no final solution to the difficulty'. (Hayek, 1933, p. 223)

25. 'Thus the disturbances described as resulting from changes in the *value* of money form only a small part of the much wider category of deviations from the static course of events brought about by changes in the volume of money' (Hayek, 1933, p. 121). Hayek made it quite clear that inside money was central to the argument and that the observed price changes were *effects*, not *causes* of cyclical fluctuation: 'A starting-point for such explanations should be found in the possibility of alterations in the quantity of money occurring automatically and in the normal course of events, under the present organization of money and credit, without the need for violent or artificial action by some external agency' (Hayek, 1933, p. 109). He *excluded* price level changes as causal in explaining cyclical fluctuations. (See below, notes 32 and 33.)

26. A more thorough discussion of the precise nature of (external) increasing returns in his scheme would have saved Schumpeter much of this criticism.

27. 'To investigate the effects of changes in the data is the task posed for the theory by the business cycle' (Lutz, 1932, p. 167). It seems fair to say that Lutz's criticism 'won' the day. Shortly after his book had been published, however, the debate was cut short: none of the participants could, or wanted, to remain in Germany, or Austria, after Hitler's rise to power.

28. 'Coming into town to-day by an unaccustomed road, I saw a notice-board displaying the word 'trade cycles repaired'. But in spite of this curious omen, I do not propose to do here anything of the kind...'. (Hayek, 1938, p. 578).

29. 'There are, of course, certain typical theoretical problems raised by any attempt to explain a particular crisis or depression ... But the question is whether it is legitimate to fit the

different theorems by which these questions are answered, into one single scheme for which it can be claimed that it will explain all or most industrial fluctuations'. (Hayek, 1938, p. 578).

30. Cf. Trautwein (1992 and in this volume) for a critical discussion of Wicksell and Hayek, including (but not confined to) the points addressed above.

31. The argument is also reminiscent of the old distinction between 'income-' and 'business money' with credit creation starting to increase the volume of IOU's during the boom: cheques are used as means of payment between capitalists, i.e. of prime importance during the initial process of expanding productive capacity, whereas their use diminishes as more final goods are traded. (Hayek was quite familiar with Thomas Tooke's work, parts of which he edited.)

32. To rely on arbitrary 'mistakes' was not considered good theory, anyway: 'The "wrong" prices, on the other hand, which lead to wrong dispositions, cannot in turn be explained by a mistake. Within this framework of explanation in which ... prices are merely expressions of a necessary tendency towards a state of equilibrium, it is not permissible to reintroduce the old Sismondian idea of the misleading effect of prices on production without first bringing it into line with the fundamental system of explanation' (Hayek, 1933, p. 85).

33. Another difference to Lucas: '... general price changes are no essential feature of a monetary theory of the Trade Cycle; they are not only inessential, but they would be completely irrelevant if only they were completely "general" – that is if they affected all prices at the same time and in the same proportion' (Hayek, 1933, p. 123).

34. 'We must turn our attention to the importance in Trade Cycle theory on *errors of forecast* ... Here, as elsewhere in our investigations, we shall only be concerned with those theories which are *endogenous*, i.e. which explain the origin of general under- and over-estimation from the economic situation itself, and not from some external circumstance such as weather changes, ... [that] present no problem to economic theory' (Hayek, 1933, pp. 82–3).

References

Burchardt, F. (1928), 'Entwicklungsgeschichte der monetären Konjunkturtheorie', *Weltwirtschaftliches Archiv*, **28** (II).

Cassel, G. (1921), *Theoretische Sozialökonomie*, 2nd ed., Leipzig: C.F. Winter.

Desai, M. (1982), 'The Task of Monetary Theory', in M. Baranzini (ed.), *Advances in Economic Theory*, London: Macmillan.

Hayek, F. A. von (1975) [1933], *Monetary Theory and the Trade Cycle*, Clifton: Augustus M. Kelley (German edition 1929).

Hayek, F. A. von (1938), 'Discussion on the Trade Cycle', *Journal of the Royal Statistical Society*, Part III.

Harberger, A. (1993), 'The Search for Relevance in Economics', *American Economic Review. Papers and Proceedings*, May.

Hicks, J. (1939), *Value and Capital. An Inquiry into Some Fundamental Principles of Economic Theory*, Oxford: Clarendon Press.

Juglar, C. (1889), *Des crises commerciales et de leur retour periodique en France, en Angleterre et aux Etats-Units*, 2nd ed., Paris: Guillaumin.

Kohn, M. (1986), 'Monetary Analysis, the Equilibrium Method, and Keynes' "General Theory"', *Journal of Political Economy*, **94**.

Kydland, F. and E. Prescott (1982), 'Time to Build and Aggregate Fluctuations', *Econometrica*, **50**.

Kydland, F. and E. Prescott (1991), 'The Econometrics of the General Equilibrium Approach to Business Cycles', *Econometrica*, **93**.

Laidler, D. (1986), 'The New Classical Contribution to Macroeconomics', *Banca Nazionale del Lavoro – Quarterly Review*, No. 136.

Leijonhufvud, A. (1983), 'What would Keynes have thought of Rational Expectations?' in D.

Worswick and J. Trevithik (eds), *Keynes and the Modern World*, Cambridge: Cambridge University Press.

Löwe, A. (1925), 'Der gegenwärtige Stand der Konjunkturtheorie in Deutschland', *Die Wirtschaftswissenschaft nach dem Krieg. Festschrift für L. Brentano*, Vol. 2, Berlin: Duncker & Humblot.

Löwe, A. (1926), 'Wie ist Konjunkturtheorie überhaupt möglich?', *Weltwirtschaftliches Archiv*, **2**.

Löwe, A. (1926a), 'Weitere Bemerkungen zur Konjunkturforschung', *Wirtschaftsdienst*, 37.

Lucas, R. (1977), 'Understanding Business Cycles', in K. Brunner and A. Meltzer (eds), *Stabilization of the Domestic and International Economy*, Amsterdam: North-Holland.

Lucas, R. (1987), *Models of the Business Cycle*, Oxford: Basil Blackwell.

Lutz, F. (1932), *Das Konjunkturproblem in der Nationalökonomie*, Jena: Gustav Fischer.

Nell, E. (1993), 'The Old and the New Trade Cycle'. ms., New School for Social Research.

Oppenheimer, F. (1924), *System der Soziologie, Vol. 3: Theorie der reinen und politischen Ökonomie* (5th ed.), Jena: Gustav Fischer.

Romer, P. (1986), 'Increasing Returns and Long-Run Growth', *Journal of Political Economy*, **94**.

Rühl, C. (1994a), 'Equilibrium Analysis', in P. Arestis and M. Sawyer (eds), *The Elgar Companion to Radical Political Economy*, Aldershot: Edward Elgar.

Rühl, C. (1994b), 'Der Beitrag deutschsprachiger Ökonomen zur konjunkturtheoretischen Debatte der Zwischenkriegszeit', in H. Hagemann (ed.), *Die deutschsprachige wirtschaftswissenschaftliche Emigration nach 1933*, Marburg: Metropolis.

Samuelson, P. (1982), 'Evaluating Schumpeter's Zero-Interest-Rate Doctrine', in H. Frisch (ed.), *Schumpeterian Economics*, Eastbourne.

Schumpeter, J. (1917/18), 'Das Sozialprodukt und die Rechenpfennige. Glossen und Beiträge zur Geldtheorie von heute', *Archiv für Sozialwissenschaften und Statistik*, **44**.

Schumpeter, J. (1926), *Theorie der wirtschaftlichen Entwicklung*, München und Leipzig: Duncker & Humblot (1st ed. 1911).

Schumpeter, J. (1927), 'The Explanation of the Business Cycle', *Economica*, **7**.

Schumpeter, J. (1928), 'The Instability of Capitalism', *The Economic Journal*, **38**.

Tichy, G. (1989), 'Neuere Entwicklungen im Rahmen der Gleichgewichtskonjunkturtheorie', Austrian Institute of Economic Research, *Working Paper*, No. 30.

Trautwein, M. (1992), 'Kredit, Zins und Güterpreise: über produktive Unklarheiten bei Wicksell und Hayek', *Diskussionsbeiträge aus dem Institut für Volkswirtschaftslehre*, No. 69, Universität Hohenheim.

10 Hayek and modern business cycle theory

Richard Arena

During the last two decades, macroeconomists have contributed greatly to the revival of business cycle theory. One of the main indications of this revival was the emergence of the so-called 'new classical theory'. A general agreement seemed to appear among commentators, to consider this theory as the heir of the Austrian and, especially, of the Hayekian approach. Laidler (1982, p. IX), for instance, characterized the former as the 'modern version' of the latter, preferring to use the term 'neo-Austrian' than 'new classical' to define the 'body of doctrine' of 'Robert E. Lucas Jr, Robert J. Barro, Thomas J. Sargent, and Neil Wallace (...) [who] place themselves firmly in the intellectual tradition pioneered by Ludwig von Mises and Friedrich von Hayek'. Hoover (1988, ch. 10, p. 237) also noticed that 'the similarities between the Austrian and the new classical research programmes are striking'. Focusing on business cycle theory, Scheide (1986, p. 595) confirmed this common view:

> The discussions of both approaches showed that it would not be appropriate to claim that Austrians have developed the *only* theory of business cycles which refers to individual behavior and choice. New classicals have rediscovered this approach and used many of the tenets for their explanation. This is not to say that new classical theory completely follows Austrian traditions. But many of the differences appear to be small or are only semantic in character.

Now, our paper is precisely devoted to the discussion of this widely accepted opinion, which we do not consider at all to be self-evident. The discussion will, however, slightly differ from the one offered by Laidler, Hoover and Scheide.

First, we shall not deal with the Austrian approach as a whole, but rather concentrate on Hayek's specific theory of business cycles. Therefore, the works of von Mises or of modern Austrians (e.g. Kirzner and Lachmann) will not be considered. The attention paid to business cycle theory in Hayek also involves the usual question of the intellectual homogeneity and continuity of this author's attempt. From this point of view, it is clear that Hayek's business cycle theory sensibly evolved if we consider its emergence at the end of

*The author wishes to thank all the participants in the conference for their comments and suggestions. The usual caveats apply.

the 1920s and the second phase of the author's research, which began in the 1940s. When it appears necessary, we shall refer to this intellectual evolution. However, our purpose here is not philological and, therefore, we shall focus rather on the homogeneity of Hayek's message than on its chronological variations. Moreover, we fully agree with Colonna (1990, p. XXI), when she notes that

> these 'changes of view', often emphasized by the author himself, concern less the theoretical explanation of increasing inflation and crisis, or the mechanism of the effects of money supply changes, than the kind of policy which is able to contribute more efficiently to the eradication of these evils. (our translation)

Second, we shall not limit our investigation to new classical business cycle theory. This is the reason for the expression 'modern business cycle theory' in the title of our paper. Obviously, it will be irrelevant to compare Hayek's theory with the modern theories of endogenous or of non-linear determinist business cycles. These theories indeed often belong to the approach of Keynes, Kalecki, Kaldor or Goodwin, which Hayek always explicitly rejected. In comparison with this type of approach, Hayek's clearly refers to the tradition of exogenous business cycle theory, according to which the origin of the cycle is not to be found within the natural working of the economic system but in the occurrence of exogenous disturbances.[1]

This view might be considered contradictory with some passages in which Hayek understates the place of original disturbances:

> It must be emphasized first and foremost that there is no necessary reason why the initiating change, the original disturbance eliciting a cyclical fluctuation in a stationary economy, should be of monetary origin. Nor, in practice, is this even generally the case. The initial change need have no specific character at all, it may be any one among a thousand different factors which may at any time increase the profitability of any group of enterprises. For it is not the occurrence of a 'change of data' which is significant, but the fact that the economic system, instead of reacting to this change with an immediate 'adjustment' (Schumpeter) – i.e. the formation of a new equilibrium – begins a particular movement of 'boom' which contains, within itself, the seeds of an inevitable reaction. (Hayek, 1966, pp. 182–3)

However, even if they are 'any one among a thousand different factors', original disturbances are necessary to generate a cycle, according to the exogenous business cycle theory tradition. By the way, this specific feature of Hayek's theory confirms the relevance of a comparison with the new classical approach since it belongs to the same tradition. However, the reference to Lucas among the modern revivers of business cycle theory would be insufficient. We must also consider the other branch of the modern exogenous cycle tradition, that is real business cycle theory. This reference might be surprising if we have in mind the monetary character of Hayek's approach. We shall see, however, that this first impression is superficial.

Having defined the terms of our comparison, it is now time to focus on the main themes which establish analogies and differences between Hayek's and modern exogenous business cycle theories.

Methodology

From the beginning of his research on business cycles, Hayek insisted upon the necessity of building a deductive approach which would not differ methodologically from the one offered by price theory. Thus, in one of his first articles, he had already complained about the fact that economists, focusing on empirical research on business cycles,

> do not begin from a definite basic theoretical conception of the economic process, but content themselves with gaining as detailed as possible a picture of the typical course of a cycle with the aid of detailed statistical investigation of the behaviour of the individual factors in each phase of the cycle (...). The result is a type of *symptomatology* of the course of the cycle (...). [This type of approach] does not offer the comprehensive understanding attainable with a theory derived from general economic principles. It is of little help when what is at issue is not detailed interconnections but the cause of cyclical fluctuations in general. (Hayek, 1984, pp. 6–7)

These doubts about the utility of empirical research became stronger in *Monetary Theory and the Trade Cycle*:

> Just as no statistical investigation can prove that a given change in demand must necessarily be followed by a certain change in price, so no statistical method can explain why all economic phenomena present that regular wave-like appearance which we observe in cyclical fluctuations. This can be explained only by widening the assumptions on which our deductions are based, so that cyclical fluctuations would follow from these as a necessary consequence, just as the general propositions of the theory of price followed from the narrower assumptions of equilibrium theory. (Hayek, 1966, p. 30)

This necessity to build a deductive theory of business cycles was combined by Hayek with the characterization of 'criteria of correctness', which were two:

> Firstly, [trade cycle theory] must be deduced with unexceptionable logic from the fundamental notions of the theoretical system; and secondly, it must explain by a purely deductive method those phenomena with all their peculiarities which we observe in the actual cycle. (Hayek, 1966, pp. 32–3)

These views did not imply, however, a refusal to do any statistical research. On the contrary, Hayek devoted a part of his *Monetary Theory* to consider and discuss what are 'the problems for statistical investigations' (Hayek, 1966, pp. 231ff). However, the 'problems' raised were predominantly technical and their investigation did not change Hayek's position on the necessity of building first a deductive theory: 'even as a means of verification, the statistical examination of the cycles has only a very limited value for trade cycle theory' (Hayek, 1966, p. 32).

Hayek's view clearly contrasts with Lucas's. If Lucas indeed criticizes some usual models of econometric cycles, his critique concerns their specific features. It does not reveal general scepticism with regard to the use of econometrics in business cycle research. Lucas's interest for the use of econometrics is instead checked by the progress of econometric techniques involved in the debates within new classical and real business cycle approaches. Modern business cycle theorists use alternatively analytical as well as empirical methods and do not give to the former a pre-eminent role, as was the case in Hayek.

Microfoundations of macroeconomics?

Hayek's reference to a deductive theory of business cycles is related to his vision of economics. According to this conception, price theory indeed provides some universal tools which might be adapted to investigate other areas of research, including business cycle analysis. Therefore, the principles and the characterization of agents which prevail within price theory also occur elsewhere:

> We cannot superimpose upon the system of fundamental propositions comprised in the theory of equilibrium, a Trade Cycle theory resting on unrelated logical foundations (...)
> [That regular wave-like appearance which we observe in cyclical fluctuations] (...) can be explained only by widening the assumptions on which our deductions are based, so that cyclical fluctuations would follow from these as a necessary consequence, just as the general propositions of the theory of price followed from the narrower assumptions of equilibrium theory. (Hayek, 1966, pp. 28, 30)

This pre-eminent role given to equilibrium price theory and Hayek's defence of methodological individualism combine to explain his refutation of macroeconomics, seen as an autonomous or an aggregate level of analysis:

> [Lorsque nous essayons d'établir des relations causales directes entre la quantité totale de monnaie, le niveau général de l'ensemble des prix et éventuellement la production totale], aucune de ces grandeurs en tant que telle n'exerce jamais d'influence sur les décisions des individus; pourtant, les principales propositions de la théorie économique non monétaire sont fondées sur l'hypothèse d'une

connaissance des décisions individuelles. Nous devons notre compréhension, quelles qu'en soient ses limites, des phénomènes économiques à cette méthode 'individualiste'. (Hayek, 1975, p. 63)

Therefore, as it was the case for price theory, the heterogeneity and the interdependence of agents have to be taken explicitly into account, in order to build what we could call a microeconomic theory of business cycles. This attempt implies some important consequences.

Hayek first gives up using the notions of volume of money and general level of prices. This renunciation, which is necessary for 'further progress' (Hayek, 1975, p. 62), means discarding quantity theory:

> Si la théorie monétaire essaie encore d'établir des relations causales entre agrégats ou moyennes générales, c'est à cause de son retard sur le développement de la science économique en général. En fait, ni les agrégats ni les moyennes ni les moyennes n'interagissent, et il ne sera jamais possible d'établir entre eux des relations systématiques de cause à effet, comme on peut le faire pour des phénomènes individuels, des prix individuels, etc. (Hayek, 1975, p. 63)

But this rejection of aggregate analysis also appears in the theory of capital. Hayek indeed expresses his doubts with regard to the treatment of capital goods as a single homogeneous quantity. He writes:

> the problems that are raised by any attempt to analyse the dynamics of production are mainly problems connected with the interrelationships between the different parts of the elaborate structure of productive equipment which man has built to serve his needs. But all the essential differences between these parts were obscured by the general endeavour to subsume them under one comprehensive definition of the stock of capital. (Hayek, 1976, p. 6)

Here also, Hayek's position is different from equilibrium and real business cycle theories. Lucasian theory indeed gives an important and, often, a crucial role to aggregates such as the volume of money or the stock of capital and to averages such as the general level of prices. The volume of money in Lucas is the variable which is struck by the original exogenous stock of the cycle. In the same way, the level of prices is the result of exogenous decisions of monetary authorities that individual agents try unsuccessfully to expect. Real business cycle theorists do not always refer to macroeconomic monetary magnitudes but they use real aggregates such as the national income or the stock of capital, which are also considered meaningless by Hayek.

These differences are not surprising. They derive from the fact that modern equilibrium or real business cycle theorists use representative agents, whereas Hayek refers to individual agents and develops a pure microeconomic perspective.

Information and expectations

Hayek faced explicitly the problem of 'errors of forecast' within the context of business cycle theory (Hayek, 1966, ch. II, para. VII). He indeed considered what he called 'psychological theories', that is theories for which 'an overestimate of future demand can occasion a development of the productive apparatus so excessive as automatically to lead to a reaction, unprecipitated by other psychological changes' (Hayek, 1966, p. 83). Hayek's position is sharp and clear. The author excludes the possibility of systematic errors. He notices that

> no one would deny, of course, that errors can arise as regards the future movements of particular prices. But it is not permissible to assume without further proof that the equilibrating mechanism of the economic system will begin its work only when the excessively increased product due to these mistaken forecasts actually comes on the market, the disproportional development continuing undisturbed up to that time. At one point or another, all theories which start to explain cyclical fluctuations by miscalculations or ignorance as regards the economic situation fall into the same error as those naive explanations which base themselves on the 'planlessness' of the economic system. They overlook the fact that, in the exchange economy, production is governed by prices, independently of any knowledge of the whole process on the part of individual producers, so that it is only when the pricing process is itself disturbed that a misdirection of production can occur. The 'wrong' prices on the other hand, which lead to 'wrong' dispositions, cannot in turn be explained by a mistake. (Hayek, 1966, pp. 84–5)

This conception of agents' behaviour is obviously supported by Hayek's belief in the existence of a natural tendency of the economy towards equilibrium. The reason why agents cannot make the same mistakes over and over again is that they learn from market experiments. Hayekian agents are indeed learning more than rational ones; they '*cannot* know more than a tiny part of the whole of society, and ... therefore all that can enter into [their] motives are the immediate effects which [their] actions will have in the spheres [they] know' (Hayek, 1946, p. 14).

Therefore, interindividual market relations provide the opportunity for the diffusion of private knowledge which forms 'the unlimited variety of human gifts and skills' (Hayek, 1946, p. 15) and which is *a priori* unequally distributed among agents. From this point of view, the main problem of agents is the *discovery* of new information through the economic signals revealed by the market process. Prices are some of these signals but, as Hayek expressed it,

> price expectations and even the knowledge of current prices are only a very small section of the problem of knowledge as I see it. The wider aspect of the problem of knowledge with which I am concerned is the knowledge of the basic fact of how the different commodities can be obtained and used, and under what condi-

tions they are actually obtained and used, that is, the general question of why the subjective data to the different persons correspond to the objective facts. (Hayek, 1937, p. 51)

These remarks are already sufficient to cast some doubt on the possibility of comparing Hayekian and new classical conceptions of agents' behaviour. Serious differences indeed make it impossible.

On the one hand, Hayek's and Lucas's conceptions of individual behaviour near equilibrium are clearly different. Lucas refers to the traditional conception of economic rationality, which Hayek describes, using the term 'pure logic of choice':

the assumptions from which the Pure Logic of Choice starts are facts which we know to be common to all human thought. They may be regarded as axioms which define or delimit the field within which we are able to understand or mentally to reconstruct the processes of thought of other people. They are therefore universally applicable to the field in which we are interested – although, of course, where *in concreto* the limits of this field are is an empirical question. They refer to a type of human action (what we commonly call 'rational' or even merely 'conscious', as distinguished from 'instinctive' action) rather than to the particular conditions under which this action is undertaken. (Hayek, 1937, p. 47)

On the other hand, Hayek's conception is neither axiomatic nor universal. He notes that

apparently subsidiary hypotheses or assumptions that people do learn from experience, and about how they acquire knowledge ... constitute the empirical content of our propositions about what happens in the real world. (Hayek, 1937, p. 46)

Therefore, agents' behaviour essentially concerns the creation of knowledge through experience and not the use of given natural endowments.

Moreover, Hayek describes economic activity as a process in time. He considers equilibrium as an ideal normative benchmark compatible with real disequilibria. He refutes the concept of a representative agent forming rational expectations:

since equilibrium relations exist between the successive actions of a person only in so far as they are a part of the execution of the same plan, any change in the relevant knowledge of the person, that is, any change which leads him to alter his plan, disrupts the equilibrium relation between his actions taken before and those taken after the change in his knowledge. In other words, the equilibrium relationship comprises only his actions during the period in which his anticipations prove correct. Second, ... since equilibrium is a relationship between actions, and since the actions of one person must necessarily take place successively in time, it is obvious that the passage of time is essential to give the concept of equilibrium any meaning. (Hayek, 1937, p. 37)

On the contrary, the case describes an economy ruled by a market-clearing assumption. Equilibrium is seen as a timeless state of affairs and a representative agent forms macrorational expectations.

The conception of knowledge provides a further opportunity to differentiate Hayekian and new classical approaches. According to Hayek,

> Another misleading phrase, used to stress an important point, is the famous presumption that each man knows his interest best. In this form the contention is neither plausible nor necessary for the individualist's conclusions. The true basis of his argument is that nobody can know *who* knows best, and that the only way by which we can find out is through a social process in which everybody is allowed to try and see what he can do. (Hayek, 1946, p. 15)

The preceding remarks do not exhaust the problem of information in a comparison between Hayekian and exogenous business cycle theories. We indeed know that the emergence and persistence of cycles in Lucas's theory are strongly related to his theory of incomplete information. Now, such a theory is completely absent from the Hayekian theoretical framework. Therefore, Lucas's remark according to which 'the Austrian over investment theory was based on the same idea of investment errors implied by false price signals' (Lucas, 1977, p. 13) is misleading.

However, as we have already noted, the Lucasian version of modern exogenous business cycles theory is not the only one. Now, we may immediately verify that, from the point of view of information, real business cycle agents cannot make forecast errors. They are subjected to real exogenous shocks and they always give to them optimal answers through their intertemporal choices of consumption and production. From this point of view, the similarity is greater between Hayekian and real business cycle theories than between Hayek's and Lucas's theories.

Equilibrium

The insistence of Hayek on the concept of equilibrium, even within the business cycle theory context, led some authors to describe Hayek and Lucas as Walrasian theorists. Hoover, for instance, notes that

> equilibrium theory for Hayek is best represented in the Walrasian school's analysis of the general interdependence of economic quantities. Lucas sees new classical theory as a movement away from Keynesian analysis and as a technically superior but natural extension of the interwar views represented by Hayek. (Hoover, 1988, p. 253)

Moreover, Hayek himself wrote that we 'have to make use of the logic of equilibrium theory', adding in a footnote:

By 'equilibrium theory' we here primarily understand the modern theory of the general interdependence of all economic quantities, which has been most perfectly expressed by the Lausanne School of theoretical economics. (Hayek, 1966, p. 42)

In spite of this reference to Walras or to the Lausanne school, the view according to which Hayek would have been a follower of Walras, and Lucas a follower of Hayek, appears to be superficial.

We might first note that the footnote in *Monetary Theory and the Trade Cycle*, often quoted, is incomplete. Hayek adds a final sentence: '...The significant basic concept of this theory was contained in James Mill's and J.B. Say's *Théorie des Débouchés*. Cf. L. Miksch, *Gibt es eine allgemeine Uberproduktion*?, Jena, 1929.'

This sentence clearly means that, in Hayek's mind, equilibrium theory includes James Mill as well as Say or Walras. Now, those three authors have developed drastically different theories of prices. The reference to equilibrium is therefore more general than a kind of intellectual oath of allegiance to Walras. It visibly refers again to Hayek's belief that there is a natural tendency in the economic system to clear markets. This is much but not more.

Our view is immediately confirmed, since Hayek adds after his footnote:

Yet this logic, properly followed through, can do no more than demonstrate that such disturbances of equilibrium can come only from outside – i.e. that they represent a change in the economic data – and that the economic system always reacts to such changes by its well-known methods of adaptation, i.e., by the formation of a new equilibrium. (Hayek, 1966, pp. 42–3)

In other words, after having referred to 'the logic of equilibrium', Hayek notes its inability to take economic fluctuations into account. The same critique is developed, when Hayek explains why the Walrasian–Paretian approach cannot cope with business cycles. Let us indeed recall that for Walras or Pareto, as well as for their follower in the 1930s, Henry Moore, dynamics was described as a succession of 'moving' or temporary equilibria disturbed by recurrent changes of the data.[2] No evidence is given *a priori* which confirms that this succession will take the shape of a cycle.

Evidently, Hayek does not agree with this conception. This is already clear when we compare the Walrasian and the Hayekian processes of reaching equilibrium. There is little common room between Walras's *tâtonnement* and Hayek's market discovery. But Hayek does not even accept the notion of stationary state with which Schumpeter and others interpreted Walras (Donzelli, 1986; Arena, 1992) during the 1920s and 1930s:

> Since equilibrium is a relationship between actions, and since the actions of one person must necessarily take place successively in time, it is obvious that the passage of time is essential to give the concept of equilibrium any meaning. (Hayek, 1937, pp. 36–7)

Hayek did not always conform to this critique of stationary states. Thus, in *Prices and Production* he accepted this notion, writing:

> Si nous voulons procéder de façon systématique, nous devons partir d'une situation déjà suffisamment analysée par le corps général de la théorie économique. Et seule la situation dans laquelle toutes les ressources disponibles sont employées, satisfont ce critère. (Hayek, 1975, p. 98)

But in *Monetary Theory and the Trade Cycle* and in *The Pure Theory of Capital*, Hayek replaced the notion of stationary state by the concept of intertemporal equilibrium. This replacement was necessary to fulfil the objectives of building a capital theory and to take time seriously into account:

> [An effective discussion of the problems of capital theory] must *not* be confined to the stationary state, because here *ex definitione* most of the problems with which the theory of capital must be concerned have disappeared. The main problems are to explain what types of instruments will be produced under given conditions, and what will be the consequences of producing particular instruments. And these problems will of course be non-existent if we assume from the beginning that the same stock of instruments will be constantly reproduced. The impossibility of treating the problems of capital adequately within the framework of a stationary equilibrium becomes, of course, even more obvious as soon as we include, as we must, the problems relating to what are usually described as 'saving' and (new) 'investment', since these are activities which imply by definition that the persons undertaking them want to alter their future position and consequently will do in the future something different from what they are doing in the present. (Hayek, 1976, pp. 15–16)

Having characterized Hayek's equilibrium according to its temporal dimension, it is now necessary to examine the notion in more detail. We have already introduced the notion of 'market discovery'. Beyond this, Donzelli (1986, p. 192) has shown that the Hayekian notion of equilibrium is better understood if we associate it with the notion of 'economic order' (Hayek, 1976). The idea is that Hayek's equilibrium offers a direction for the natural tendency of the economy. On this path intertemporal disequilibria can appear but, if they are not 'too large', they can be included in an 'order' which corresponds to the normal working of the economic system. Obviously, such an 'order' is vaguer than a Walrasian equilibrium and cannot be formalized through a *tâtonnement* process.

The equilibrium is therefore a norm in regard to which disequilibria might be estimated:

if we want to predict at all, it must be on the basis of the plans which entrepreneurs are likely to make in the light of their present knowledge, and of an analysis of the factors which in the course of time will determine whether they will be able to carry out these plans or whether they will have to alter them. It seems natural to begin by constructing, as an intellectual tool, a fictitious state under which these plans are in complete correspondence without, however, asking whether this state will ever, or can ever, come about. (Hayek, 1976, pp. 22–3)

The path of the economy towards the equilibrium cannot be investigated analytically, as is the case in a *tâtonnement* process:

Its justification is not that it allows us to explain why real conditions should ever in any degree approximate towards a state of equilibrium, but that observation shows that they do to some extent so approximate, and that the functioning of the existing economic system will depend on the degree to which it approaches such a condition. (Hayek, 1976, pp. 27–8)

It is easy to understand this view if we have in mind the distinction introduced by Hayek between 'logical (or axiomatic) and empirical (or causal) analysis' (Klausinger, 1990, p. 66). Now the proposition according to which there exists a 'natural tendency towards equilibrium' is clearly of the second type, in sharp contrast with the Walrasian view:

Whatever may occasionally have been said by over-pure economists, there seems to be no possible doubt that the only justification [to admit the fictitious state of equilibrium] is the supposed existence of a tendency towards equilibrium. It is only with this assertion that economics ceases to be an exercise in pure logic and becomes an empirical science ... The assertion of the existence of a tendency towards equilibrium is clearly an empirical proposition, that is, an assertion about what happens in the real world which ought, at least in principle, to be capable of verification. (Hayek, 1937, p. 45)

The concept of equilibrium, therefore, as it appears to be in the previous lines, is strongly different from Lucas's. If an analogous concept of intertemporal equilibrium plays a role in Lucas as in Hayek, however, the assumption of constant market clearing changes its nature. Lucasian equilibrium is always assumed to be realized in time and does not admit durable disequilibria. It is, however, unsafe to assimilate Lucasian and Walrasian equilibria because the problem of reaching the equilibrium is not really faced by Lucas. Therefore, there is no process of *tâtonnement*, no learning process which can explain how equilibrium is attained. In the same way, rational expectations are macroeconomic and, therefore, the question of the possible diversity or heterogeneity of opinions is not investigated. We are thus far from the more interesting notion of *rational expectations equilibrium*. The same point could be developed concerning real business cycle theory.

Money and cycles

Money takes an important part in the origin and the persistence of economic fluctuations. This is certainly one of the main reasons which leads commentators to compare Hayekian and new classical approaches. Hayek emphasized the role of money as a condition of cycles, while Lucas considered stochastic injections of money as the main factor in fluctuations. However, more precise investigation allows us to stress the differences and not only the analogies.

We have already noted that, in a Hayekian barter economy, there was a natural tendency towards the equilibrium between supply and demand:

> so long, at least, as disturbing monetary influences are not operating, we have to assume that the price which entrepreneurs expect to result from a change in demand or from a change in the conditions of production will more or less coincide with the equilibrium price. (Hayek, 1966, p. 69)

The introduction of money changes the working of economic activity:

> in a barter economy, interest forms a sufficient regulator for the proportional development of the production of capital goods and consumption goods, respectively. If it is admitted that, in the absence of money, interest would effectively prevent any excessive extension of the production of production goods, by keeping it within the limits of the available supply of savings, and that an extension of the stock of capital goods which is based on a voluntary postponement of consuments' demand into the future can never lead to disproportionate extensions, then it must also necessarily be admitted that disproportional developments in the production of capital goods can arise only through the independence of the supply of free money capital from the accumulation of savings; which in turn arises from the elasticity of the volume of money. (Hayek, 1966, pp. 91–2)

We know that referring to the Wicksellian tradition, Hayek locates the origin of the cycle in an increase in the equilibrium rate of interest (the Wicksellian 'natural' rate) associated either with a decrease in the ratio of voluntary saving of individuals or with an increase in the investment demand of firms.

The first case corresponds to an intertemporal substitution of present for future consumptions. The second derives from the implementation of technical changes within the firms of the economy.

Still in compliance with Wicksell's theory, if we are in a monetary economy, the market rate of interest ceases to move according to the self-regulatory principles which rule the working of a barter economy. The equilibrium rate of interest increases while the market rate remains fixed.

What is happening then is a change in the volume of money, as an answer to the preceding variations of saving or investment. Now, 'a change in the volume of money ... represents as it were a one-sided change in demand, which is not counterbalanced by an equivalent change in supply' (Hayek, 1966, p. 93).

We can therefore see that the causes of the cycle can be real as well as monetary. Money, in any case, is a necessary condition of the cycle because it prevents the self-regulating working of the economy.

But the original shock of the working of the money market is not sufficient to ensure the permanence of fluctuations. As Hayek noted 'the successive changes in the real structure of production [...] constitute those fluctuations' (Hayek, 1966, p. 17). The effect of the variation of the volume of money is not indeed a change in the general level of prices but a change in the relative prices of goods, according to their places in the structure of production. For instance, if the voluntary saving of agents increases, the prices of production goods will increase in proportion to the prices of consumers goods.

This interpretation is confirmed by Hayek's *Profits, Interest and Investment* – a book which, however, is often interpreted as the locus of a drastic change in Hayek's approach to business cycles. Commentators frequently stressed Hayek's description of the natural rate of interest as rate of profit (Hayek, 1939, pp. 3–4) and his insistence on real more than on monetary causes of fluctuations:

> We have seen that if the rate of interest fails to keep investment within the bounds determined by people's willingness to save, a rise in the rate of profit in the industries near consumption will in the end act in a way very similar to that in which the rate of interest is supposed to act, because a rise in the rate of profit beyond a certain point will bring about a decrease in investment just as an increase in the rate of interest might do. (1939, p. 64)

However, the necessary and logical condition of the existence of business cycles is the short-term rigidity of the monetary rate of interest:

> If the rate of interest were allowed to rise as profits rise (*i.e.* if the supply of credit were not elastic), the industries that could not earn profits at this higher rate would have to curtail or stop production, and incomes and the demand for consumers' goods and profits in the consumers' goods industries would cease to rise. (1939, p. 32)

We might interpret this assumption of a rigid short-term rate of interest as a concession to the Keynesian context of the epoch. But this is not the important point. It is the fact that in a monetary economy, the profit and interest rates do not move simultaneously and, therefore, imply the possible occurrence of business cycles. The explanation of the stickiness of the monetary rate of interest might be Wicksellian (banks' behaviour), or Keynesian (distinction between short and long periods) but, in both cases, the monetary characteristic of the rate of interest remains and allows the birth of cycles.

Lucas's story is very different. First, its beginning is not a variation of the equilibrium rate of interest but a set of stochastic injections of money units. Their global volume and the general level of prices are taken into account as such, in contradiction with Hayek's views. Then, intertemporal substitution effects might occur between present consumption and saving. However, these effects do not enter into the realm of production, as they do in Hayek's model, when he defines the structure of different stages of productive activity.

If we focus now on real business cycle theory, original shocks are close to Hayekian ones, either on consumer preferences, or on technology. Moreover, the persistence of instability does not depend on forecast errors of agents relative to the general level of prices, as is the case with Lucas. In compliance with Hayek's approach, individual answers are optimal and take the shape of intertemporal choices between consumption and production. Some of the models even authorize a multisectoral framework and, therefore, the appearance of several goods. However, the missing actor is money and the introduction of liquidity constraints or of financial intermediaries does not play a crucial role.

Conclusion

The results of our investigation are predominantly negative. Hayekian and modern exogenous business cycle theories belong to a common great tradition but, on many crucial points, their similarities are more apparent than real. The history of economic analysis is more complex than some commentators might think *a priori* and it is not sufficient to use the term 'new classical' to revive the 'classical' theories which preceded Keynes's approach.

Now, modern business cycle theory is probably more convincing for mainstream economists than the Hayekian one. Technically, it appears to be clearer and more rigorous and, conceptually, one of its great merits is simplicity. These might be good reasons which lead many economists to consider Hayek's business cycle theory as a first imperfect version of the modern one.

Things might appear to be different for unorthodox economists. From their point of view, Hayek might be credited with having tried to cope with a monetary production economy, with the stricture of production and its temporal changes, with the market viewed as a process. However, to do this, Hayek used a particular version of the traditional theory of prices based on the symmetrical laws of supply and demand, i.e., an approach which was perhaps ill-equipped to fulfil his purposes.

Therefore, for most contemporary economists, Hayek's attempt appears to have been unsuccessful. The paradox is however that, today, unorthodox economists have perhaps more to learn from Hayek than their mainstream colleagues.

Notes

1. This distinction between 'endogenous' and 'exogenous' business cycle theories must not be confused with the one to which, after Bouniatian, Hayek refers, using the same terms (Hayek, 1966, pp. 143–4).
2. See Raybaut (1991, vol. 7, pp. 37–56 and 1992).

References

Arena, R. (1989), 'Keynes après Lucas: quelques enseignements récents de la macroéconomie monétaire', *Economies et Sociétés*, Série 'Economie Monétaire, 4–5.

Arena, R. (1992), 'Schumpeter after Walras: "économie pure" or "stylized facts"?' in S. Todd Lowry (ed.), *Perspectives in the History of Economic Thought, Volume VIII*, Aldershot, Hants: Edward Elgar.

Colonna, M. (1990), 'Introduzione' to F.A. Hayek,: *Prezzi e produzione*, Napoli: Edizioni Scientifiche Italiane.

Donzelli, F. (1986), *Il concetto di equilibrio nella teoria economica neoclassica*, Roma: Nuova Italia Scientifica.

Hayek, F.A. von (1937) 'Economics and knowledge', reprinted in F.A. von Hayek, *Individualism and Economic Order*, London: Routledge and Kegan Paul, 1949.

Hayek, F.A. von (1939), *Profits, Interest and Investment*, London, Routledge and Kegan Paul.

Hayek, F.A. von (1946), 'Individualism: true and false', reprinted in F.A. von Hayek, *Individualism and Economic Order*, op. cit.

Hayek, F.A. von (1966), *Monetary Theory and the Trade Cycle*, New York: Augustus M. Kelley. First published 1933.

Hayek, F.A. von (1975), *Prix et production*, Paris: Calmann-Levy (with an introduction to the French edition), first published 1931.

Hayek, F.A. von (1976), *The Pure Theory of Capital*, London: Routledge and Kegan Paul. First published 1941.

Hayek, F.A. von (1984), 'The monetary policy of the United States after the recovery from the 1920 crisis', in F.A. von Hayek, *Money, Capital and Fluctuations*, London: Routledge and Kegan Paul. First published 1925.

Hoover, K. (1988), *The New Classical Macroeconomics: a Skeptical Inquiry*, Oxford: Basil Blackwell.

Klausinger, H. (1990), 'Equilibrium methodology as seen from a Hayekian perspective', *Journal of History of Economic Thought*, **12**, (1) Spring.

Laidler, D. (1982), *Monetarist perspectives*, Oxford: Philip Allan.

Lucas, R. (1977), 'Understanding business cycles', in K. Brunner and A. Meltzer (eds), *Stabilization of the Domestic and International Economy*, Amsterdam: North Holland.

Raybaut, A. (1991), 'Cycles et instabilité: traditions et renouveau dans la théorie des fluctuations économiques', Thèse de Doctorat ès Sciences Economiques, University of Nice, Sophia-Antipolis.

Raybaut, A. (1992), 'L'Economie synthétique d'H.L. Moore' *Revue d'Economie Politique*, **101**, (6).

Scheide, J. (1986), 'New classical and Austrian business cycle theory', *Weltwirtschaftliches Archiv*, **3**.

Index